A Research Agenda for Terrorism Studies

Elgar Research Agendas outline the future of research in a given area. Leading scholars are given the space to explore their subject in provocative ways, and map out the potential directions of travel. They are relevant but also visionary.

Forward-looking and innovative, Elgar Research Agendas are an essential resource for PhD students, scholars and anybody who wants to be at the forefront of research.

Titles in the series include:

A Research Agenda for Intelligence Studies and Government
Edited by Robert Dover, Huw Dylan and Michael S. Goodman

A Research Agenda for Financial Crime
Edited by Barry Rider

A Research Agenda for Small and Medium-Sized Towns
Edited by Heike Mayer and Michela Lazzeroni

A Research Agenda for Social Welfare Law, Policy and Practice
Edited by Michael Adler

A Research Agenda for Organisation Studies, Feminisms and New Materialisms
Edited by Marta B. Calás and Linda Smircich

A Research Agenda for Terrorism Studies
Edited by Lara A. Frumkin, John F. Morrison and Andrew Silke

A Research Agenda for Terrorism Studies

Edited by

LARA A. FRUMKIN

Senior Lecturer, School of Psychology and Counselling, The Open University, UK

JOHN F. MORRISON

School of Law and Criminology, Maynooth University, Ireland

ANDREW SILKE

Professor of Terrorism, Risk and Resilience, Cranfield Forensic Institute, Cranfield University, UK

Elgar Research Agendas

Edward Elgar
PUBLISHING

Cheltenham, UK • Northampton, MA, USA

Published by
Edward Elgar Publishing Limited
The Lypiatts
15 Lansdown Road
Cheltenham
Glos GL50 2JA
UK

Edward Elgar Publishing, Inc.
William Pratt House
9 Dewey Court
Northampton
Massachusetts 01060
USA

A catalogue record for this book
is available from the British Library

Library of Congress Control Number: 2022950546

This book is available electronically in the **Elgar**online
Political Science and Public Policy subject collection
http://dx.doi.org/10.4337/9781789909104

ISBN 978 1 78990 909 8 (cased)
ISBN 978 1 78990 910 4 (eBook)

Printed and bound by CPI Group (UK) Ltd, Croydon, CR0 4YY

This work is dedicated to our colleague Chandra Lekha Sriram, who passed away far too young in 2018. An unforgettable character, Chandra was a passionate researcher and prolific writer on conflict resolution and transitional justice, with a keen interest in research methodologies, human rights and ethics. She conducted fieldwork on conflicts in many troubled corners of the world, including Sierra Leone, Sudan, Colombia and Sri Lanka.

Contents

Editors and contributors

Editors

Lara A. Frumkin is Senior Lecturer in the School of Psychology and Counselling at The Open University. Lara's research explores psychological factors such as catastrophising, anxiety and ethnocentrism as they relate to coping with terrorist threat. She works with law enforcement in examining the role they can play in mitigating the public's perceived threat of terrorist attacks and counterterrorism policing legitimacy. Lara's research has been funded by the Home Office and the Engineering and Physical Sciences Research Council. Previously Lara has worked in policy and for the United States (US) Government.

John F. Morrison is based at the School of Law and Criminology at Maynooth University, Ireland. He holds a BA in psychology from University College Dublin, an MA in forensic psychology from University College Cork and a PhD in international relations from the University of St Andrews. John is an associate editor of two leading academic journals in terrorism studies, *Perspectives on Terrorism* and *Behavioral Sciences of Terrorism and Political Aggression*, and sits on the editorial board of *Terrorism and Political Violence*. He is also the host and developer of the *Talking Terror* podcast. John's research interests include organisational splits in terrorist groups, the role of trust in terrorist involvement, violent dissident Irish republicanism, the psychology of terrorism, expert–novice differences in terrorist offenders and the social ecology of radicalisation.

Andrew Silke is Professor of Terrorism, Risk and Resilience at Cranfield University. He has a background in forensic psychology and criminology and has worked both in academia and for government. He is the author/editor of many books on terrorism and counterterrorism, with recent volumes including *Terrorism: All That Matters* (2014), *Historical Perspectives on Terrorism* *and Organised Crime* (2018) and *The Routledge Handbook of Terrorism and Counterterrorism* (2019). He tweets at @AndrewPSilke.

Contributors

Shirley Achieng' is a Kenyan national and recipient of a New Zealand Commonwealth doctoral scholarship. She is a PhD candidate at the University of Otago's National Centre for Peace and Conflict Studies. Her academic background is in political science and international relations, specialising in diplomacy and foreign policy. Her professional background is in policy drafting and interpretation of statutory instruments, having worked with the legislative arm of the Nairobi County Government. Her research interests include indigenous counterterrorism approaches and decolonial perspectives. She is currently working on her doctoral thesis titled 'Towards an Indigenous African Approach to Counterterrorism in Kenya'.

Gary A. Ackerman's research focuses on understanding how terrorists and other adversaries make tactical, operational and strategic decisions, particularly with regard to innovating in their use of weapons and tactics. In addition to his faculty position as Associate Professor in the College of Emergency Preparedness, Homeland Security and Cybersecurity at the State University of New York, Ackerman is Director of the Center for Advanced Red Teaming and Founding Director of the Unconventional Weapons and Technology Division at the National Consortium for the Study of Terrorism and Responses to Terrorism (START). Previous positions have included research director and special projects director at START and before that director of the Weapons of Mass Destruction Terrorism Research Program at the Center for Non-Proliferation Studies in Monterey, California.

Eke Bont has a background in psychology and her PhD research at Royal Holloway, University of London focuses on moral injury in Republican ex-prisoners from the Northern Ireland conflict. She is currently a social researcher at the United Kingdom (UK) Ministry of Justice.

Katherine E. Brown is a reader in religion and global security at the University of Birmingham, UK. Her research examines the role of gender in Islamist extremism and counterterrorism. This is the focus of her book *Gender, Religion, Extremism* (2020). Her policy work addresses gender mainstreaming in preventing and countering extremism and screening, prosecution, rehabilitation and reintegration for those affiliated with terrorist organisations.

Julie Chernov Hwang is Associate Professor of Political Science and International Relations at Goucher College. She is the author of *Why Terrorists Quit: The Disengagement of Indonesian Jihadists* (2018), *Peaceful Islamist Mobilization in the Muslim World: What Went Right* (2009) and the co-editor of *Islamist Parties and Political Normalization in the Muslim World* (2014). Her articles have been published in *Political Psychology, Terrorism and Political Violence, Asian Survey, Contemporary Southeast Asia, Asia-Pacific Issues, Southeast Asia Research* and *Nationalism and Ethnic Politics*. Her new book project, *Becoming Jihadis: Radicalization and Commitment in Southeast Asia*, explores how and why Indonesian and Filipino Muslims join, commit and take on high-risk roles as part of Islamist extremist groups.

Meghan Conroy is an investigator with the US House of Representatives specialising in the spread of reactionary narratives through both legacy and new media.

Celia Davies is Director of International Programmes and Ethics at Moonshot, leading interventions and safeguarding programming to reduce violent extremism and gender-based violence.

Ludovica Di Giorgi is Programme Manager at Moonshot, overseeing the delivery of insight projects and development of new methodologies to improve understanding of online harms.

Anastasia Filippidou is Lecturer at the Cranfield Forensic Institute, Cranfield University, and is Course Director of the MSc Counterterrorism. Her research and publications focus on terrorism, intelligence, and conflict resolution. She is the author/editor of *Deterrence - Concepts and Approaches for Current and Emerging Threats* (2020), *The Role of Leadership in Transitional States: the cases of Lebanon, Israel-Palestine* (2014). She has professionally engaged with a variety of governmental departments in the UK and abroad, including the Ministry of Defence, NATO, law enforcement and security forces in Lebanon, Palestine, Uruguay, Brazil, Morocco and Pakistan.

Paul Ford completed his masters in applied criminology at Selwyn College, University of Cambridge and specialises in police legitimacy and counterter-rorism research. Paul is the counterterrorism thematic lead for the UK Society of Evidenced-Based Policing and vice-chair of the UK Counterterrorism Evidenced-Based Review Group. Paul has over 15 years experience in coun-terterrorism policy writing. He is Member of the Security Institute, Fellow of the Chartered Management Institute and Fellow of the Royal Society of Arts.

Ross Frenett is Chief Executive Officer and Founder of Moonshot, a private company which carries out paid terrorism research on behalf of a wide range of clients, including US Agency for International Development, US State Department, UK Home Office, Public Safety Canada, Google and Facebook.

Carolyn Hoyle is Director of Global Strategy at Moonshot, responsible for overseeing programmes across different online harms, including violent extremism, disinformation, hate speech, human trafficking and child sexual exploitation and abuse.

Richard Jackson is Professor of Peace Studies and Director of the National Centre for Peace and Conflict Studies at the University of Otago, New Zealand. He is Editor-in-Chief of the journal *Critical Studies on Terrorism* and the author/editor of numerous books on critical terrorism studies.

Stephen Johnson is an academic, forensic scientist, military reservist and policeman with a record in providing strategic advice, training and education to government, armed forces, academia and industry on chemical, biological, radiological, nuclear and explosives (CBRNE), intelligence and forensics. Educated at Cambridge University and Cranfield University, he has received broad training across policing and counterterrorism, with specialisation in CBRNE. At Cranfield University he is Course Director for the MSc in forensic explosive and explosion investigation and runs courses and research on CBRN, fire and explosions, explosives and terrorism. He was recently appointed to the professorial committee of the University of Tor Vergata on their CBRNE Protection Master of Engineering programme, where he has also taught on explosives, CBRN and crisis communication.

Ashton Kingdon is Criminologist at the University of Southampton. She is also an Advisory Board member at the Accelerationism Research Consortium, a research fellow at Vox-Pol, a core member of the Extremism and Gaming Research Network and former head of technology and research ethics at the Centre for Analysis of the Radical Right. Her research is interdisciplinary, combining criminology, history and computer science to explore the ways in which extremists utilise technology for recruitment and radicalisation, while giving equal weight to the subcultural elements of the users of this technology. In addition, she examines the various ways history is being manipulated and weaponised to fuel contemporary extremist narratives. In addition to extremists' use of technology to recruit and radicalise, her expertise lies in analysing the relationship between terrorism and climate change.

Orla Lynch is Senior Lecturer in Criminology and Associate Dean of Graduate Studies at University College Cork, Ireland. Until 2015 she was Director of Teaching and Lecturer in Terrorism Studies at the Centre for the Study of Terrorism and Political Violence at the University of St Andrews. Orla's background is in international security studies and applied psychology; her primary training is as a social psychologist. Orla's current research focuses on victimisation, trauma and political violence in relation to the direct victims of violence, but also the broader psychosocial impact of victimisation and the perpetrator–victim complex. Her books include *Nothing about Us without Us* (2021), *Reflections on Irish Criminology* (2020) and *Applying Psychology: The Case of Terrorism and Political Violence* (2018, with Carmel Joyce).

Stuart Macdonald is Professor of Law at Swansea University's Hillary Rodham Clinton School of Law. He is Director of the University's Cyber Threats Research Centre and the lead organiser of the biennial Terrorism and Social Media Conference. Stuart has been a visiting scholar at universities in the US, Australia and France and in 2016/2017 was the holder of a Fulbright Cyber Security Award.

Sarah Marsden is Senior Lecturer at the Centre for the Study of Terrorism and Political Violence at the University of St Andrews. Sarah's research examines contemporary counterextremism and counterterrorism policy and practice, focusing on disengagement and deradicalisation processes. She engages widely with policymakers and practitioners in the UK and internationally, and her research has been funded by the Home Office, the Economic and Social Research Council and Public Safety Canada, among others. Her last book *Reintegrating Extremists: Deradicalisation and Desistance* was published in 2017.

Asta Maskaliūnaitė is Director of the Department of Political and Strategic Studies at the Baltic Defence College, a NATO accredited professional military education institution of the three Baltic countries located in Tartu, Estonia. She holds a PhD from the Central European University, completed in 2007 with a thesis that discussed the construction of terrorism threat in Spain. She has been focusing on terrorism and its study since 1999, paying particular attention to the development of the idea of terrorist violence, its definitional aspects and the role of theory in terrorism studies.

Samwel Oando is an Associate Researcher at the Institute for the Study of African Realities (ISAR) of the Africa International University (AIU), Kenya. He recently completed a PhD in Peace and Conflict Studies at the University of Otago, New Zealand. His thesis is entitled: 'Enhancing space for African women in tackling violent extremism: Engendering Afrocentrism in conflict transformation in Kenya'. His current research interests include gender perspectives and African voices in knowledge production, conflict transformation, peacebuilding and countering violent extremism. His publications include 'Peacemaking in Africa and Nobel Peace Prize 2019: Role of Ahmed Abiy Ali in resolving the Ethiopia–Eritrea cross-border conflict' and 'An

Indigenous African framework to counterterrorism: Decolonising Kenya's approach to countering "Al-Shabaab-ism"'.

Elizabeth Pearson is Lecturer in Criminology at Royal Holloway, University of London, based within the Conflict, Violence and Terrorism Research Centre. Elizabeth specialises in gender, extremism and countering extremism and was previously part of the team at the Cyber Threats Research Centre at Swansea University. Her European Social Research Council-funded PhD was awarded by King's College London and focused on masculinities and radical right and Islamist activism in the UK. She has also written on gender and the jihadist group Boko Haram. Elizabeth is Associate Fellow at the Royal United Services Institute and author of *Countering Violent Extremism: Making Gender Matter* (2021, with Emily Winterbotham and Katherine Brown). Before academia Elizabeth spent more than 15 years with BBC Radio where she worked in production, reporting and feature making, mainly for BBC Radio 4.

Daniela Pisoiu is Senior Researcher at the Austrian Institute for International Affairs and Lecturer at the University of Vienna. She completed her PhD at the Centre for the Study of Terrorism and Political Violence, University of St Andrews. Her research focuses on radicalisation processes, terrorism and extremism in Europe. She is the author of *Islamist Radicalisation in Europe: An Occupational Change Process* and co-author of *Theories of Terrorism: An Introduction*, among others.

Nic Rees is Design Manager at Moonshot. He studied graphic design at Falmouth University and is responsible for Moonshot's branding and ethical data visualisation.

Catriona Scholes is a former Metropolitan Police detective and current Director of Insight at Moonshot, overseeing the development of new methodologies and technologies to improve understanding of online harms.

Bart Schuurman is Associate Professor at Leiden University's Institute of Security and Global Affairs. His work has looked at contemporary terrorism and counterterrorism from a variety of perspectives, including the role of public support in determining counterterrorism success or failure, the causes of home-grown jihadism and the state of the field of research. His current research project studies the differences between individuals who radicalise to extremism but do not use terrorist violence, and those who do.

Ryan Scrivens is Assistant Professor in the School of Criminal Justice at Michigan State University. He is also Associate Director at the International CyberCrime Research Centre at Simon Fraser University and Research Fellow at the VOX-Pol Network of Excellence. He conducts problem-oriented interdisciplinary research with a focus on the local, national and international threat of terrorism, violent extremism and hatred as it evolves online and offline. In the past five years, he has published over 40 peer-reviewed journal articles, books, book chapters, conference proceedings and policy notes. He is the recipient of the 2022 Early Career Impact Award from the American Society of Criminology Division on Terrorism and Bias Crimes.

Harmonie Toros is Reader in International Conflict Analysis at the University of Kent, UK. Her research lies at the crossroad between conflict transformation, peace studies and terrorism studies, developing a critical theory-based approach to terrorism and examining the transformation of conflicts marked by terrorist violence. She has carried out extensive field research in Europe, the Middle East, Southeast Asia and Africa. She has advised numerous governments, international organisations (NATO and United Nations in particular) and international non-governmental organisations on non-violent responses to terrorism, particularly negotiations with groups who use terrorist violence. She trained as a historian before working in international journalism for eight years. She returned to academia in 2003. She has recently been named Deputy Director of the Institute of Cyber Security for Society at the University of Kent.

Joe Whittaker is Lecturer in the Department of Criminology at Swansea University. He is also a research fellow at the International Centre for Counter-Terrorism. Joe focuses on the online behaviours of terrorists and extremists, assessing the role of the internet in radicalisation. He also researches whether recommendation algorithms promote extremist content, as well as the deployment of online counternarratives.

Emma Ylitalo-James is a psychologist and visiting research fellow at Cranfield University. She holds an MSc in war and psychiatry from King's College London and a PhD in defence and security from Cranfield University. Her research focuses on the psychological drivers and decision-making processes of escalation from sympathetic to active violent extremist roles. Prior research areas have been behaviour and perception distortion in high-pressure, time-critical environments.

1 Contemplating a research agenda for terrorism studies

Andrew Silke, Lara A. Frumkin and John F. Morrison

Research on terrorism has come a long way. The past 20 years in particular have seen a transformation in research in this area. Yet, terrorism and counterterrorism have always been challenging subjects to study. Emotive and controversial, throughout the twentieth century the study of both lurked on the fringes of scientific research. There were few scholars willing to commit their careers to the area, funding was extremely limited and inside and outside academia there were plenty who questioned whether terrorism and counterterrorism were even appropriate subjects for scientific study, and questioned too the motives of any researcher willing to explore such potentially divisive issues. The attacks of 9/11 heralded a huge increase in political, public and academic interest in terrorism and counterterrorism. The 'global war on terror' and its various legacies dominated international politics in the opening two decades of the twenty-first century. Never before in history has terrorism and how it should be combatted attracted so much attention and controversy. The study of terrorism itself has been catapulted from academic obscurity to a subject routinely taught at most universities. Terrorism studies now produces an unprecedented level of research and writing, though the quality of a great deal of this still leaves much to be desired, often suffering from weak research methods, conceptual confusion and political bias. Yet, while there are certainly problems, overall, terrorism research is still remarkably vibrant and prolific, and amid a herd of mediocre studies in many areas there is a growing amount of high-quality research offering findings of genuine progress and insight. Overall, it is likely that future scholars will look back at this period as an important and transformational phase in our understanding of terrorism and counterterrorism, perhaps even as a golden age (Silke & Schmidt-Petersen, 2017).

Bearing in mind this rich and varied context, the need for an accessible and comprehensive overview on many of the controversial issues and challenges facing contemporary terrorism studies remains profound. This then is the motivation behind this current volume: to provide a wide-ranging overview of the current state of academic analysis and research on terrorism and counter-terrorism, as well as informed assessment of the future directions of terrorism studies.

When definitions matter and when they don't

It is a well-established trope that most books on terrorism research open with an exploration of the long-running definitional question. The definition problem has plagued terrorism studies from the very beginning, and a universally agreed definition of what constitutes terrorism has stubbornly resisted attempts to be pinned down. The reasons for the failure are well recognised, but this has not stopped several attempts to concoct a universal definition. Alex Schmid, for example, has led a prominent, career-long effort to identify a consensus definition (e.g. Schmid & Jongman, 1988; Schmid, 1992, 2011, 2012). He has come as close as any, though the final results have still not achieved the elusive consensus status.

Perhaps unexpectedly for a book focused on setting a research agenda for terrorism studies, we do not argue for a particular definition here. On the contrary, given that several decades have already been spent on a fruitless quest, we are much more inclined to recommend largely abandoning the search for a *consensus* definition. Resolution is almost certainly impossible and there is little to be gained in trying to convince readers of any one particular preferred interpretation. Rather than attempt to sell a definition, then, we are focused instead on selling the argument that researchers do not need to all sign up to the same definition. It is sufficient if they simply outline in their work what definition they have used.

Definitional ambiguity is a feature of many fields of study and is not unique to terrorism studies. As terrorism studies has discovered, definitional uncertainty is not automatically a barrier to the development or accumulation of knowledge. Haziness around conceptual edges does not have to impede scientific progress. On the contrary, it can be an indication of disciplinary, theoretical and methodological richness. This does not mean that no definition is needed but rather that researchers just need to be clear on what definition *they* have used in a particular study. Others can then judge if that focus means the findings are relevant (or not) in terms of frameworks they later use for subsequent work.

Consider, for example, research into the causes of terrorism. Different studies looking at causes vary in terms of how they define terrorism. This means, for example, that case studies which are considered legitimate for inclusion in one study are not considered relevant in another. One study might have a very narrow focus, only exploring instances of terrorism perpetrated by lone actors; another might focus instead on conflicts which could potentially also be regarded as insurgencies or civil wars; while a third study might be examining state-level use of terrorism. All three studies might in theory be looking at *the causes of terrorism* but what each means by 'terrorism' is very different. Inevitably, the studies come to different conclusions. Similar problems apply in terms of research on counterterrorism: exactly what type of terrorism is being countered? This is not always clearly spelt out with the predictable result that there can be confusion and mixed findings around what works and what doesn't. Factors which are identified as critically important in one case are entirely absent or have no effect in another. Thus, we have to be alert to how past research has defined terrorism, what acts and actors are included and what has been left out.

Although conceptual clarity is certainly needed at a grand level in relation to how terrorism is defined, it also applies in more applied contexts. For example, how research has engaged with the phenomenon of lone actor terrorism gives us an excellent case to consider. Much of the research on lone actors has focused on building datasets of lone actor attacks and/or the characteristics of the perpetrators (e.g. Clemmow, Bouhana & Gill, 2020). These datasets are usually based on information gathered from open sources including court reports, scholarly articles, autobiographical accounts and media news reports. However, there has been considerable variation between the datasets in terms of the criteria used to determine who counts as a lone actor terrorist. At the strictest level is the work of Hamm and Spaaij (2017) who uncompromisingly noted that 'a lone wolf terrorist does not conspire with anyone in their attempt to commit political violence. There is no second party, no third party or more. The lone wolf acts totally alone' (p.8).

In contrast, most other datasets apply looser guidelines than this and are often willing to consider dyads and in some cases even triads in their samples (e.g. Ellis et al., 2016). Some will also include perpetrators who have had significant contact and engagement with a terrorist group, including in some cases command and control links with that group (e.g. Kenyon, Baker-Beall & Binder, 2021). Spaaij and Hamm (2015) have criticised such flexibility arguing that it can artificially 'inflate the incidence' of lone actor terrorism making it appear more common than is really the case. They also flag that by casting a wider net for the databases, this 'can render invisible important differences and nuances that … policymakers need to keep in mind as they develop inter-diction and prevention strategies'.

There is evidence that Spaaij and Hamm are right to be concerned. For the most part, research based on the databases which use more flexible inclusion criteria do not report any differences found between the different categories of 'lone actors' within their samples. One rare exception to this trend has been provided by Gill, Horgan and Deckert (2014). Their database used a relatively broad definition of lone actor which included not just individual terrorists with no links to a terrorist group but also individuals who have command and control links with a terrorist group, and individuals who are part of what are termed 'isolated dyads', i.e. pairs of terrorists working together to plan and carry out attacks. The researchers admit that this did mean that some of the cases in their sample were then 'not technically "lone" actors'.

Gill et al. (2014) reported some significant differences between the lone actors who have no links with a terrorist group versus those who did have a connec-tion and the dyads. Notably, the individuals with no links were significantly more likely to have past criminal convictions and to 'be characterized as socially isolated, and have a history of mental illness'. Unfortunately, very few other studies using the more flexible definitional criteria have provided similar breakdowns, though it seems very likely that significant differences would still exist.

These experiences with regard to how different studies have examined lone actor terrorism give us a useful illustration of how definitions can significantly impact research findings, account for some important differences between the findings of different studies and affect the potential wider impacts of the research.

Ultimately, we are not calling for only one definition to be used across all studies. Whether we are dealing with high-level terms such as terrorism, extremism or radicalisation or more applied contexts such as with lone actors as discussed above, expecting or requiring universally agreed definitions or criteria is unrealistic. It is also unnecessary. Rather, the priority is to have clarity on the specific definitions and criteria used in individual studies. We do not have to have agreement across the field as to what each term means and applies to. Instead, clarity on what is meant within the context of each specific study will suffice.

The evolution of terrorism studies

As a distinct area of research, terrorism studies effectively first emerged in the 1970s. This was the decade in which the first journal devoted to terrorism research was formed. The research community overall remained very small and by the end of the 1990s there were still fewer than 150 researchers for whom terrorism was a major long-term focus of their work (Phillips, 2021). The area did however attract large numbers of transient researchers whose main interests lay elsewhere but who published one article on terrorism and then effectively vanished from the field never to return. This transient work, alas, was often poorly aware of the work which had already been done in the area and perhaps inevitably for the most part struggled to leave much if any mark on the state of knowledge and understanding of terrorism.

While initially small in size, the field has always shown an appetite for reflecting on the overall state of terrorism research and considering how this could be improved. Reviews carried out first by Reid (1983), Gurr (1988), Schmid and Jongman (1988), McCauley (1991) and Reid (1997) all highlighted problems with the state of terrorism research. Schmid and Jongman's (1988) review was particularly influential and their conclusion that most researchers were really not producing substantively new data or knowledge was quite damning (and largely also endorsed by the other reviews). As one respondent to Schmid and Jongman's survey bleakly assessed the situation, there were really only about five researchers who actually 'knew what they were talking about' and the rest were simply 'integrators of literature'. Their survey led Schmid and Jongman (1988) to conclude that 'there are probably few areas in the social science literature in which so much is written on the basis of so little research. Perhaps as much as 80 percent of the literature is not research-based in any rigorous sense' (p.179).

A review by Silke (2001) effectively found that Schmid and Jongman's bleak assessment continued to apply in the run-up to 9/11, but change did follow. While research before 9/11 was wallowing – starved of funding and limited by a small pool of committed researchers – one impact of Al Qaeda's attacks that day in 2001 was an enormous increase in both researchers wanting to seriously commit to examining the subject and, crucially, a major uplift in funding for terrorism research to match that interest. The result was an extensive and sustained increase in terrorism research in the decades which followed.

Not only was there a very substantial increase in research activity overall, a number of reviews which have followed have also found that the nature of that research has changed over time. In the first few years post-9/11 terrorism research was generally very similar to how it had been pre-9/11, though there were some subtle positive shifts (Silke, 2007). In particular there was an increase in collaborative research, an increase in more sophisticated statistical analysis and a small shift away from relying heavily on literature review methodologies (Silke, 2009).

Schuurman (2020a) found that those encouraging initial trends deepened over the next ten years. Reviewing research between 2007 and 2016 and casting a wider net than the earlier reviews, he found that the shift away from relying on literature review methodologies had continued and that terrorism research was now embracing a much greater variety of data-gathering techniques. Silke (2001) reported that literature review methodologies were the sole source of data for 62 per cent of research by 2000. Schuurman found that by 2007 this had dropped to 42 per cent and was down to 33 per cent by 2016. Statistical analysis was also more prominent, growing from a rate of just 19 per cent by 2000 to 28 per cent by 2016. This partly reflected the wider range of data which was available to researchers by 2016 due to a greater variety in methodologies.

Although Marc Sageman (2014) famously talked about research stagnating during this same period, the reality was that a combination of a wider range of methodologies and increased sophistication around data analysis were producing some very high-quality studies. Silke and Schmidt-Petersen (2017), for example, argued that instead of stagnating this period was witnessing 'a powerful renaissance period for the scientific study of terrorism'. That conclusion was based on a review of the growing number of high-impact, high-quality research papers which were being published, many of which were part of the trend for using the wider range of data-gathering methods and statistical analysis.

Nevertheless, some problems remained. The reviews all recognised that much research was still of mediocre or poor quality. Further, while the trends were generally heading in a positive direction, this was often coming from an extremely low base. Schuurman (2020a), for example, found that most research between 2007 and 2016 was still the work of a single author (just 25 per cent was collaborative) and most was still being produced by transient authors who published only one article in the field and then disappeared.

The picture looked a little better outside of the main terrorist studies journals which both Silke and Schuurman focused on in their reviews. Phillips (2021), for example, did a review based on a search of all articles in Web of Science with 'terrorism' or 'terrorist' in the title. He found that the average number of collaborators per article moved to 2.1 after 9/11 and stayed at roughly that level over the next 18 years. On the downside, Phillips' review suggested even more of the literature was the work of transients – perhaps as much as 83 per cent of the papers were from one-timers who would never again write on the topic. More encouragingly, he calculated that the overall number of more committed terrorism researchers had risen considerably from approximately 140 in 2000 to well over 500 by 2015. Commitment in this case was determined by the researchers having multiple journal publications with 'terrorist' or 'terrorism' in the title, a metric Phillips recognised was likely to significantly underestimate the true number of researchers actively engaged in and committed to terrorism research.

A research agenda?

As we think about a research agenda for terrorism studies, the first issue to consider is what are the questions that the field can and should focus on? The second issue is what are the research methodologies which can and should be used to provide answers to these and other questions? Ultimately, two key problems dominate terrorism studies and they can arguably be boiled down to first, why do people become involved in terrorism? And second, why do they cease involvement? Issues around the causes of terrorism and how it might be prevented, mitigated and resolved all at heart relate back to these two core questions.

The causes of terrorism have long been a source of critical concern to policymakers and of intense interest to researchers. Understanding the causes opens avenues to preventing the emergence of future conflicts and of safely diverting individuals from pathways towards extremist violence. It also offers the potential to mitigate the severity of ongoing conflicts and of possibly facilitating a resolution to violence. Recent decades have witnessed enormous research effort to identify the factors, processes and environments which drive radicalisation, and have produced a range of sometimes very different models and perspectives for understanding the issue.

Limitations with the available evidence, however, have had significant consequences in terms of theory and model development, most of which have traditionally been based on very limited empirical evidence. In 2005, for example, Victoroff warned there appeared to be more theories on terrorism and violent extremism than there were empirical studies and that almost none of the theories and models had 'been tested in a systematic way. They are overwhelmingly subjective [and] speculative' (Victoroff, 2005, pp.33, 38). Borum (2011) largely agreed with this assessment, noting specifically that for theories and models relating to terrorist radicalisation: 'each model remains underdeveloped: none of them yet has a very firm social scientific basis as an established "cause" of terrorism, and few of them have been subjected to any rigorous scientific or systematic inquiry' (p.37).

The advances increasingly noted in a variety of recent reviews of the literature suggest that the situation regarding evidence is improving (e.g. Lösel, King, Bender & Jugl, 2018; Franc & Pavlović, 2021). Yet, despite that progress, important questions still remain to be addressed. For example, researchers have repeatedly drawn attention to the specificity problem (e.g. Silke, 1998; Horgan, 2005; Sageman, 2014; Dawson, 2019; Schuurman, 2020b). This asks, why do only a few people radicalise when much larger numbers appear to have been exposed to at least some (and often many) of the causes? Alex Schmid referred to this question as 'perhaps the greatest mystery' facing terrorism studies (Schmid, 2013, p.31). Certainly its importance cannot be overstated. A perceived lack of progress in answering this question was the basis for Marc Sageman's (2014) famous cry of stagnation in terrorism research. In the long term, increasing our understanding of the specificity question could certainly help to prevent the emergence of terrorism overall and to identify better safeguards for those vulnerable to terrorist pathways.

We seem much better placed today to tackle these questions than before. As Schuurman (2020a) concluded after reviewing recent research trends in terrorism studies:

> In terms of the use of primary data, statistics, methods of data collection other than the literature review, and the degree of collaboration, there are signs of gradual and continuing improvement … Particularly in terms of the use of primary sources, these figures indicate that considerable progress has been made. From a field of study in which experts mostly talked amongst themselves, endlessly referencing books, articles, and media reports, the study of terrorism has developed to a point where a (slim) majority of articles do use primary data. Moreover, there is a steady upward trend in the use of such data. The lack of research based on primary sources, one of the most enduring and detrimental problems to face the field, finally appears to be abating.

With a fundamental shift in the nature and scale of research activity and analysis unfolding, terrorism studies is opening up fresh avenues for tackling many long-standing questions. For example, on the specificity question, one promising avenue for more research looks beyond the biographical backgrounds and contexts of the perpetrators of terrorist violence (who traditionally attract most effort) to also focus attention on those individuals who support terrorism but who do not become directly involved in terrorist offending. A resolution to the specificity problem depends not just on developing a better understanding of terrorists, but equally on developing a fuller understanding of compatriots who share many of the same traits, characteristics and contexts, but who did not progress to involvement in terrorism. Such work would finally allow us 'to bring to light what sets both apart in terms of personal background characteristics, involvement-process dynamics and the influence of group as well as structural-level variables' (Schuurman, 2020b). Growing recognition of the need for such insight has led to research increasingly scrutinising role variation within terrorist movements (e.g. Horgan, Shortland & Abbasciano, 2018) and also to consider differences between supporters, non-violent radicals and violent terrorists (e.g. Ylitalo-James & Silke, 2022).

In thinking about the research methodologies that can be used to help provide answers to these and other important questions it is worth reflecting on the multidisciplinary nature of terrorism studies. There will not be one methodological solution to the area's unanswered questions but rather multiple pathways to a better understanding. Some of these pathways will utilise well-established research methodologies while others will be more innovative in approach.

For example, a notable recent strand of research has involved using neuroimaging methodologies to shed additional light on the processes involved in radicalisation. Hamid et al. (2019) carried out a neuroimaging analysis of 30 male supporters of the militant group Lashkar-et-Taiba. This shed fresh light on the role of sacred values in radicalisation and confirmed findings from previous research using other methodologies which had identified that sacred values are resistant to negotiation. When an individual is making decisions in relation to a sacred value, the imaging showed that there was 'less activation of brain regions previously associated with cognitive control and cost–benefit calculations'. Thus the decision-making processes individuals display when sacred values are involved are not the same as those seen for non-sacred issues. Going forward we are likely to see more research using such innovative approaches which can help to shed fresh light and data on a wide range of issues.

A final point worth reflecting on relates to the issue of data sharing and transparency in terrorism research. Traditionally, the field did not have an impressive track record in this regard. Researchers were often extremely loathe to share datasets and attempts to replicate previous research were rare. In a context where primary source data was scarce this is perhaps understandable. It took considerable time and effort to gather such data, and that in itself made replication efforts less likely. The substantial increase in funding for terrorism studies has helped to change the landscape in this regard. Data have become more obtainable and many funders have expectations about facilitating data sharing and transparency which has also helped. A lack of access to data has historically been a major obstacle in terrorism research and the field's growing ability to test and retest existing research findings can only strengthen the quality of research in general and wider confidence in the reliability of findings which can sometimes have serious implications in terms of policy and practice.

Structure of this volume

The current volume is the result of a deliberate effort to pull together thinking, theory and methodologies in a broad agenda for terrorism studies. Given both the ongoing critical relevance of the subject and the sustained growth in research, we have tried to take a holistic and wide-ranging perspective to relevant research approaches, methodologies, theoretical frameworks and debates. While the final book is a fairly large volume (indeed, one of the largest within the Elgar Research Agendas series), we still recognise that it is not complete and more could be said on many topics. Nevertheless, we do hope the assembled chapters go some way in outlining a helpful framework for research in this area.

Part I of the volume focuses on some of the overarching perspectives which can be taken in terrorism studies. In Chapter 2, Sarah Marsden looks at those who carry out acts of terrorism. Within her analysis Marsden addresses the central questions of why people become involved in, and ultimately leave terrorism. This chapter considers what it means to be a 'terrorist', including a critical assessment of the contemporary dominance of a radicalisation-based understanding of terrorist involvement. As with other chapters within this volume Marsden emphasises the pluralistic nature of contemporary terrorism research, noting that there is no longer one dominant explanatory model of involvement in terrorism, even if much of this area of study seems subsumed by radicalisation. Marsden concludes the chapter by outlining how terrorism studies can and will benefit from methodological and theoretical innovation which can assist in driving research in new directions.

An often ignored part of terrorism studies is the analysis of the impact of terrorism on direct and indirect victims. In her contribution Orla Lynch examines the research that exists on victims of terrorism, including the assessment of the impact on interpersonal and intergroup relations, the damage to the sense of identity and well-being of society. To get the most holistic understanding of the impact of terrorism on victims Lynch looks at research conducted both within and surrounding terrorism studies. This analysis considers issues around the framing of victims and trauma while addressing issues surrounding victims' pursuit of a voice in the aftermath of terrorist violence. This chapter takes a psycho-social perspective to present an introduction to some core themes surrounding victims of terrorism and outlines core ways this analysis can and should move forward.

Within the twenty-first century one of the factors which has changed terrorism research most significantly is the emergence of critical terrorism studies (CTS). In their chapter, Shirley Achieng', Samwel Oando and Richard Jackson chart the establishment, impact and contribution of CTS over the past decade. The chapter highlights how the normative and analytical concerns of critical security studies have been applied to the analysis of terrorism over the past decade or so. This has led to the establishment of CTS. Within this contribution it is emphasised that CTS was developed in reaction to scholarly concerns about terrorism studies' perceived state centrism, pro-Western bias and complicity with violent forms of counterterrorism. While outlining the strengths of this approach to the analysis of terrorism the authors also clearly engage with some of the criticisms of CTS and helpfully chart what future direction CTS could take within its next phase of development.

Part II of the book is around the assessment of theory, methods and approaches in researching terrorism. This part starts with a chapter from Daniela Pisoiu on applying theory to research with a focus on the discipline of international relations (IR). It is argued that as terrorists are considered non-state actors, they tend to be excluded from IR research. This chapter notes that by considering terrorist organisations as those that act strategically, we can use IR theory to understand terrorism. The chapter then explores a number of IR theories in relation to understanding terrorism, borrowing from disciplines such as psychology, to further illustrate the importance of interdisciplinary social science research. There is a discussion about the role of popular culture in IR studies. From here, an argument is made that terrorism studies should consider the role of power, ideology and identity. The chapter concludes with the idea that IR of 'ordinary people' might be useful in trying to understand terrorism.

Is terrorism studies a discipline? Asta Maskaliūnaitė considers this and related issues in Chapter 6. 'Interdisciplinarity' features prominently here and it is also a term that reoccurs elsewhere throughout this volume. Interdisciplinarity is frequently praised as a concept, but Maskaliūnaitė highlights that true interdisciplinarity requires a high degree of integration between disciplines, either on methodological and/or theoretical levels. There are, she argues, signs of significant methodological integration but theoretical integration is much more poorly developed. Perhaps unexpectedly, she reaches the conclusion that in order to be a truly successful interdisciplinary project, terrorism studies should actually become more robust as a discipline in itself. This could allow more systematic theorising on the phenomenon, which could truly integrate various disciplinary approaches.

In the next chapters the volume moves to considering specific research methodologies in more detail. Ethnographic approaches have played a significant part in terrorism research and, in Chapter 7, Anastasia Filippidou examines the strengths and challenges of the ethnographic approach. She draws on her own fieldwork experiences investigating violent ethnonational conflicts, predominantly from the cases of Spain/Basque Country, France/Corsica, United Kingdom/Ireland and Israel/Palestine. She argues that ethnographic approaches can provide a very useful umbrella research method for terrorism studies, with the capacity to deal with a range of critical themes. A key recommendation is the importance and utility of a pragmatic empathetic ethnographic approach in researching terrorism and political violence.

Following on from this, in Chapter 8, Julie Chernov Hwang uses her extensive research with Islamist extremists in Indonesia to explore the role of guides when conducting interviews for data collection and the importance of working with ethics committees. She starts by considering how guides provide an 'in' for the researcher as the guide already has the trust of the community. Building on this while developing a researcher–community relationship is essential. The chapter goes on to describe the importance of trust when conducting interviews and how repeat visits with interviewees is a crucial aspect of rapport building. This allows the researcher to hear the person's narrative and gauge when setbacks and progress are made in collecting usable data. The chapter also emphasises the importance of working with ethics committees. Julie describes the importance of such committees as essential aspects of academic work by underscoring the importance of an open dialogue when developing and undertaking research on terrorism.

More and more terrorism research is focusing on online sources of information. In the first of two chapters which look at how such sources can be utilised in terrorism research, Ashton Kingdon and Emma Ylitalo-James focus particularly on the opportunities and challenges presented with research focused on social media. Social media has, alas, become a well-established virtual forecourt for extremists who seek to radicalise, recruit and disseminate propaganda. Social media research, however, offers a rich repertoire of methods through which to capture data to aid researchers in their understanding of extremist and terrorist activity. Kingdon and Ylitalo-James outline some key approaches including the use of online interviews, social network analysis, and open source intelligence, and assess the affordances and limitations of each. They argue that social media both necessitates and requires methodological innovation, specifically in relation to adapting traditional research methods and developing new ones specifically tailored to examining extremism in the virtual environment.

Chapter 10 tackles further how online data may be used by terrorism researchers to undertake their work. Stuart Macdonald, Elizabeth Pearson, Ryan Scrivens and Joe Whittaker consider three types of online data available for researchers. First, they look at machine learning and its use when considering the vast amount of data available to detect indicators of involvement in terrorism. Next the authors consider case studies and their use when addressing 'how' and 'why' questions. Given the difficulty of research with this population, case studies lend themselves to analysis of an individual terrorist's behaviour. Finally, netnography (an ethnographic study of online communities) is reviewed with the argument that it has furthered our understanding of radicalisation. This area of research considers the intersection of online and offline relationships in mobilising people towards radicalisation. The chapter concludes with a review of the benefits and weaknesses of these different online research methods.

The final chapter in this part examines the important role of databases in terrorism research. The proliferation of empirical research in terrorism studies has certainly been facilitated by the advent of a wide variety of databases. While these databases are of huge benefit to the advancement of this area of research they are not without their challenges. In their chapter, Stephen Johnson and Gary Ackerman look at the problems and solutions with a sample of databases. Within this they outline what they believe the metrics of a 'good database' are, highlighting factors around scope, transparency, error handling, consistency and availability. Following on from this they outline their good practice guide to utilising terrorism data. Their assessment of the utility of these databases will allow students and scholars of terrorism to approach their analysis in a thorough and systematic manner.

Part III of the book considers the controversies and debates around studies of terrorism. One of the most significant debates in terrorism studies in the last decade has been the stagnation debate kicked off by Marc Sageman in 2014. We have already discussed this earlier in this chapter, but Bart Schuurman dives deeper into the issues involved in Chapter 12. Schuurman has already provided some of the key evidence in the debate and he follows up on that here by focusing on the health of terrorism studies. The quantity of output, and the prominence that the subject obtained after 9/11, are contrasted with widespread concerns about its quality. This chapter provides an overview of the main issues of contention and how terrorism researchers' perception of them has changed over time. The discussion focuses specifically on several methodological concerns, including a long-established overreliance on secondary sources, and on worries over the degree to which state-centric biases have affected the field's research agenda. After years in which pessimistic assessments were prevalent, a more optimistic attitude has taken hold, spurred in part by more use of primary data and a broader focus in terms of research designs.

One of the most significant developments in terrorism studies over the past decade has been a revolution in how gender is considered, approached and positioned. One of the key researchers helping to lead this transformation is Katherine Brown, who in Chapter 13 explores how gender has been traditionally neglected in the field and what the benefits of the recent renaissance are already proving to be. She notes that feminist and gender approaches to the study of terrorism were largely sidelined by the mainstream of the field until the rise of Islamic State. When Islamic State started and sustained a strategic recruitment of women this forced both researchers and policymakers to rethink gender-blind and frequently sexist assumptions. In the chapter, Brown gives readers insight into 30 plus years of research into gender and terrorism, highlights core debates in the field and points to significant trends for future research in this area. She concludes with an admonition to remember that there is no one approach to the study of gender and terrorism.

In Chapter 14, Lara Frumkin and police officer Paul Ford address the benefits and challenges of academic researchers working with law enforcement personnel to consider good practice for countering terrorism. They start the chapter by reviewing the events of the London Bridge attack in 2017 and then discuss some of the recent progress made in working collaboratively following lessons learned from the attack. By building on positive working relationships and collaboration borne from tragedies such as London Bridge, a push for a multi-disciplinary and cross-sector approach is evidenced. The chapter highlights a growing trend of the creation of research centres supporting interdisciplinary academic and government projects while noting some potential stumbling blocks. The chapter finishes with a review of select common analytical practices used by law enforcement working on counterterrorism.

In their chapter, Ross Frenett and colleagues from Moonshot provide a detailed overview of research practices in the private sector. From the outset they emphasise that much of the research on terrorism will never appear in prestigious journals and does not originate from learned institutions. The majority of research is actually taking place outside of academia, carried out by government and private-sector analysts. Within their chapter they outline how they approach decision-maker-focused research and ethical safeguards in a client-centric industry. Within this they address the methodologies and processes utilised to produce the highest-quality rapid response research. They emphasise the importance of bringing in people from diverse backgrounds to enhance the work produced, alongside the importance of thorough risk assessment and risk mitigation processes.

Across this volume, and within this introduction, it has been emphasised that there has been a proliferation of primary data-led research in contemporary terrorism studies. With this comes ethical responsibilities. In the final chapter of Part III, John Morrison, Eke Bont and Andrew Silke talk about the ethical challenges and issues frequently faced in terrorism research. As part of the discussion, the authors discuss the development of the Framework for Research Ethics in Terrorism Studies. This was designed by the authors to assist researchers, ethics reviewers and ethics committee chairs in the development and review of ethics applications related to terrorism studies research. The authors challenge the readers to think critically about how we assess ethical risks. Within this there has to be equal care and attention paid to participants' and researchers' rights, safety and vulnerability. The chapter concludes by emphasising that when done properly the ethical review of research proposals should enhance rather than diminish the quality of the research.

The final part of the volume concludes with a chapter on the future of terrorism studies. Harmonie Toros explains why making future predictions for the field is difficult but we can explore aspirations for the field. She then illustrates the three research areas she hopes will be considered over the next several years. First, she presses for the need for interdisciplinarity in research. This is not for fields to borrow frameworks from other disciplines but rather to engage in long-term collaborations reaching across fields. Second is the aspiration for research to truly become global. This is particularly important as many of the terrorist attacks do not occur in the Global North but theory is driven by researchers living in it. Finally, an argument that terrorism studies takes a less central role to the study of insurgency is made. All in all, this chapter provides an insight into some new directions for consideration by terrorism researchers.

A research culture for terrorism studies?

It feels appropriate to end this chapter by considering the research culture in terrorism studies. Does terrorism studies have one? And if it doesn't, should it? Overall, we are not aware of any explicit discussion of a specific research culture within terrorism studies to date. But given both the focus of this volume and the growing overall size of terrorism studies, this is perhaps as good a moment as any to reflect on what such a research culture might be and what it could be.

Terrorism research has arguably entered something of a golden age marked by very high levels of output and a significant increase in high-quality research (Silke & Schmidt-Petersen, 2017). The number of researchers committed to working in this area has grown significantly compared to just 20 years ago (Phillips, 2021). There are other indications of a thriving scholarship, such as the now well-established Society for Terrorism Research, as well as the emergence of various bespoke frameworks for helping new and developing researchers to tackle a range of research challenges in this area (e.g. the Framework for Research Ethics in Terrorism Studies; Morrison, Silke & Bont, 2021).

These, and other welcome developments, are genuinely positive indicators for terrorism studies as a whole, though they do not mask that academic research and scholarship overall are facing a range of serious problems.

Indeed, there are growing signs of crisis in academia. This has been marked by widespread changes in the nature of academic research as a profession, changes which primarily seem to be heading in negative directions. Within the sector there is rising job insecurity, increasing use of short-term contracts (especially among early-career researchers), workloads which are becoming more onerous but which have been accompanied by stagnation or reduction in pay and benefits and national-level strikes are becoming increasingly common. Promotion and career progression opportunities appear to be more restricted and competition for the posts and funding which is available is intense. These trends have been especially marked in the United States and United Kingdom, the two countries with the longest history of terrorism research and which both historically and currently have provided the professional homes for most terrorism researchers. These wider trends have been associated with increasing dissatisfaction among academic researchers, growing levels of work-based stress and mental health problems, as increasing numbers of researchers burn out with apparently growing numbers abandoning academia entirely for careers in other fields.

As these pressures and stresses have risen, it is not difficult to find stories and accounts of researchers being the victims and targets of bad behaviour, including bullying and harassment. This can come from outside academia (especially given the focus of much terrorism research) but sadly also seems increasingly common within academic institutions. Certainly there seem to be increasing reports of bad behaviour by researchers themselves towards colleagues, external researchers and students. Sometimes this appears at least partly connected to a wider deterioration in the overall work environment, with growing pressure to secure stable employment and funding in an increasingly uncertain and competitive atmosphere, and where negative approaches, attitudes or working practices have become established and entrenched. The meltdown experienced at the Centre for Analysis of the Radical Right, for example, in early 2022, with mass resignations following the publication of a provocative blog, seems to have been at least partly connected to the organisation's working practices, processes and orientation. This case is discussed in more detail in Chapter 16.

There is a further perception that female researchers and researchers from minority backgrounds are disproportionately affected. Again, such trends are hardly unique to terrorism studies but the field has become much more diverse in the past two decades. In his recent review of terrorism research, Phillips (2021) noted increasing diversification among terrorism researchers. This included growing internationalisation of researchers, with a wider range of countries represented among the published researchers. He also reported a change in the gender of researchers over time. Pre-9/11, female researchers made up only 5 to 13 per cent of published authors. By 2015, however, this had risen to 30 per cent of researchers. Such diversification is very welcome and more is needed. Researchers being targeted, harassed or bullied on account of their background is not.

Although there has been a bleak feel to much of this discussion on culture so far, there are also promising signs. A review of terrorism studies social media, for example, provides many examples of positive approaches, engagement and conduct. Bad behaviour is increasingly called out by the wider community and not accepted. Norms and expectations around appropriate behaviour and interaction are repeatedly emphasised and are coalescing around several positive principles. These include fostering support and respect for diversification, encouraging and sustaining the work of female researchers and researchers from minority and underrepresented backgrounds. There has been notable improvement on these fronts in many regards, though some areas are still neglected. The Global South, for example, is not incorporated in the way it should be.[1] There is also growing recognition of the many challenges facing early-career researchers (especially important for those early-career research-ers who are in institutions where there is no senior terrorism research pres-ence) and how important it is to encourage and nurture researchers in what seems to be an increasingly arduous work environment.

The challenge going forward will be to capture and sustain the positive ele-ments and to continue to isolate and erode the more toxic traits. Twenty years ago a fundamental question facing terrorism studies was whether the post-9/11 surge would or could last. What type of future should the field aim for given the uncertainties around that increase? If the surge simply ebbed away terror-ism studies would revert to the shoestring existence of the twentieth century; as one of the editors of this volume once wrote, doomed to a peripheral existence in the cracks between the great academic disciplines. But the surge did not ebb.

Now, two decades later, terrorism studies remains a substantial and vibrant field. Questions around the future shape of the area can be approached with more confidence. The foundations for the future look promising and what is built now feels like it will still exist and have form in coming decades. The investment in such an endeavour looks worth it. In thinking about the culture that we would like to build today and leave to future researchers to inherit, fundamentally a culture which nurtures and values the many positive trends already flagged in this chapter, as well as others which will be highlighted in the coming chapters, represents an obvious way forward. The good news is that the appetite to do just this across the various researcher communities within wider terrorism studies seems very real. In many respects it already feels like the course the field is flowing towards (albeit with occasional detours and setbacks). There are worse foundations to build from.

---

[1]   It is perhaps telling that one of the chapters which we particularly wanted in the volume was to have been focused on terrorism research and the Global South and written by authors based there. This was one of the very first chapters confirmed for the volume but, alas, the contributors had to pull out very close to the end. It was too late at that point for alternative authors to be brought in. It is normal for any edited book to lose chapters along the way – and we lost others here too – but this is the one we regretted not having the most. The case illustrates something of the challenges at play and underlined that researchers based in and working on the Global South can face additional burdens and pressures on top of those com-monly faced by their compatriots in the Global North.

References

Borum, R. (2011). Radicalization into violent extremism II: A review of conceptual models and empirical research. *Journal of Strategic Security*, 4(4), 37–62.

Clemmow, C., Bouhana, N., & Gill, P. (2020). Analyzing person-exposure patterns in lone-actor terrorism: Implications for threat assessment and intelligence gathering. *Criminology and Public Policy*, 19(2), 451–482.

Dawson, L. (2019). Clarifying the explanatory context for developing theories of radicalization: Five basic considerations. *Journal for Deradicalization*, 18, 146–184.

Ellis, C., Pantucci, R., de Roy van Zuijdewijn, J., Bakker, E., Smith, M., Gomis, B., & Palmobi, S. (2016). Analysing the processes of lone-actor terrorism: Research findings. *Perspectives on Terrorism*, 10(2), 33–41.

Franc, R., & Pavlović, T. (2021). Inequality and radicalisation-systematic review of quantitative studies. *Terrorism and Political Violence*, 1–26. DOI: 10.1080/09546553.2021.1974845

Gill, P., Horgan, J., & Deckert, P. (2014). Bombing alone: Tracing the motivations and antecedent behaviors of lone-actor terrorists. *Journal of Forensic Sciences*, 59(2), 425–435.

Gurr, T. (1988). Empirical research on political terrorism: The state of the art and how it might be improved. In R. Slater & M. Stohl (Eds). *Current Perspectives on International Terrorism* (pp.115–154). London: Macmillan.

Hamid, N., Pretus, C., Atran, S., Crockett, M. J., Ginges, J., Sheikh, H., Toben, A., Carmona, S., Gomez, A., Davis, R., & Vilarroya, O. (2019). Neuroimaging 'will to fight' for sacred values: An empirical case study with supporters of an Al Qaeda associate. *Royal Society Open Science*, 6(6), 181585.

Hamm, M. S., & Spaaij, R. (2017). *The Age of Lone Wolf Terrorism*. New York: Columbia University Press.

Horgan, J. (2005). *The Psychology of Terrorism*. New York: Routledge.

Horgan, J., Shortland, N., & Abbasciano, S. (2018). Towards a typology of terrorism involvement: A behavioral differentiation of violent extremist offenders. *Journal of Threat Assessment and Management*, 5(2), 84–102.

Kenyon, J., Baker-Beall, C., & Binder, J. (2021). Lone-actor terrorism: A systematic literature review. *Studies in Conflict & Terrorism*. DOI: 10.1080/1057610X.2021.1892635

Lösel, F., King, S., Bender, D., & Jugl, I. (2018). Protective factors against extremism and violent radicalization: A systematic review of research. *International Journal of Developmental Science*, 12(1–2), 89–102.

McCauley, C. (1991). Terrorism, research and public policy: An overview. *Terrorism and Political Violence*, 3(1), 126–144.

Morrison, J., Silke, A., & Bont, E. (2021). The development of the Framework for Research Ethics in Terrorism Studies (FRETS). *Terrorism and Political Violence*, 33(2), 271–289.

Phillips, B. J. (2021). How did 9/11 affect terrorism research? Examining articles and authors, 1970–2019. *Terrorism and Political Violence*. DOI: 10.1080/09546553.2021.1935889

Reid, E. (1983). *An Analysis of Terrorism Literature: A Bibliometric and Content Analysis Study*. Los Angeles, CA: University of Southern California.

Reid, E. (1997). Evolution of a body of knowledge: An analysis of terrorism research. *Information Processing and Management*, 33(1), 91–106.

Sageman, M. (2014). The stagnation in terrorism research. *Terrorism and Political Violence*, 26(4), 565–580.

Schmid, A. P. (1992). The response problem as a definition problem. *Terrorism and Political Violence*, 4(4), 7–13.

Schmid, A. P. (2011). The definition of terrorism. In A. Schmid (Ed.). *The Routledge Handbook of Terrorism Research* (pp.57–116). London: Routledge.

Schmid, A. P. (2012). The revised academic consensus definition of terrorism. *Perspectives on Terrorism*, 6(2), 158–159.

Schmid, A. P. (2013). Radicalisation, de-radicalisation, counter-radicalisation: A conceptual discussion and literature review. *ICCT Research Paper*, 97(1).

Schmid, A. P., & Jongman, A. (1988). *Political Terrorism: A New Guide to Actors, Authors, Concepts, Databases, Theories and Literature*. Amsterdam: North-Holland Publishing.

Schuurman, B. (2020a). Research on terrorism, 2007–2016: A review of data, methods, and authorship. *Terrorism and Political Violence*, 32(5), 1011–1026.

Schuurman, B. (2020b). Non-involvement in terrorist violence. *Perspectives on Terrorism*, 14(6), 14–26.

Silke, A. (1998). Cheshire-cat logic: The recurring theme of terrorist abnormality in psychological research. *Psychology, Crime and Law*, 4(1), 51–69.

Silke, A. (2001). The devil you know: Continuing problems with research on terrorism. *Terrorism and Political Violence*, 13(4), 1–14.

Silke, A. (2007). The impact of 9/11 on research on terrorism. In M. Ranstorp (Ed.). *Mapping Terrorism Research: State of The Art, Gaps and Future Direction* (pp.76–93). London: Routledge.

Silke, A. (2009). Contemporary terrorism studies: Issues in research. In R. Jackson, M. B. Smyth & J. Gunning (Eds). *Critical Terrorism Studies: A New Research Agenda* (pp.34–48). London: Routledge.

Silke, A., & Schmidt-Petersen, J. (2017). The golden age? What the 100 most cited articles in terrorism studies tell us. *Terrorism and Political Violence*, 29(4), 692–712.

Spaaij, R., & Hamm, M. S. (2015). Key issues and research agendas in lone wolf terrorism. *Studies in Conflict and Terrorism*, 38(3), 167–178.

Victoroff, J. (2005). The mind of the terrorist: A review and critique of psychological approaches. *Journal of Conflict Resolution*, 49(1), 3–42.

Ylitalo-James, E., & Silke, A. (2022): How proximity and space matter: Exploring geographical and social contexts of radicalization in Northern Ireland. *Studies in Conflict and Terrorism*. DOI: 10.1080/1057610X.2022.2083932

PART I

Major perspectives in terrorism studies
research

2   Terrorists

Sarah Marsden

Introduction

This chapter focuses on those who carry out acts of terrorism. It cannot do justice to the depth and breadth of scholarship that has sought to address questions about how, where and to what effect people become involved in terrorism. Instead, what follows traces the evolving debate over why people become involved in, and disengage from, terrorism. This misses out a wide range of research on tactics, targets and strategies and the modalities, contexts and organisations implicated in terrorism. However, by concentrating on efforts to explain involvement in terrorism, a number of features of the research literature are revealed. The chapter reflects on these dynamics and considers their implications for future research in the field.

Discussion first considers the terrorist concept, asking what the use of the terrorist label makes visible and what it overlooks. The chapter then traces the evolution of efforts to interpret why people become involved in terrorism. Beginning with the primarily strategic approach adopted in the 1960s, discussion traces the debate about the role of individual psychology and mental health problems, going on to consider how these were challenged by rational choice approaches as the century reached its close, before the emergence of the radicalisation concept in the early 2000s. Since then, radicalisation has become the dominant paradigm for explaining how and why people become involved in terrorism. It has come to encompass explanations that consider the role of social networks and social psychology, and those which focus on ideology as a driving motivation, through to more recent multi-dimensional approaches. Exploring these developments, the chapter describes how the radicalisation construct opened the way for deradicalisation under an ever widening rubric of initiatives to counter and prevent violent extremism.

In tracing the evolution of efforts to explain why people become involved in terrorism, the chapter draws attention to a number of features of the evidence base. First, the field is more pluralistic than in the past. There is no dominating explanatory model, as there was, for example, with mental health or rational

23

choice perspectives. Instead, the field is characterised by vibrant research streams that take account of a wide range of theoretical and empirical perspectives, albeit much of it subsumed under the concept of radicalisation. Research on what causes people to engage in terrorism is developing greater methodological rigour and is increasingly data driven. Following policy and practice, research is heavily focused on individual, micro-level processes. Although the social embeddedness of terrorism is acknowledged in the literature, less attention has been paid to social-ecological, subcultural and cultural factors. This, in part, helps to explain why there have been relatively few attempts to integrate explanations across micro, meso and macro levels. There have also been only relatively modest efforts to test the range of models that have been developed in order to understand which factors or approaches are most helpful in explaining why people become involved in, or disengage from, terrorism.

The next generation of research has a range of new directions to pursue, some of which are described towards the end of the chapter. This effort will benefit from methodological and theoretical innovation, and by ensuring terrorism studies remains a space of interdisciplinary engagement, able to draw on and adapt theories and approaches from fields where the evidence base is more mature. In this way, the field will be able to develop more compelling and nuanced explanations about why, how and under what circumstances people turn to terrorism.

Conceptualising the 'terrorist'

Who is considered a terrorist is inevitably bound up in the definition of terrorism. Rather than rehearsing the definitional debate, it is perhaps more fruitful to consider what the terrorist label does analytically and how the boundaries of the terrorist concept have evolved, as well as reflecting on how the changing nature of the threat has shaped the ways in which research, and policy and practice, have approached the subject of the 'terrorist'.

One of the challenges of the terrorist label is that it can flatten out individual identities and characteristics by foregrounding the use of a particular form of violence. This can overlook the range of other identities and practices people involved in terrorism engage in. As well as terrorists, they may be mothers, brothers, employees or students, and belong to different communities and social groups. They may be central or peripheral to the production of violence. Individuals may fundraise, produce propaganda, write songs or focus on operational security. Although studies are beginning to refine our understanding of the 'terrorist', focusing on the roles that people engage in (Marchmont and Gill, 2020), and disaggregating between different types and trajectories of extremist actors, including non-violent and violent extremists (Knight et al., 2019), research often treats terrorist actors homogenously, not going far enough to differentiate between their motivations and behaviours.

In order to develop more compelling explanations about why and how people become involved in terrorism, understanding and differentiating between identities, roles and activities is important and invites judicious use of the 'terrorist' denotation. As Charles Tilly has argued, 'the terms terror, terrorism, and terrorist do not identify causally coherent and distinct social phenomena but strategies that recur across a wide variety of actors and political situations' (2004, p.5). Acknowledging this demands that research seeks, as far as possible, to understand the particularities that inform how different people come to engage in this specific form of violence.

Taking care with the use of the terrorist label draws attention to the appropriate boundary of the concept and how this has evolved. In more concrete terms, the question is one of defining the dependent variable. Do those who have been convicted of a terrorism offence constitute terrorists? Are those who are in the process of deepening their involvement in violent networks terrorists? Or is it only those who perpetrate violence that should properly be described as such? These questions matter for the purposes of academic enquiry as they tell us what to study and how. They are also central to questions of policy.

There is an increasing emphasis on the concept of extremism, a move which has widened the scope for intervention and legislation beyond terrorist violence. This raises the question of whether and on what basis to defend the boundaries of the terrorism concept and how to differentiate it from extremism (Bjørgo and Ravndal, 2019). Central to this analytical distinction is the question of when, how and under what circumstances involvement in extremism might lead to engagement in violence, and whether that violence is appropriately designated as terrorism. These issues have been given momentum, at least in part, by a focus on policies that seek to interrupt the process of radicalisation, which are themselves an important aspect of contemporary research. This chapter traces some of these debates and explores the evolution of research seeking to explain why people engage in terrorism over the last 50 years, drawing attention to the most promising new research directions and some of the challenges that remain.

Explaining involvement in terrorism: An evolving debate

Explanations for why people become involved in terrorism have evolved in different directions over the last half century. At the risk of oversimplifying a multi-disciplinary and dynamic research field, it is possible to trace how a series of contrasting approaches have dominated the debate at different times. The earliest iteration of work on terrorism stepped off from a wider body of research on counterinsurgency (Stampnitzky, 2013). Informed by this approach and influenced by the socio-political context of the 1960s and 1970s, early research interpreted the dynamics of terrorism from a broadly strategic perspective. With the increase in violence in Europe from those motivated by nationalist, separatist, extreme-left and extreme-right ideas, or what has been described as 'classical' terrorism (Wieviorka, 2020), researchers began focusing on terrorism as a discrete phenomenon that required its own explanations.

In an effort to explain why people carried out such extreme acts of violence, attention turned to the role of psychopathology. A number of researchers in the 1970s argued that terrorism's perpetrators must be mentally ill; motivated to join militant organisations because of psychological vulnerabilities, personality traits or because of a pathological desire to inflict violence on others (Weatherston and Moran, 2003). Over the coming years, there was a relatively robust push-back against causal explanations that centred the role of mental health problems. This was informed, in part, by a methodological shift towards collecting data directly from those involved in terrorism, providing first-hand evidence that mental health did not seem to be a primary cause of terrorism (Corner and Gill, 2015). Researchers went on to repeatedly emphasise the normality of terrorists (Crenshaw, 1981; Silke, 2003), arguing that those involved in terrorism were largely rational actors (Pape, 2006); there was no 'terrorist personality' (Laqueur, 2000); and that terrorism could usefully be understood as a strategic choice (Crenshaw, 1998), consistent with rational choice perspectives (Shugart, 2011).

From there, explanations focused more heavily on group dynamics and the role of social psychological factors (Post, 2005) and social networks (Wiktorowicz, 2004; Sageman, 2011), considering how peers and small group processes shaped the potential for violence. Researchers also considered wider structural causes, and there was an effort to identify the root causes of terrorism, with different research strands examining the role of socio-economic factors, social inequality, repression and demographic changes (Bjørgo, 2004; Newman, 2006). As the war on terror gathered momentum through the 2000s, explanations that foregrounded the role of ideology and belief came to prominence (Kepel, 2002; Juergensmeyer, 2009). Here, research sought to understand whether and how ideology motivated violence, what role it played in mobilisation processes and how it interacted with the range of other personal and political factors that pushed people towards terrorism.

More recently, the role of the internet and information communication technology has generated a significant amount of research, from earlier work that sought to understand whether the internet had become a 'virtual training ground' (Stenersen, 2008), and research that considered the propaganda and information-sharing opportunities the internet provided (Rogan, 2006), to research that borrowed from other fields to ask if online spaces should be understood as subcultures distinct from violent extremist organisations (Ramsay, 2013). Researchers have also considered the function that online extremist communities serve in sharing information and engendering support for violence (Bowman-Grieve, 2009), alongside ongoing efforts to understand the role of social media in mobilisation processes (Klausen, 2015).

As this brief review of the generations of research seeking to explain involvement in terrorism demonstrates, the popularity of different explanations as to why people become involved in terrorism has ebbed and flowed over time. Despite this diversity, over the last 20 years or so, explanations about why people come to use terrorism have become increasingly subsumed into the debate about radicalisation, and more recently still, the idea of extremism (Richards, 2015; Onursal and Kirkpatrick, 2019). This more recent body of research is increasingly pluralistic, encompassing a wide range of explanations, many of which echo previous generations of research. The field is also becoming increasingly specialised, with researchers working on ever more detailed questions about radicalisation, extremism and terrorism.

For example, contemporary research has looked with greater rigour at the role that mental health problems might play in terrorism, describing a complex picture that highlights the importance of interactions between mental health problems and other kinds of risk factors (Gill et al., 2021). Similarly, research is paying increased attention to the importance of social relations and socio-spatial settings in shaping extremist networks (Malthaner, 2018). Studies seeking to understand the wider structural factors or 'root causes' that might create the context for terrorism are deriving important insights into the complex, often non-linear relationships between terrorism and economic factors (Verwimp, 2016), repression (Piazza, 2017) and governance (Asongu et al., 2018), while the debate over the role of ideology in radicalisation and extremism continues to play out, with strong views on both sides (Kepel, 2017; Roy, 2017).

Research on the role of the internet is growing ever more sophisticated. Work is increasingly challenging the dichotomy between online and offline processes by observing how the internet is interwoven into daily life (Gill et al., 2017). This has led to the exploration of 'onlife' approaches which try to interpret how and to what effect people's engagement in extremism is shaped through interactions across online and offline spaces (Valentini et al., 2020).

This ever growing body of research on terrorism is characterised by an increase in quality and a more data-driven approach. Researchers are generating more primary data, using increasingly robust methodologies and deploying a greater diversity of methods (Morrison, 2020; Schuurman, 2020). Always a multi-disciplinary field, research in terrorism studies continues to reflect a diverse set of disciplinary approaches drawing on theories and methods rooted in everything from communication studies, history, sociology, criminology, psychology, internet studies, linguistics, theology, political science and international relations (Youngman, 2020). This informs the more pluralistic approach that characterises contemporary research, with vibrant bodies of work looking across the full range of explanations that have previously dominated the debate over what causes people to engage in terrorism.

Knowledge is also becoming increasingly well synthesised, providing a valuable platform for the next generation of researchers. Recent systematic reviews have catalogued the evidence on risk and protective factors in relation to violent extremism (Lösel et al., 2018; Wolfowitz et al., 2020); how mental health problems relate to terrorism (Gill et al., 2021); personality traits (Corner et al., 2021); the effectiveness of counternarrative initiatives in CVE programming (Carthy et al., 2020); the impact of exposure to online extremist content (Hassan et al., 2018); lone actor terrorism (Kenyon et al., 2021); the factors that inform radicalisation to violence (Vergani et al., 2020) and more. These studies and the wider commitment to better-quality and more robust methodological standards demonstrate that terrorism studies has come a long way in overcoming the challenges it faced in its early days (Schuurman, 2020).

Important questions remain across a wide range of research topics, some of which are discussed later in this chapter, but when tracing the evolution of terrorism research, it is also worth considering some of the broader dynamics that have informed the field. Efforts to explain who and why people come to engage in terrorism still largely track state agendas (Schuurman, 2019). Problem solving remains the dominant paradigm, and although the work of critical scholars continues to act as an important counterweight (Martini, 2020), this dialectic has not necessarily fostered the evolution of a more independent research agenda (Marsden et al., 2018). This is perhaps not surprising. Given its devastating consequences, researchers will inevitably share an interest in explaining contemporary terrorism and how best to respond to it. However, the structural reasons why research and state interests coincide, including the provision of funding which prioritises particular kinds of research (Richards, 2011), can have more systematic influences on academic priorities. Similarly, engagement between policymakers and researchers can have more subtle influences, shaping researchers' subjective perspectives and creating the conditions that privilege particular kinds of approaches to the study of terrorism and radicalisation.

From radicalisation to deradicalisation and countering violent extremism

A particularly prominent site of cross-over between research and policy has emerged in the context of the preventing and countering violent extremism (P/CVE) agenda, which aims to discourage involvement in, or support disengagement from, terrorism and extremism. P/CVE is intertwined with the genesis of the radicalisation construct, a common argument about which is the context it provided for early intervention on the path towards terrorism (Martin, 2021). By focusing attention on the process leading up to violence, a new set of questions and an alternative range of policy options came to the fore which have coalesced into a body of policy, practice and research on P/CVE (Stephens et al., 2021). A core feature of this work is the concept of deradicalisation, an idea which foregrounded the attitudinal changes that, if altered, are believed to reduce the risk of terrorism (Horgan, 2009).

Research on deradicalisation, disengagement and desistance from violent extremism has followed a comparable, if less high-profile, trajectory to work on radicalisation. Beginning with efforts directed at degrading terrorist organisations through arresting, incapacitating or providing inducements to their members, policies evolved to focus on ideology, socio-psychological support and community-based efforts (Silke, 2011). Tracing the evolution of counterterrorism and later counterextremism initiatives in this way illustrates an early emphasis on degrading violent oppositional groups through force, echoing the strategic logic of early policies. These were followed by a growing focus on bargaining and the provision of incentives to encourage disengagement, for example, in the context of the *dissociati* programme set up in Italy to encourage the Brigate Rosse to confess and reject violence in return for better conditions (Jamieson, 1990). Or efforts in Spain to support the 'social reinsertion' of members of Euskadi Ta Askatasuna who were willing to renounce their violent past (Alonso, 2011). The types of policies adopted in Spain, Italy and later in Scandinavia to deal with far-right extremism (Daugherty, 2020) followed a largely rational choice logic. States provided practical incentives to encourage people to move away from terrorism, often once a prison sentence had been served.

As Islamist terrorism came to dominate the agenda in the early 2000s, attention moved from practical support for disengagement based on an assumption of rational actors who could be incentivised to make different choices to a focus on the role of ideology. Much has been written about the exceptionalism with which particular religious identities have been treated in relation to contemporary security policy (Mandaville, 2017). One feature of this is the privileging of ideological motivations which saw the role of ideology become one of the central strands of research and practice on deradicalisation in the 2000s. Early initiatives in Saudi Arabia and Yemen (Boucek, 2008; al-Hadlaq, 2015) were joined by a growing set of initiatives in Western Europe, many of which foregrounded the question of how to address religion and ideology (Koehler, 2016).

Relatively swiftly, research and practice came to recognise that the reasons for engaging in terrorism, and hence the factors that might support disengagement, encompassed a much wider set of issues than ideology (Marsden, 2017). Emphasis shifted to consider the importance of peers and social networks, economic conditions and psychosocial factors on deradicalisation and disengagement (Koehler, 2016). Now there is widespread recognition of the individualised nature of these processes, and the importance of taking a multi-dimensional approach which considers social, psychological, ideological, economic and political drivers (Ellis et al., 2021).

In a comparable way to research on radicalisation, efforts to explain why people move away from terrorism have become increasingly pluralistic, acknowledging the need for approaches which can take account of the complex and dynamic nature of decisions to disengage from terrorism. To understand these processes, contemporary research has examined the push and pull factors relevant to disengagement and deradicalisation (Altier et al., 2020); the types of interventions that might support this effort (Zeuthen, 2021); who is best placed to carry out P/CVE work (Parker and Lindekilde, 2020); the barriers to disengagement (Jensen et al., 2020a); and what causes people to re-engage in terrorism (Altier et al., 2019).

Although not as extensive as research on radicalisation, work on deradicalisation and P/CVE is growing in strength. There are increasingly sophisticated efforts to address challenging methodological questions such as how to eval-uate P/CVE programmes (Baruch et al., 2018; Lewis et al., 2020). A greater range of theoretical perspectives are being deployed, including narrative-based approaches (Copeland, 2019; Graef et al., 2020); quantitative methods (Altier et al., 2020); comparative analyses (Webber et al., 2018); and the role of emotion (Simi et al., 2019). There is also a modest but growing body of theoretical and conceptual work (Kruglanski et al., 2014; Khalil et al., 2019). This evolving evidence base is opening up new, fruitful lines of enquiry which promise new insights into how and why people move towards and away from terrorism.

New research directions

In developing research on radicalisation and deradicalisation there are oppor-tunities to deepen existing lines of enquiry and open up new ones, both by drawing on theory and methods from other disciplines and in response to the evolving nature of terrorism and extremism. There are also gains to be made by more rigorous testing and, where appropriate, synthesis of existing models and approaches in order to consolidate the research that has been undertaken to date.

In a seminal article published in 1981, Martha Crenshaw argued that to develop more cogent explanations about the causes of terrorism, it was necessary to bring together explanations across different levels of analysis. Despite attempts to conceptualise the macro-, meso- and micro-level processes that inform violence developed over the years (Post, 2005; McCauley and Moskalenko, 2017), this call remains valid today and is echoed by Cardeli et al. when they argue that 'few studies of radicalization adopt a systematic and comprehensive approach to capture the dynamic interplay of individuals with their environment' (2019, p.4).

It is perhaps understandable why research has not yet met the challenge of developing more compelling multi-level explanations. There are obvious chal-lenges when seeking to develop a framework able to encapsulate the complex, dynamic and emergent processes that inform why people become involved in violence. Although the field is known for its multi-disciplinarity, integrating accounts that draw on often contrasting research methods, types of expertise and forms of data can be difficult. Hence, there are relatively few examples of truly interdisciplinary attempts to synthesise the different factors that shape involvement in terrorism (Youngman, 2020). This issue is made more acute given the comparative neglect of the social and ecological factors that shape radicalisation.

Although efforts to develop more compelling multi-level explanations are gaining momentum (Dawson, 2017; Bouhana, 2019), there has been a comparative neglect of the social contexts relevant to interpreting trajectories through extremism (Marsden, 2017; Bouhana, 2019), and efforts to interrupt or counter this process (Stephens et al., 2021). Existing approaches have paid less attention to interpreting the environmental or contextual factors that shape the risk of involvement in terrorism (Desmarais et al., 2017). Instead, they have been described as reflecting a 'strong form of methodological individualism where the ultimate explanation and arena for intervention and change are located in the individual, personal space' (Knudsen, 2020, p.44). As a result, there are numerous lists of individualised risk factors but few theoretically robust accounts of how they relate to wider social processes (Corner et al., 2019). Further work to develop and test conceptual and theoretical tools able to accommodate different levels of analysis is needed to produce more holistic explanations about radicalisation and deradicalisation.

It will also be important to invest more effort into empirically testing the array of models of radicalisation that have been developed over the last two decades (Borum, 2011; Hafez and Mullins, 2015). Doing so would provide a more solid foundation for the next generation of work by determining which models are most helpful in explaining radicalisation processes. Research is beginning to do this, by mapping out different pathways and the factors that seem to be relevant in explaining why violence emerges (Campelo et al., 2018; Jensen et al., 2020b). However, there is more to do to interpret causal processes and determine the most discriminating models and factors.

Part of the work to test existing approaches involves determining not just where particular risk factors are present, but when they are relevant. That is, going beyond aggregate analyses of the range of things that seem to be present in the life histories of those who use violence, to look in depth, using qualitative methods, to understand how and why particular factors, experiences or events are relevant (Corner et al., 2019; Gill et al., 2021). Doing so will move the field closer to addressing the specificity problem, that is, why, despite the apparent ubiquity of many risk factors, only some people become involved in terrorism (Dawson, 2019).

The same point about going beyond the presence to the relevance of particular influences can be made in relation to protective factors, or those things which mitigate or moderate the impact of risk factors. Before this can happen, more work is needed to develop the comparatively weak evidence base on protective factors (Lösel et al., 2018). Research needs to establish both which protective factors are reflected in the lives and contexts of violent extremists and how they work at the micro, meso and macro levels. Research has begun to examine the constraints on violence extremism at the subcultural and group levels (Ramsay and Marsden, 2015), by looking at the internal breaks that operate in militant groups (Busher et al., 2019) and by raising questions about non-involvement in terrorism (Schuurman, 2020). However, there is much more to do to explain why violence often fails to emerge from what might otherwise appear to be radicalising settings (Malkki, 2020).

It also remains important not to neglect how life choices and chances are informed by socio-cultural and historical events, such as experiences of discrimination, repression or the legacy of political violence. Given the increasing focus on often apolitical, individual-level risk factors, such as low self-control or mental health problems, in radicalisation research, asking this question foregrounds how political and historical factors are implicated in radicalisation. Taking this approach asks not only when and how certain factors seem important in explaining or understanding involvement in terrorism, but why people come to embody them in the first place. Research on the relationship between trauma and violent extremism is beginning to explore this question (Lewis and Marsden, 2021), by considering how individual and collective experiences of adversity might inform involvement in terrorism (Ellis et al., 2015; Rousseau et al., 2019), and how grievances might mediate community-level experiences of trauma and the path to violence (Siegel et al., 2019).

As the field develops, it will be important to track the evolving nature of extremism to understand the implications for research on radicalisation and deradicalisation. Some of the more contemporary dynamics that warrant attention include the growth of syncretic or idiosyncratic ideologies that combine features of different ideological traditions (Norris, 2020; Regehr, 2020). The increasing concern about far-right extremism and terrorism requires the field to consider what is genuinely novel in the contemporary far right, and what insights from existing research might help interpret its dynamics (Copeland and Marsden, 2020). The interactions between misogyny, hypermasculinity and terrorism require further attention from researchers, not least so that the concept of gender is extended beyond women in terrorism. This effort can include further analysis of Incel communities, links between the far right and male supremacism or the ways in which misogyny manifests in support for violent extremism (Diaz and Valji, 2019; Johnston and True, 2019).

There is a small but growing body of work on children and terrorism. This is particularly urgent in relation to children who have been exposed to political violence (Weine et al., 2020). However, given the growing number of young people becoming involved in extremism, and the ongoing need to understand the processes and outcomes of interventions that engage with young people, there is sensitive work to be undertaken to understand these dynamics (Vicente, 2020).

The role of information communication technology is likely to remain an ongoing preoccupation for researchers and practitioners. Despite rapid progress and increasingly sophisticated methodological approaches (Baele et al., 2020), a range of interesting and important research directions remain open (see Scrivens et al., 2020). Finally, the ongoing effort to problematise and critically analyse how the discourses and policies associated with radicalisation, extremism and terrorism are deployed by states, and to what ends, remains an important avenue of research (Jarvis, 2019).

Looking ahead to the research agenda for work on deradicalisation, there are parallels with the next steps for work on radicalisation, including concern with the role of social contexts in shaping deradicalisation and disengagement. Although people's social ecology, and how this might create the conditions that support or hinder reintegration and deradicalisation, is a growing research area, there is much to learn about how individual and social factors interact and to what effect (Kruglanski and Bertelsen, 2020). Promising lines of enquiry include building on work that has examined how exposure to norms and the diversity of an individual's social networks can impact attitudes towards violent extremism (Kaczkowski et al., 2020), and how community-level conditions might generate resilience to violent extremism (Grossman et al., 2020). More research is needed to understand the circumstances under which people might intervene to help someone they believe is at risk of engaging in extremism or violence (Puigvert et al., 2020; Thomas et al., 2020; Williams et al., 2020), while the opportunities the online space provides to intervene when people are seeking out extremist material is likely to remain a prominent area of research (Carthy et al., 2020). There is also more to do to understand how 'onlife' interventions might be deployed and to what effect (Valentini et al., 2020).

A broader dynamic that warrants attention is the process and impact of the internationalisation of the P/CVE research and policy agendas. Echoing the trajectory of harder forms of counterterrorism, where states, largely located in the Global North, have deployed force to pursue their security agenda, there is increasing momentum behind work that exports and embeds the P/

CVE agenda in different national contexts. The questions for research in this area are only just beginning to be addressed and revolve around how to bring research and practice developed in the Global North into dialogue with differing local and national contexts where the background conditions, such as commitment to human rights, political stability and state fragility, may differ. There is also a need to foreground the negative or unintended consequences of these initiatives given the increasing scope of the global counterterrorism apparatus (Aolain, 2019). The insights that can be derived from initiatives in the Global South in the North have also yet to be fully understood.

Conclusion

Charting the trajectory of research on why people become engaged in terrorism, this chapter has drawn attention to a number of dynamics including the increasingly rigorous and specialised nature of research; the growing pluralism of disciplines and research streams that make up terrorism studies; and the way the field has evolved to focus ever more on individual-level processes, and increasingly, on the precursors to violence by foregrounding the concept of extremism. The preceding discussion on future research directions has suggested some of the ways this body of work might evolve. There is much more to do to understand how and why people become involved in terrorism, and what enables the move away from violent settings. The more future research is informed by a reflexive approach to exploring new approaches and rigorously testing the utility of existing theories and methods, the greater the chance that this body of work sustains the momentum it has developed to date. In this way, the field will be better placed to consolidate an independent research agenda able to develop ever more robust and wide-ranging accounts of why and under what circumstances terrorism emerges.

References

al-Hadlaq, A. 2015. Saudi efforts in counter-radicalisation and extremist rehabilitation. In R. Gunaratna and M. Bin Ali (Eds), *Terrorist Rehabilitation: A New Frontier in Counter-Terrorism* (pp.21–39). Imperial College Press.

Alonso, R. 2011. Why do terrorists stop? Analyzing why ETA members abandon or continue with terrorism. *Studies in Conflict and Terrorism, 34*(9), pp.696–716.

Altier, M.B., Leonard Boyle, E. and Horgan, J.G. 2019. Returning to the fight: An empirical analysis of terrorist reengagement and recidivism. *Terrorism and Political Violence*, pp.1–25.

Altier, M.B., Boyle, E.L. and Horgan, J.G. 2020. Terrorist transformations: The link between terrorist roles and terrorist disengagement. *Studies in Conflict and Terrorism*, pp.1–25.

Aolain, F.N. 2019. How can states counter terrorism while protecting human rights. *Ohio Northern University Law Review*, 45, p.389.

Asongu, S., Tchamyou, V., Asongu, N. and Tchamyou, N. 2018. The comparative African economics of governance in fighting terrorism. *African Security*, 11(4), pp.296–338.

Baele, S.J., Brace, L. and Coan, T.G. 2020. Uncovering the far-right online ecosystem: An analytical framework and research agenda. *Studies in Conflict and Terrorism*, pp.1–21.

Baruch, B., Ling, T., Warnes, R. and Hofman, J. 2018. Evaluation in an emerging field: Developing a measurement framework for the field of counter-violent-extremism. *E valuation*, 24(4), pp.475–495.

Bjørgo, T. (Ed.). 2004. *Root Causes of Terrorism: Myths, Reality and Ways Forward*. Routledge.

Bjørgo, T. and Ravndal, J.A. 2019. *Extreme-Right Violence and Terrorism: Concepts, Patterns, and Responses*. International Centre for Counter-Terrorism.

Borum, R. 2011. Radicalization into violent extremism, I: A review of social science theories. *Journal of Strategic Security*, 4(4), pp.7–36.

Boucek, C. 2008. Jailing Jihadis: Saudi Arabia's special terrorist prisons. *Terrorism Monitor*, 6(2).

Bouhana, N. 2019. The moral ecology of extremism: A systemic perspective. Paper prepared for the UK Commission for Countering Extremism.

Bowman-Grieve, L. 2009. Exploring 'Stormfront': A virtual community of the radical right. *Studies in Conflict and Terrorism*, 32(11), pp.989–1007.

Busher, J., Holbrook, D. and Macklin, G. 2019. The internal brakes on violent escalation: A typology. *Behavioral Sciences of Terrorism and Political Aggression*, 11(1), pp.3–25.

Campelo, N., Bouzar, L., Oppetit, A., Pellerin, H., Hefez, S., Bronsard, G., Cohen, D. and Bouzar, D. 2018. Joining the Islamic State from France between 2014 and 2016: An observational follow-up study. *Palgrave Communications*, 4(1), pp.1–10.

Cardeli, E., Bloom, M., Gillespie, S., Zayed, T. and Ellis, B.H. 2019. Exploring the social-ecological factors that mobilize children into violence. *Terrorism and Political Violence*, pp.1–23.

Carthy, S.L., Doody, C.B., Cox, K., O'Hora, D. and Sarma, K.M. 2020. Counter-narratives for the prevention of violent radicalisation: A systematic review of targeted interventions. *Campbell Systematic Reviews*, 16(3), 1106.

Copeland, S. 2019. Telling stories of terrorism: A framework for applying narrative approaches to the study of militant's self-accounts. *Behavioral Sciences of Terrorism and Political Aggression*, 11(3), pp.232–253.

Copeland, S. and Marsden, S.V. 2020. *Right-Wing Terrorism: Pathways and Protective Factors*. Lancaster University and University of St Andrews, Centre for Research and Evidence on Security Threats. Available at https:// crestresearch .ac .uk/ resources/ right-wing-terrorism-pathways-and-protective-factors/

Corner, E. and Gill, P. 2015. A false dichotomy? Mental illness and lone-actor terrorism. *Law and Human Behavior*, 39(1), pp.23–34.

Corner, E., Bouhana, N. and Gill, P. 2019. The multifinality of vulnerability indicators in lone-actor terrorism. *Psychology, Crime and Law*, 25(2), 111–132.

Corner, E., Taylor, H., Van Der Vegt, I., Salman, N., Rottweiler, B., Hetzel, F., Clemmow, C., Schulten, N. and Gill, P. 2021. Reviewing the links between violent extremism and personality, personality disorders, and psychopathy. *Journal of Forensic Psychiatry and Psychology*, pp.1–30.

Crenshaw, M. 1981. The causes of terrorism. *Comparative Politics*, 13(4), pp.379–399.

Crenshaw, M. 1998. The logic of terrorism: Terrorist behavior as a product of strategic choice. In W. Reich (Ed.), *Origins of Terrorism: Psychologies, Ideologies, Theologies, States of Mind* (pp.7–24). Woodrow Wilson Center Press.

Daugherty, C.E. 2020. Deradicalization and disengagement: Exit programs in Norway and Sweden and addressing neo-Nazi extremism. *Journal for Deradicalization*, 21, pp.219–260.

Dawson, L. 2017. *Sketch of a social ecology model for explaining homegrown terrorist radicalisation*. ICCT Research Note. International Centre for Counter-Terrorism.

Dawson, L. 2019. Clarifying the explanatory context for developing theories of radicalization: Five basic considerations. *Journal for Deradicalization*, 18, pp.146–184.

Desmarais, S.L., Simons-Rudolph, J., Brugh, C.S., Schilling, E. and Hoggan, C. 2017. The state of scientific knowledge regarding factors associated with terrorism. *Journal of Threat Assessment and Management*, 4(4), pp.180–209.

Diaz, P.C. and Valji, N. 2019. Symbiosis of misogyny and violent extremism. *Journal of International Affairs*, 72(2), pp.37–56.

Ellis, B.H., Abdi, S.M., Horgan, J., Miller, A.B., Saxe, G.N. and Blood, E. 2015. Trauma and openness to legal and illegal activism among Somali refugees. *Terrorism and Political Violence*, 27, pp.857–883.

Ellis, B.H., Miller, A.B., Schouten, R., Agalab, N.Y. and Abdi, S.M. 2021. The challenge and promise of a multidisciplinary team response to the problem of violent radicalization. *Terrorism and Political Violence*, pp.1–18.

Gill, P., Corner, E., Conway, M., Thornton, A., Bloom, M. and Horgan, J. 2017. Terrorist use of the internet by the numbers: Quantifying behaviors, patterns, and processes. *Criminology and Public Policy*, 16(1), pp.99–117.

Gill, P., Clemmow, C., Hetzel, F., Rottweiler, B., Salman, N., Van Der Vegt, I., Marchment, Z., Schumann, S., Zolghadriha, S., Schulten, N. and Taylor, H. 2021. Systematic review of mental health problems and violent extremism. *Journal of Forensic Psychiatry and Psychology*, 32(1), pp.51–78.

Graef, J., Da Silva, R. and Lemay-Hebert, N. 2020. Narrative, political violence, and social change. *Studies in Conflict and Terrorism*, 43(6), pp.431–443.

Grossman, M., Hadfield, K., Jefferies, P., Gerrand, V. and Ungar, M. 2020. Youth resilience to violent extremism: Development and validation of the BRAVE Measure. *Terrorism and Political Violence*, pp.1–21.

Hafez, M. and Mullins, C. 2015. The radicalization puzzle: A theoretical synthesis of empirical approaches to homegrown extremism. *Studies in Conflict and Terrorism*, 38, pp.958–975.

Hassan, G., Brouillette-Alarie, S., Alava, S., Frau-Meigs, D., Lavoie, L., Fetiu, A., Varela, W., Borokhovski, E., Venkatesh, V., Rousseau, C. and Sieckelinck, S. 2018. Exposure to extremist online content could lead to violent radicalization: A systematic review of empirical evidence. *International Journal of Developmental Science*, 12(1–2), pp.71–88.

Horgan, J.G. 2009. *Walking away from Terrorism: Accounts of Disengagement from Radical and Extremist Movements*. Routledge.

Jamieson, A. 1990. Entry, discipline and exit in the Italian Red Brigades. *Terrorism and Political Violence*, 2(1), pp.1–20.

Jarvis, L. 2019. Terrorism, counter-terrorism, and critique: Opportunities, examples, and implications. *Critical Studies on Terrorism*, *12*(2), pp.339–358.

Jensen, M.A., James, P. and Yates, E. 2020a. Contextualizing disengagement: How exit barriers shape the pathways out of far-right extremism in the United States. *Studies in Conflict and Terrorism*, pp.1–29.

Jensen, M.A., Atwell Seate, A. and James, P.A. 2020b. Radicalization to violence: A pathway approach to studying extremism. *Terrorism and Political Violence*, *32*(5), pp.1067–1090.

Johnston, M. and True, J. 2019. Misogyny and violent extremism: Implications for preventing violent extremism. Monash University. Available at https://arts.monash .edu/__data/assets/pdf_file/0007/2003389/Policy-Brief_VE_and_VAW_V7t.pdf

Juergensmeyer, M. 2009. *Global Rebellion: Religious Challenges to the Secular State from Christian Militias to Al Qaeda*. University of California Press.

Kaczkowski, W., Swartout, K.M., Branum-Martin, L., Horgan, J.G. and Lemieux, A.F. 2020. Impact of perceived peer attitudes and social network diversity on violent extremist intentions. *Terrorism and Political Violence*, pp.1–19.

Kenyon, J., Baker-Beall, C. and Binder, J. 2021. Lone-actor terrorism: A systematic literature review. *Studies in Conflict and Terrorism*, pp.1–24.

Kepel, G. 2002. *Jihad: The Trail of Political Islam*. Harvard University Press.

Kepel, G. 2017. *Terror in France: The Rise of Jihad in the West* (Vol. 64). Princeton University Press.

Khalil, J., Horgan, J. and Zeuthen, M. 2019. The attitudes-behaviors corrective (ABC) model of violent extremism. *Terrorism and Political Violence*, pp.1–26.

Klausen, J. 2015. Tweeting the Jihad: Social media networks of Western foreign fighters in Syria and Iraq. *Studies in Conflict and Terrorism*, *38*(1), pp.1–22.

Knight, S., Keatley, D. and Woodward, K. 2019. Comparing the different behavioral outcomes of extremism: A comparison of violent and non-violent extremists, acting alone or as part of a group. *Studies in Conflict and Terrorism*, pp.1–22.

Knudsen, A.R. 2020. Measuring radicalisation: Risk assessment conceptualisations and practice in England and Wales. *Behavioral Sciences of Terrorism and Political Aggression*, *12*(1), pp.37–54.

Koehler, D. 2016. *Understanding Deradicalization: Methods, Tools and Programs for Countering Violent Extremism*. Taylor and Francis.

Kruglanski, A.W. and Bertelsen, P. 2020. Life psychology and significance quest: A complementary approach to violent extremism and counter-radicalisation. *Journal of Policing, Intelligence and Counter Terrorism*, *15*(1), pp.1–22.

Kruglanski, A.W., Gelfand, M.J., Bélanger, J.J., Sheveland, A., Hetiarachchi, M. and Gunaratna, R. 2014. The psychology of radicalization and deradicalization: How significance quest impacts violent extremism. *Political Psychology*, *35*, pp.69–93.

Laqueur, W. 2000. *The New Terrorism: Fanaticism and the Arms of Mass Destruction*. Oxford University Press.

Lewis, J. and Marsden, S.V. 2021. *Exploring Historical Trauma and Violent Extremism*. University of St Andrews, Centre for Research and Evidence on Security Threats.

Lewis, J., Marsden, S.V. and Copeland, S. 2020. *Evaluating Programmes to Prevent and Counter Extremism*. Lancaster University and University of St Andrews, Centre for Research and Evidence on Security Threats. Available at https://crestresearch.ac.uk/ resources/evaluating-programmes-to-prevent-and-counter-extremism/

Lösel, F., King, S., Bender, D. and Jugl, I. 2018. Protective factors against extremism and violent radicalization: A systematic review of research. *International Journal of Developmental Science*, *12*(1–2), pp.89–102.

Malkki, L. 2020. Learning from the lack of political violence. *Perspectives on Terrorism*, *14*(6), pp.27–36.

Malthaner, S. 2018. Spaces, ties, and agency: The formation of radical networks. *Perspectives on Terrorism*, *12*(2), pp.32–43.

Mandaville, P. 2017. Designating Muslims: Islam in the western policy imagination. *Review of Faith* and *International Affairs*, *15*(3), pp.54–65.

Marchmont, Z. and Gill, P. 2020. Psychological and criminological understanding of terrorism: Theories and models. In C.A. Ireland, M. Lewis, A. Lopez and J.L. Ireland (Eds), *The Handbook of Collective Violence: Current Developments and Understanding* (pp.100–111). Routledge.

Marsden, S.V. 2017. *Reintegrating Extremists: Deradicalisation and Desistance*. Springer.

Marsden, S., Zick, A., Malkki, L. and Schuurman, B. 2018. Radicalisation research: The state of the art. Paper presented at the Society for Terrorism Research 12th Annual International Conference, Liverpool.

Martin, T. 2021. The radical ambitions of counter-radicalization. *British Journal of Sociology*, *72*(2), pp.270–285.

Martini, A. Ed. 2020. *Bringing Normativity into Critical Terrorism Studies*. Routledge.

McCauley, C. and Moskalenko, S. 2017. Understanding political radicalization: The two-pyramids model. *American Psychologist*, *72*(3), pp.205–216.

Morrison, J.F. 2020. Talking stagnation: Thematic analysis of terrorism experts' perception of the health of terrorism research. *Terrorism and Political Violence*, pp.1–21.

Newman, E. 2006. Exploring the 'root causes' of terrorism. *Studies in Conflict* and *Terrorism*, *29*(8), pp.749–772.

Norris, J.J. 2020. Idiosyncratic terrorism: Disaggregating an undertheorized concept. *Perspectives on Terrorism*, *14*(3), pp.2–18.

Onursal, R. and Kirkpatrick, D. 2019. Is extremism the 'new' terrorism? The convergence of 'extremism' and 'terrorism' in British parliamentary discourse. *Terrorism and Political Violence*, pp.1–23.

Pape, R.A. 2006. *Dying to Win: The Strategic Logic of Suicide Terrorism*. Random House.

Parker, D. and Lindekilde, L. 2020. Preventing extremism with extremists: A double-edged sword? An analysis of the impact of using former extremists in Danish schools. *Education Sciences*, *10*(4), art.111.

Piazza, J.A. 2017. Repression and terrorism: A cross-national empirical analysis of types of repression and domestic terrorism. *Terrorism and Political Violence*, *29*(1), pp.102–118.

Post, J.M. 2005. When hatred is bred in the bone: Psycho-cultural foundations of contemporary terrorism. *Political Psychology*, *26*(4), pp.615–636.

Puigvert, L., Aiello, E., Oliver, E. and Ramis-Salas, M. 2020. Grassroots community actors leading the way in the prevention of youth violent radicalization. *PloS One*, *15*(10), 0239897.

Ramsay, G.A. 2013. *Jihadi Culture on the World Wide Web*. A&C Black.

Ramsay, G.A. and Marsden, S.V. 2015. Leaderless global jihadism: The paradox of discriminate violence. *Journal of Strategic Studies*, *38*(5), pp.579–601.

Regehr, K. 2020. In(cel)doctrination: How technologically facilitated misogyny moves violence off screens and on to streets. *New Media and Society*.

Richards, A. 2015. From terrorism to 'radicalization' to 'extremism': Counterterrorism imperative or loss of focus? *International Affairs*, *91*(2), pp.371–380.

Richards, A. 2011. The problem with 'radicalization': The remit of 'Prevent' and the need to refocus on terrorism in the UK. *International Affairs*, *87*(1), pp.143–152.

Rogan, H. 2006. *Jihadism Online: A Study of How al-Qaida and Radical Islamist Groups Use the Internet for Terrorist Purposes.* FFI.

Rousseau, C., Hassan, G., Miconi, D., Lecompte, V., Mekki-Berrada, A., El Hage, H. and Oulhote, Y. 2019. From social adversity to sympathy for violent radicalization: The role of depression, religiosity and social support. *Archives of Public Health, 77*, pp.1–12.

Roy, O. 2017. *Jihad and Death: The Global Appeal of Islamic State.* Oxford University Press.

Sageman, M. 2011. *Leaderless Jihad: Terror Networks in the Twenty-First Century.* University of Pennsylvania Press.

Schuurman, B. 2019. Topics in terrorism research: Reviewing trends and gaps, 2007–2016. *Critical Studies on Terrorism, 12*(3), pp.463–480.

Schuurman, B. 2020. Research on terrorism, 2007–2016: A review of data, methods, and authorship. *Terrorism and Political Violence, 32*(5), pp.1011–1026.

Scrivens, R., Gill, P. and Conway, M. 2020. The role of the internet in facilitating violent extremism and terrorism: Suggestions for progressing research. In T.J. Holt and A.M. Bossler (Eds), *The Palgrave Handbook of International Cybercrime and Cyberdeviance* (pp.1417–1435). Palgrave.

Shugart, W.F. 2011. Terrorism in rational choice perspective. In W.F. Shugart and F. William (Eds), *The Handbook on the Political Economy of War* (pp.126–153). Edward Elgar Publishing.

Siegel, A., Brickman, S., Goldberg, Z. and Pat-Horenczyk, R. 2019. Preventing future terrorism: Intervening on youth radicalization. In C.W. Hoven, L.V. Amsel and S. Tyano (Eds), *An International Perspective on Disasters and Children's Mental Health, Integrating Psychiatry and Primary Care* (pp.391–418). Springer.

Silke, A. 2003. Becoming a terrorist. In A. Silke (Ed.), *Terrorists, Victims and Society: Psychological Perspectives on Terrorism and Its Consequences,* (pp.29–54). Wiley.

Silke, A. 2011. Disengagement or deradicalization: A look at prison programs for jailed terrorists. *CTC Sentinel, 4*(1), pp.18–21.

Simi, P., Windisch, S. Harris, D. and Ligon, G. 2019. Anger from within: The role of emotions in disengagement from violent extremism. *Journal of Qualitative Criminal Justice and Criminology, 7*(2), pp. 3–28.

Stampnitzky, L. 2013. *Disciplining Terror: How Experts Invented 'Terrorism'.* Cambridge University Press.

Stenersen, A. 2008. The internet: A virtual training camp? *Terrorism and Political Violence, 20*(2), pp.215–233.

Stephens, W., Sieckelinck, S. and Boutellier, H. 2021. Preventing violent extremism: A review of the literature. *Studies in Conflict and Terrorism, 44*(4), pp.346–361.

Thomas, P., Grossman, M., Christmann, K. and Miah, S. 2020. Community reporting on violent extremism by 'intimates': Emergent findings from international evidence. *Critical Studies on Terrorism, 13*(4), pp.638–659.

Tilly, C. 2004. Terror, terrorism, terrorists. *Sociological Theory, 22*(1), pp.5–13.

Valentini, D., Lorusso, A.M. and Stephan, A. 2020. Onlife extremism: Dynamic integration of digital and physical spaces in radicalization. *Frontiers in Psychology, 11*, art.524.

Vergani, M., Iqbal, M., Ilbahar, E. and Barton, G. 2020. The three Ps of radicalization: Push, pull and personal. A systematic scoping review of the scientific evidence about radicalization into violent extremism. *Studies in Conflict and Terrorism, 43*(10), pp.854–854.

Verwimp, P. 2016. Foreign fighters in Syria and Iraq and the socio-economic environment they faced at home: A comparison of European countries. *Perspectives on Terrorism*, *10*(6), pp.68–81.

Vicente, Á. 2020. How radicalizing agents mobilize minors to jihadism: A qualitative study in Spain. *Behavioral Sciences of Terrorism and Political Aggression*, *14*(4), pp.1–27.

Weatherston, D. and Moran, J. 2003. Terrorism and mental illness: Is there a relationship? *International Journal of Offender Therapy and Comparative Criminology*, *47*(6), pp.698–713.

Webber, D., Chernikova, M., Kruglanski, A.W., Gelfand, M.J., Hettiarachchi, M., Gunaratna, R., Lafreniere, M.A. and Belanger, J.J. 2018. Deradicalizing detained terrorists. *Political Psychology*, *39*(3), pp.539–556.

Weine, S., Brahmbatt, Z., Cardeli, E. and Ellis, H. 2020. Rapid review to inform the rehabilitation and reintegration of child returnees from the Islamic State. *Annals of Global Health*, *86*(1), art.64.

Wieviorka, M. 2020. From the 'classic' terrorism of the 1970s to contemporary 'global' terrorism. In D. Jodelet, J. Vala and E. Drozda-Senkowska (Eds), *Societies under Threat* (pp.75–85). Springer.

Wiktorowicz, Q. Ed. 2004. *Islamic Activism: A Social Movement Theory Approach.* Indiana University Press.

Williams, M.J., Horgan, J.G., Evans, W.P. and Bélanger, J.J. 2020. Expansion and replication of the theory of vicarious help-seeking. *Behavioral Sciences of Terrorism and Political Aggression*, *12*(2), pp.89–117.

Wolfowicz, M., Litmanovitz, Y., Weisburd, D. and Hasisi, B. 2020. A field-wide systematic review and meta-analysis of putative risk and protective factors for radicalization outcomes. *Journal of Quantitative Criminology*, *36*(3), pp.407–447.

Youngman, M. 2020. Building 'terrorism studies' as an interdisciplinary space: Addressing recurring issues in the study of terrorism. *Terrorism and Political Violence*, *32*(5), pp.1091–1105.

Zeuthen, M. 2021. *Reintegration: Disengaging Violent Extremists: A Systematic Literature Review of Effectiveness of Counter-Terrorism and Preventing and Countering Violent Extremism Activities.* Ministry of Foreign Affairs of the Netherlands and RUSI. Available at https://english.iob-evaluatie.nl/binaries/iob-evaluatie-eng/documents/sub-studies/2021/02/01/literature-studies-%E2%80%93-counterterrorism-and-preventing-and-countering-violent-extremism/Rusi_Reintegration_disengaging_violent_extremists_202102.pdf

3 Victims and victimhood: the case of terrorism and political violence

Orla Lynch

Introduction

Terrorism is a highly contested, divisive and overtly politicised term. The *terrorist* is by extension conceptualised by incorporating these frames. However, terrorism is also a behavioural and communicative act, carried out by a range of actors, that can be understood by examining the context in which it occurs, and especially the surrounding social and political pathology and disorder that enables it (Blanco, Blanco and Díaz, 2016; Schmid, 2012). Terrorism is an act of theatre, the aim is to deliver a message. Brian Jenkin's maxim that terrorists want a lot of people watching not a lot of people dead sums up the fact that the audience for terror is not the victims, but the broader community or wider society. While terrorism is a profound personal tragedy for the direct victims, the survivors and their families, the impact of the trauma goes beyond those direct and indirect victims to have an existential impact on the communities it targets, and it can even impact upon the sense of identity and well-being of society more broadly. Interpersonal and intergroup relations suffer in the aftermath of terrorism when the attribution of blame is politicised, victims are politicised and guilt by association based on ethnic and religious identity becomes a malignant barrier to social harmony. For example, in the aftermath of the Bataclan attacks there was an ideological shift in the way minority groups were treated in French society, while the emergence of the so-called Separatism Bill opened the door for discrimination of non-Christian communities. In addition, the terrorist attacks shifted the balance between security and civil liberties towards the former, further extending the impact of terrorism on French society (Rubin and Peltier, 2017).

The catastrophic and dramatic nature of certain terrorist attacks is almost guaranteed to capture the attention of a variety of audiences in the aftermath of an attack (Schmid, 2012). This is due to the highly mediated nature of the phenomenon, the impact of social media as a platform to share personalised accounts of the violence in real time and the manipulation of social media by attackers (for example in the case of the Christchurch perpetrator), but also the fundamental nature of terrorism as a communicative act (Schmid, 2004). Terrorism, by its very nature, is about the omnipresent threat of violence, the belief that anyone, at any time, can be victimised. A probabilistic analysis of risk will point out that the likelihood of being a victim of terrorism is phenomenally rare but such an approach fundamentally misses the point (Global Terrorism Database, 2020; Shaver, 2015). The mere threat of being the victim of a *random* attack, of being in *the wrong place at the wrong time* and having no control over our fate targets our fundamental sense of safety and triggers emotional and ideological reactions in any population who perceives they are at *risk* (Butler, Panzer and Goldfrank, 2003).

Apart from the reaction of society to terrorist attacks, it is important to note that terrorist actors seek to manipulate social and political conditions in order to enhance the impact on their victims and wider audiences. In particular, perpetrators seek to manipulate the sense of risk. For example, regarding perceptions of risk, in the case of crime, a variety of factors impact on an individual's perception of risk of being a victim: age, gender, previous victimisation, socioeconomic status, etc. (Walklate, 2018). In the case of terrorism, the *threat* of violence is used to instil an omnipresent sense of fear in a population and increase the perception among an audience that they are at significant risk of violence. The infamous Provisional Irish Republican statement issued in the aftermath of the failed 1984 attack on the British Prime Minister epitomises the sentiment: 'We only have to be lucky once, you have to be lucky everytime' (Thomas, 1984).

By facilitating the belief that terrorism can touch anyone at any time, the perception of risk is skewed and a heightened fear is created. In recognition of this, the consensus definition of terrorism compiled by Schmid and Jongman (1988) includes both violence and the *threat* of violence as key elements. As well as the manipulation of the emotions of an audience prior to the perpetration of an attack, in the aftermath of violence, terrorist actors also seek to manipulate the victims and multiple audiences. They have been known to intimidate and threaten their victims and victims' families into silence, thus removing any recognition that the victims may receive, any support they might be entitled to and blackening the memory of their victims. For example, in the case of Northern Ireland, *disappearance* was used as a tool by paramilitary groups as a means of punishment but also as a form of community control. In many cases after the individual was disappeared, the paramilitary groups denied involvement, spread rumours about the victim, threatened and silenced the families. In some cases it was more than 40 years before families received confirmation that their loved one had been killed by a paramilitary group (Peake and Lynch, 2016).

The complexity and centrality of victims' issues for our understanding of terrorism often go unnoticed; victims are often treated as unfortunate collateral damage. In the field of terrorism studies, victims are considered exceptional and as a result isolated from the significant bodies of relevant work that exists outside of the field. In an effort to address these issues, this chapter will examine how the victims of terrorism and political violence (TPV) are impacted and understood by focusing on a few key issues. This work will examine how terrorism manipulates feelings of fear, our sense of risk, community relations, notions of innocence and social identity. By exploring the research that exists on victims of TPV both within and surrounding the field known as terrorism studies this chapter reflects on how victims and victimhood should be fundamental to our understanding of the impact of terrorism, but also our reactions and responses to terrorism. In addition, this chapter will explore the framing of victims, issues of trauma at a personal and community level and explore how victims of TPV seek to be heard in the aftermath of terrorist violence. Finally, this chapter will address narratives of victimhood and how they are relevant to the motivation to engage in and desist from TPV.

Research on victims of terrorism

Victimhood and victims' issues remain under-researched in the terrorism literature (Downing, 2019). While there is an entire field of study that focuses on victimhood (i.e. victimology), terrorism per se has never been a significant focus of this work. There is however a growing body of literature that focuses specifically on the impact of terrorism on victims and society. There are a selection of occasional papers (e.g. Hoffman and Kasupski, 2007), European Union reports (e.g. Lynch and Argomaniz, 2013), government reports (e.g. the Radicalisation Awareness Papers (RAN); De Saint Marc et al., 2016) as well as academic publications available (see Alonso, 2017; Downing, 2019; Fominaya and Barberet, 2018; Jupp, 2019; Lynch and Argomaniz, 2015, 2018; Madina, Bilbao and Bermudez, 2020; Morrison and Horgan, 2016; Parkin, Freilich and Chermak, 2015; Peake and Lynch, 2016; Weinberg, Pedahzur and Canette-Nisim 2003; Wilson, 2020). Also there are a range of autobiographical publications written by the victims themselves (see Dewilde, 2016; Knatchbull, 2010; Travers, 2007; Tullock, 2006). In addition, a substantial number of papers has emerged focusing on the medical and psychological consequences of terrorism, but these feature in psychological, psychiatric, medical and social work journals rather than terrorism-focused publications (Levav, 2006; Gregory et al. 2019; Eyre, 2019; Hersh, 2013; Blanco et al., 2016; Neria and Sullivan, 2011; Schuster et al., 2001; Updegraff, Silver and Holman, 2008).

While victims of terrorism have long featured in the literature on terrorism, peace studies, transitional justice and criminology, often subsumed under the label of victims of conflict, they have still received little attention compared to other topics and themes (Lawther, 2014; Rew, 2021).[1] Research on terrorism has been dominated by a focus on the perpetrators, along with our response to the perpetrators and their sponsors (Silke, 2003). From a victim perspective there are three issues with this relative neglect: it relegates the wider interpersonal context of the violence to relative insignificance; the impact of the violence on diverse segments of the population is unattended to; and the transgenerational transmission of trauma and the social conditions that allow the impact of violence to follow individuals and their descendants throughout their life is absent from any analysis (Braga, Mello and Fiks, 2012).

Recognising the wide-ranging impact of terrorism on the victims and wider society, Alex Schmid (2012) differentiated between the target (direct victim) and the audience (vicarious victim) of terrorist violence. However, recent research has shown that we should no longer be thinking in terms of this dichotomy, but consider victimhood as spreading in concentric waves from the direct to the indirect to the vicarious victims and to society more broadly (Updegraff et al., 2008). The impact on communities and societies should not be underestimated and this can be seen by the increase in support-seeking activities of individuals who were impacted but not direct victims of the violence in the aftermath of a terrorist attack (Eyre, 2019; Rew, 2021). This issue emerged in the aftermath of 9/11 when a significant number of individuals sought psychological support after witnessing (even on television) but not directly experiencing the attack on the twin towers.

Apart from the psychological impact of terrorism there are other aspects to victimhood that are highly relevant in the field of terrorism studies. Narratives of victimhood that underpin campaigns of TPV and dictate the boundaries that emerge between communities can create a transgenerational legacy of conflict (Pemberton, Mulder and Van Eck Aarten, 2018). While not advocating a simple relationship between victimhood and violence, the power of victimhood as a chosen trauma is highly relevant for the propagation of violence

---

[1]   For an overview of the literature on victims of terrorism see Price (2012).

across generations. Chosen traumas are victimising experiences usually relevant for a particular group that get passed down from generation to generation
and serve as unifying representation and in some instances serve to vilify specific out groups (Bar-Tal, Chernyak-Hai, Schori and Gundar, 2009). Similarly,
a recent study by Wilson (2020) examined how narratives of victimhood were
a *radicalising multiplier* serving to propagate and encourage the use of violence
by the extreme right. Brevik and Tarrant, the perpetrators of the 2011 Norway
and 2019 Christchurch attacks, respectively, both refer to western men being
victims, who are *least respected* in society and will suffer imminent decline.
According to Wilson (2020), this narrative of victimhood, perhaps more commonly understood as the Great Replacement or the Eurabian Conspiracy, is
converting personal grievances into political victimhood and inspiring waves
of deadly violence. This issue will be revisited later in the chapter.

The emergence of a discipline

Research on victims of terrorism is perhaps most closely conceptually aligned
with the fields of criminology or victimology, but to date it has received very
little attention from either. While for the past 80 or so years the victim has
been the focus of much research, predominantly related to crime, this focus
did not stretch to TPV. The academic study of TPV that was triggered initially
by the Oklahoma bombing by Timothy McVeigh and even more so by the
9/11 attacks led to the emergence of what is commonly called *terrorism studies*;
however, this field similarly lacked much focus on victims and victimisation.
In fact, the approach to victims and victimology that has slowly emerged
in terrorism studies over the past 20 years mirrors much of the ideological
evolution of victimology as a discipline and, problematically, many of the
foundational and now rebutted ideas in the field of victimology are alive and
well in modern-day terrorism studies. For example, the issues of victim pre-
cipitation, victim facilitation and victim vulnerability (Walklate, 2018) are still
visible in the literature on TPV, as are debates on the *causes* of involvement in
terrorism, specifically related to classist and racist societies as well as repressive
criminal justice/security systems (Le Vine, 2007; Rock, 2008). In addition, as
was witnessed in the criminology literature in the 1970s in relation to crime,
there is often a dismissal of the widespread fear of falling victim to terrorism,
labelling the fear as the result of a figment of false consciousness. For example,
we often see reference made to the greater likelihood of being attacked by
a shark or being killed falling out of bed than falling victim to a terrorist attack,
however, this approach misses the point. The very purpose of terrorism is to
cause fear to ensure everyone thinks that they may become a victim, that in the

process of going about their daily lives terrorism can strike at any point. If we consider the lasting impact of 9/11 on the American public, or the impact of the Bataclan attacks in Paris, they gave legitimate cause for the general public to be afraid; terrorism became an existential threat to their way of life and it was the dawning of the realisation that they could all be victims.

As mentioned, there is increasingly more attention paid to victims of TPV in the terrorism studies literature, however, when it is addressed, the victims are predominantly constructed as exceptional victims; exceptional in that they are *different* from other victims, that they are public and political victims, but importantly that they are *innocent* victims, individuals who were in the wrong place at the wrong time. In addition, victims and survivors are addressed in isolation from the context of their victimising experience. This is primarily due to the fact that much of the more recent literature focuses on the victims of *one-off spectacular attacks* rather than victims of terrorism that occurred as part of an ongoing conflict, but also due to the conceptual isolation of victims of terrorism issues from the literature on victims that exists in other disciplines – specifically criminology, psychology and victimology. Issues of particular relevance for victims of terrorism such as repeat victimisation, hierarchies of victimhood, competitive victimhood, politicisation, victim facilitation and social identity (Walklate, 2018) have received significant attention outside the field of terrorism studies, but less so with victims of TPV. In addition, the focus on *being in the wrong place at the wrong time* effectively focuses on chance and victim choice (e.g. routine activity) rather than the geo-sociopolitical issues of relevance, thus focusing analysis of victimhood on the individual themselves and their patterns of behaviour (Averdijk, 2014).

Developments in victimological research shed light on some of the problematic assumptions that dominate the literature on victims of terrorism. Perhaps one of the most common assumptions in the case of victims of terrorism is the issue of *innocence*, an issue that has long received attention in both criminology and victimology. The notion of innocence emerged as a desirable quality for a victim in the work of Nils Christie (1986), whereby he produced a theoretical profile of an *ideal* victim, one of whose main characteristics was that they were uninvolved in the events that led to their own victimhood but also had (vaguely defined) good moral qualities. In the case of terrorism, the issue of innocence is most likely to emerge when we talk about victims being in *the wrong place at the wrong time* and being a *random* victim of terrorism. Importantly, while this phrase implies that the individual had no control over the events that happened to them, nor had they had any *hand* in the violence that befell them, it does not imply an objective judgement but rather a reflection of broader societal bias and assumptions. Victimhood is not zero sum, but the issue of innocence is often used as a tool to disenfranchise sections of a population, to deprive them of the label victim and to create a hierarchy of victimhood.

In addition, the assumption of randomness is problematic. If we are to consider randomness as the likelihood that all segments of society are at equal risk of terrorism (Parkin, 2017) then terrorism is not random. Risk of victimisation from terrorism is related to among other things population density, attractiveness of the target and diversity of a population (Berrebi and Lakdawalla, 2007), but it is also related to an individual's identity, their group membership, their nationality, race and gender.

Another assumption in the literature is that victimisation is an event that is often sudden and unexpected, but this is not always the case. As with non-political violence, victimisation is not randomly distributed, and as mentioned, factors such as socioeconomic status, previous victimhood and routine activities are highly relevant in the likelihood that an individual will become a victim. Given the social and political conditions that some people endure (for example, living in an area of conflict or a deeply divided society) individuals can have an acute sense of risk regarding their likely victimhood. This is a significant issue in the case of terrorism both because well-being can be impacted *prior* to victimhood among those in high-risk environments but also because the nature of terrorism skews our perception of risk leading potentially to well-being impacts on a large segment of the population (Janssen, Oberwittler and Koeber, 2020) even without an attack occurring. In fact, terrorism *succeeds* exactly because it is able to project a threat without even having to carry out violence (Schmid and Jongman, 1988).

The exceptionalism with which victims of terrorism's experiences are treated is less to do with the impact of the violence on the direct and indirect victims, or the type of violence, and more to do with the definition of terrorism. We know from victimological research that the impact of crime, and particularly violence, is varied both between and within groups of victims (Shapland and Hall, 2007), and while there are risk factors that can determine the likelihood of, for example, receiving a clinical diagnosis of post-traumatic stress disorder (PTSD) after the attack (Janssen et al., 2020), there is no uniformity in how the violence is experienced. In saying that, there are commonalities in the experience of trauma across types of victimising events. The political or ideological motive of terrorism is presumed to play a role in the impact of the violence on the victim, but we know that the motive for terrorism varies from perpetrator to perpetrator and the role of ideology is variable. In addition, tactics used in terrorist attacks are often used in non-terrorist attacks, inflicting the same kinds of injuries. However, we also know that victims of interpersonal violence seek to make meaning from any attack, and making meaning for many victims involves understanding the how and why of the perpetrator and also understanding their role (i.e. victim selection, identity, etc.) in the overall event (Updegraff et al., 2008). This is where the communicative element of terrorism becomes relevant. For victims of (non-political) criminal acts, if a simplistic comparison can be made, while experiencing the same violence, they do not necessarily have a political frame that informs their experience quite so dramatically. For example, the victims of the terrorist attacks in Nice in November 2020 were almost instantly situated as victims of a *war* between France and Islamic extremists. As Neumann stated, 'the victims aren't yet cold and Le Pen is talking about the need for a war' (Neumann, 2020). This framework explains target selection, ideology motive, etc., thus serving to give a very specific meaning to the event at both the individual and societal levels.

The question then becomes how we should think about the impact of terrorism on victims and survivors and how it compares to other traumatic experiences. Research from the field of victimology acknowledges that the experience of victimisation is comparable with the incidence of other traumatic life events, however, the issue of *malign* intent is a marker of difference (Green and Pemberton, 2018) for victims of interpersonal violence. It has been suggested that malign intent makes the experience of being a victim qualitatively different due to the fact that someone is deliberately harming the victim (Green and Pemberton, 2018; Shapland and Hall, 2007). This has a particular relevance for the emotional impact on victims, particularly in terms of trust, and a lack of trust in a community or parts of society (Shapland and Hall, 2007). However, despite, or perhaps in spite of, the malign intent, meaning making is a key factor in how individuals cope with terrorism. In the context of personal trauma, while the violence poses a challenge to an individual's assumptive world (Updegraff et al., 2008), finding meaning in the event allows some individuals to reconcile a traumatic event with their worldview. Somewhat ironically, the complex and comprehensive narratives that explain terrorism may play a role in the meaning-making processes for victims in the aftermath of an attack.

Terrorism and trauma

Trauma and victimisation are not the same concepts but are often used interchangeably. Victimisation, in the criminological sense, is most often used to refer to the process of becoming a victim of a criminal act (Walklate, 2018). However, this definition has expanded to include the notion of harm, as many acts that cause harm are not necessarily criminal (Green and Pemberton, 2018). In addition, and relevant in the case of TPV, often actions of the powerful, e.g. the state, are not defined as criminal, yet still may be profoundly harmful. Trauma on the other hand is the reaction to being victimised, or more generally, the reaction to a deeply distressing event. In the literature it is mostly irrelevant what the nature of the experience is as the focus is on the psychological reaction to the event.

The impact of TPV on individuals is primarily understood through the lens of psychological trauma, be that via direct or indirect victimisation. Of course, the experiences of victims and their families are in no way uniform and reactions to terrorist violence vary between and within groups and across the lifespan, but it goes without saying that the consequences of terrorist violence are all encompassing. Devastating physical injuries are commonplace, as are long-term health implications, financial struggles and unmet complex medical needs often being the norm.

In the literature, the experience of victimisation is defined depending on the varying degrees of separation from the violence: primary victimisation (direct experience), secondary victimisation (family/friends of primary victims) and tertiary victims (first-line responders, witnesses) (Erez, 2006). As mentioned, the issue of indirect (or tertiary) victimisation has received significant attention, particularly since the September 2001 Al Qaeda attacks in the United States, given the significant number of witnesses on the ground at the attack sites and the highly mediated nature of the violence. The impact of witnessing the violence on television had a significant impact on the population and led to large numbers of indirect witnesses reporting PTSD symptoms (Neria and Sullivan, 2011). For example, in the aftermath of 9/11, Schuster et al. (2001) reported that nearly half of Americans reported symptoms of post-traumatic stress, demonstrating that the effects of the attack caused psychological problems far beyond the primary and secondary victims. This was similarly evidenced in the aftermath of the Paris Islamic State-led attacks of 2015 (Bartholomew, 2016). In terms of clinical symptomology, vicarious or tertiary victimisation is not just something that occurs in the case of terrorist violence, and the potential impact of exposure to extremely violent events was recognised in the latest iteration of the *Diagnostic and Statistical Manual*. In 2018 there was a shift in the criteria recognised as contributing to trauma-related conditions, and in the newest edition of the *Manual indirect* exposure via a friend or family member to trauma is a criterion in the diagnosis of trauma-related mental disorders (Bajo et al., 2018).

For terrorist violence, arguably one of the most mediated events in current times, the impact of the indirect experience of terrorism has implications for the reach of the terrorist message and its impact on the broader population. While *mediated* indirect exposure is not included as a specific diagnostic criteria, research has demonstrated the impact of exposure to such violence via mainstream and social media (Bajo et al., 2018). However, while clinical disorders such as PTSD are more prevalent among the population directly exposed to the violence, the broader impact on the general population cannot be ignored.

While not advocating that we are all victims based on our indirect exposure to violence, understanding the experience of tertiary and vicarious victimhood is essential to understanding the impact of terrorism on individuals and society more generally. And while indirect exposure to terrorism is seen as a significant issue for mental health and well-being, and given that events that induce a feeling of threat to one's own life are a major element of trauma reactions, understanding the underlying processes caused by indirect exposure to terrorism will help us understand the impact of terrorism and, relatedly, our political, social and psychological reactions to TPV at an individual and a group level.

The experience of terrorism should also be understood as a community or group phenomenon. When a victim is explicitly chosen because of their identity, communities may experience vicarious trauma, leading to increased in-group solidarity and allegiance to the group and an increased sense of risk leading to a reduction in well-being (Muldoon et al., 2019). Of course the experience of trauma at the individual and group levels is not directly comparable, but they are interlinked. In addition, issues such as the type of injury, the duration of the violence (acute versus chronic) and existing conceptions of victimhood are all relevant and there are within-group differences in how people react. Importantly, the concept of the layering of trauma is also relevant, and this refers to the person, community and social aspects of trauma that can simultaneously exist for individuals (UNODC, 2018). This notion of trauma layering can be better understood by reference to the concept on intersectionality whereby existing social political gender economic and racial structures are all relevant in how we understand the impact of TPV on societies and communities (Auer, Sutcliffe and Lee, 2019). Taking this concept of intersectionality, trauma manifests itself as a reflection of the individual history of the victim, their personal and family experiences and the societal implications of their identity and affiliations.

Terrorism and clinical conditions

Trauma from TPV is a profoundly personal experience, and not everyone experiences trauma, or experiences it in the same way. However, as mentioned the experience of being a victim of terrorism cannot be understood in isolation from the context in which it happens. It is important to remember that only a minority of people who experience terrorism go on to have a clinical diagnosis, e.g. PTSD, and while many people may experience short-term trauma symptoms, they mostly diminish without intervention. But that does not mean that being a victim of terrorism does not fundamentally change the social and psychological landscape for the individual victims, their families and those who rescue and support them. The impact of terrorism can cause lifelong injury, physical, social, psychological and existential that may not be reflected in a clinical diagnosis. For indirect victims, even fewer individuals go on to receive a trauma-related diagnosis, but the impact can still be significant and lifelong (Blanco et al. 2016).

Blanco et al. (2016) have developed a framework that focuses on the relevance of the different vulnerabilities, experiences and personal histories of victims of terrorism and highlight how intertwined the psychological experiences are with the environmental conditions that exist before and after the violence. These experiences are summed up in the literature as *well-being*, and research on trauma from other domains has pointed to the importance of well-being *pre-victimisation* for understanding well-being *post-victimisation*. Blanco et al. (2016) point out that man-made stressors such as poverty, inequality, persecution and exclusion are pre-trauma conditions that have implications for both the risk factor for clinical diagnosis of trauma-related conditions as well as long-term injury at all psycho-social levels. This is tied to the existence of adaptive and protective systems that are available to victims from family, community government etc. (Muldoon et al. 2019). In the case of terrorism this has serious implications for individuals who are victimised by terrorism as part of an ongoing conflict given the conditions they may endure pre-victimisation, but also for those living in a climate of fear where the terrorist threat is made relevant for everyday life.

Voices of victims

Victims of conflict and political violence over the past 30 years have achieved increasing visibility and victims and victim groups have sought to have a voice in efforts to address issues of memorialisation, compensation, policy, medical needs and also violence-prevention initiatives (Hoffman and Kasupski, 2007; Updegraff et al., 2008). However, as might be expected, the voices of victims are not all treated equally. This is largely due to the legalistic perspective that has dominated research on victims. This legalistic perspective takes the identity category of victim as *given*, one is either a victim or not a victim – it is a zero-sum situation. However, the issue of victimhood is, in circumstances of divided societies and conflict or post-conflict societies, political and politicised. In fact, victimhood is politicised even outside of conflict or post-conflict societies (Downing, 2019). Who is a victim is not self-evident. This recently played out, and in fact is still playing out, in Northern Ireland where a pension for victims of the Troubles has been held up for a number of years due to the inclusion or exclusion of individuals who were members of paramilitary organisations, or who were suspected of involvement in paramilitary activity (Moffett, 2016; O Neill, 2020). The fact of being both a victim and a perpetrator is not easily overcome. In situations like Northern Ireland, Colombia and Sri Lanka, *innocence* becomes an exclusionary and politicised concept. It is particularly relevant in the case of abductions and children being forced into violence on behalf of paramilitary groups. In transitioning societies, these victims' issues can be hugely relevant for progress, peace and stability (Lawther, 2014). But even in peaceful societies, victimhood can challenge how we construct the in group and the out group. Downing (2019) has pointed out that for Muslim victims of jihadi attacks in Europe identity lines are blurred and there emerges a good victim/bad victim dichotomy.

Activism in the aftermath of a terrorist attack often emerges in the form of victim support groups lobbying for specific needs. These groups are often linked to particular attacks (e.g. the Leopold café support group in the aftermath of the Mumbai shootings; Lynch and Argomaniz, 2015) or serve a particular area (e.g. Wave Trauma Centre, Belfast, Northern Ireland). Groups also emerge at the national and regional levels. For example, for the past ten years, the Radicalisation Awareness Network (RAN) of the European Commission working group on victims of terrorism has served as a networking and support organisation for European victims of terrorism organisations. This network has given voice to victims as individuals and as group members and has brought the issue of victims of terrorism into the spotlight, both in terms of the impact of terrorism but also regarding the role that victims can have in countering violent extremism (CVE) and preventing violent extremism (PVE) initiatives. The RAN explicitly speaks to the politicisation of victims of terrorism by recognising their *role* in defending democratic values as the antithesis of terrorism and advocating for victims' roles in CVE initiatives, especially through the use of the testimonies of survivors. This of course brings up issues of voice and visibility for victims of state terrorism or state-sponsored terrorism and is a theme that plays out globally. The issue of a hierarchy of victimhood often emerges in such circumstances where some victims are seen to be attended to more readily than others. An example is an initiative set up in the aftermath of the Warrington bombings in 1993 where an Irish women, Susan McHugh, organised a peace march in support of the victims, both of whom were children: Tim Parry and Jonathan Ball. A large rally was held in support of calls for peace, but it was remarked that the child victims of state and paramilitary groups killed around the same time in Northern Ireland did not enjoy such public recognition or support.

Outside of the European Union, victims' lobby groups have been active in many jurisdictions seeking policy change, support for victims and survivors, reparations and recognition and justice. This was evidenced in the case of the 9/11 survivors and families as they were exceptionally active in influenc-ing policy and internal affairs in the aftermath of the attack (Hersh, 2013). Along with national and international initiatives there are also a number of well-known events and programmes that practise restorative methods at a per-sonal and community level. An example of this is the public meeting of Martin McGuinness with Colin Parry, the father of Provisional Irish Republican Army victim Tim Parry at an event in Warrington in 2013 (O'Carroll, 2013). Similarly, the father of a victim of the Bataclan attacks, Lola Salines, and the father of Samy Amimour, one of the perpetrators of the attack, have come together to write a book about their experiences, in the hope of finding a way to combat terrorism. Their efforts can be described as altruism born of suffering, an attempt to ensure that the trauma they experienced becomes a force for good (Conradi, 2020).

There are ample examples of victims of TPV engaging in what might be termed peace work, focusing on preventing future violence and community division (Staub, 2003; Vollhardt, 2009). An example of this is the role of *citizen educa-tors* in Northern Ireland. The *citizen educators* work with the WAVE Trauma Centre[2] and share their stories and journeys as victims and survivors with the purpose of educating members of the community about the impact of political violence on individuals, families and communities. Similarly, across Europe and facilitated by RAN there is a range of initiatives that focus on the impor-tance of victims' testimony as a violence-prevention tool.[3] In addition, work

---

[2]   See for example http://wavetraumacentre.org.uk/course_type/strand-four/
[3]   See for example www.youtube.com/watch?v=bcPKFhgDCG4&feature=emb _logo

carried out by the Warrington Peace Centre focuses on victims and survivors and their role in education, peace and violence prevention.[4] The creation of a role for victims as public messengers for peace, as examples of forgiveness and reconciliation in action or in support of various public/security policy measures (e.g. see Martyn's Law)[5] enables victims to *make meaning* from their experience but also plays a part in what is called post-traumatic growth. Post-traumatic growth refers to the experience of personal growth that occurs after someone who has difficulty dealing with a traumatic event due to their core beliefs being challenged (Tedeschi and Calhoun, 1996). However, achieving such growth often comes at significant personal cost.

Narratives of victimhood

In the case of TPV, victimhood is predominantly seen as an *objective* descriptor but also an ideological label, as well as a narrative that serves to justify further violence. Narratives of victimhood can and are used to justify and motivate involvement in TPV. This is particularly evident in the accounts of former perpetrators of TPV when they reflect on their motives for engaging in violence (Joyce and Lynch, 2017). Victimhood is used to make sense of violence, and is often described as a radicalising factor. However, retrospective justification of involvement in terrorism is often well scripted and victimisation is most often not a sufficient cause for engaging in violence; many other factors will play a role (Pemberton and Van Eck Aarten, 2015) Narratives of victimhood are a part of the story, even if only for the purpose of justifying violence after the fact, and importantly, victimisation in these circumstances can be vicarious – it can be the trauma of a family or a community, not necessarily that of the individual that is made relevant. And while it may appear distasteful to consider victimhood as an *explainer* for involvement in violence, it is unfortunately part of the context and history of terrorism. Of course, this is not to say that there is any direct relationship between involvement in TPV and being a victim of TPV, but it is to recognise that narratives of victimhood can serve to support the use of violence (Pemberton and Van Eck Aarten, 2015).

However, narratives of victimisation also have a positive role in the prevention of violence. For example, in the case of restorative methods such as those men-

---

4   See www.peace-foundation.org.uk/support/victimsofterrorism/
5   The mother of Martyn Hett who died in the 2017 Manchester Arena bombing is lobbying government to bring in what is called Martyn's Law that addresses security measures for large-scale public events.

tioned above that happen between victims and perpetrators, the message of shared experience, understanding, forgiveness, reconciliation and *hearing the other* are important lessons that are shared. There is a limit to the role of such restorative practice, though. Increasingly there are efforts undertaken to carve out a space for victims and survivors in CVE or PVE initiatives, for example presenting victims' testimony to individuals who are in prison for terrorism offences or attempting to *deradicalise* young people on the fringes of involvement in extremism. However, research by Pemberton et al. (2018) has pointed to the fact that in the case of restorative methods, confronting individuals holding extreme beliefs may only serve to harden their position and trigger a defensive response. They similarly point out that perpetrators are generally not ignorant to the suffering of their victims, but as a means of self-protection they may engage in competitive victimhood as a justification of their actions. There is evidence to support the potentially positive role of testimony and narrative among the general population via educational and social inclusion initiatives (Lynch and Argomaniz, 2015).

Conclusion

In order to understand victimhood in the case of TPV it is important to take a psycho-social perspective. Through understanding the context to the violence, the history of the violence, the occurrence of other instances of trauma, the family legacy of trauma, in-group/out-group divisions and narratives of victimhood we can establish a greater insight into the experience of victims of terrorism, the needs of victims of terrorism and how society responds to both the threat of and the act of terrorism. Recognising the complexity of victimhood is vital in order to understand the origins and longevity of conflict and political violence and it is vital also in how we think about violence prevention, peace and beyond. The harm of terrorism is comprehensive and intergenerational and an understanding of how insidious and sustained the impact can be is vital to prevent the transmission of this harm across generations.

In terms of the literature, a more deliberate focus on the victims of terrorism is necessary to ensure that the topic is comprehensively addressed in the field of terrorism studies. In particular, the issue of the relationship between individual and communal trauma in the case of TPV is important, as well as the role of social media in impacting conceptions of risk, fear and threat of terrorism.

References

Alonso, R. (2017). Victims of ETA's terrorism as an interest group: Evolution, influence, and impact on the political agenda of Spain. *Terrorism and Political Violence*, 29(6), 985–1005.

Auer, M., Sutcliffe, A. M. and Lee, M. (2019). Framing the 'White Widow': Using intersectionality to uncover complex representations of female terrorism in news media. *Media War and Conflict*, 12(3), 281–298.

Averdijk, M. (2014). Victimization and routine activities. In A. C. Michalos (Ed.). *Encyclopaedia of Quality of Life and Well-Being Research*. Dordrecht: Springer.

Bajo, M., Blanco, A., Stavrakil, M., Gandarillas, B., Cancela, A., Requero, B. and Diaz, D. (2018). Post-traumatic cognitions and quality of life in terrorism victims: The role of well-being in indirect versus direct exposure. *Health and Quality of Life Outcomes*, 16(96), 1–9.

Bar-Tal, D., Chernyak-Hai, L., Schori, N. and Gundar, A. (2009). A sense of self perceived collective victimhood in intractable conflicts. *International Review of the Red Cross*, 91(874), 229–258.

Bartholomew, R. E. (2016). The Paris terror attacks, mental health and the spectre of fear. *Journal of the Royal Society of Medicine*, 109(1), 4–5.

Berrebi, C. and Lakdawalla, D. (2007). How does terrorism risk vary across space and time? An analysis based on the Israeli experience. *Defence and Peace Economics*, 18(2), 113–131.

Blanco, A., Blanco, R. and Díaz, D. (2016). Social (dis)order and psychosocial trauma: Look earlier, look outside, and look beyond the persons. *American Psychologist*, 71(3), 187–198.

Braga, L. L., Mello, M. F. and Fiks, J. P. (2012). Transgenerational transmission of trauma and resilience: A qualitative study with Brazilian offspring of Holocaust survivors. *BMC Psychiatry*, 12(1), 1–11.

Butler, S., Panzer, A. M. and Goldfrank, L. R. (2003). *Preparing for the Psychological Consequences of Terrorism: A Public Health Strategy*. Institute of Medicine (US) Committee on Responding to the Psychological Consequences of Terrorism. Washington, DC: National Academies Press.

Christie, N. (1986). The ideal victim. In Ezzat A. Fattah (Ed.). *From crime policy to victim policy* (pp. 17–30). Palgrave Macmillan, London.

Conradi, P. (2020). My child the terrorist killed yours. Did I fail as a father? *The Times*. www.thetimes.co.uk/article/my-child-the-terrorist-killed-yours-did-i-fail-as-a-father-nkxq36f6m (Accessed 1 November 2020).

De Saint Marc, G. D., Guglielminetti, L., Netter, J., Lacombe, S., Van De Donk, M., Galesloot, J. and Woltman, P. (2016). *Handbook – Voices of Victims of Terrorism*. Radicalisation Awareness Network. https:// ec .europa .eu/ home -affairs/ sites/ homeaffairs/ files/ what -we -do/ networks/ radicalisation_awareness_network/ about -ran/ ran -rvt/ docs/ ran_vvt_handbook_may_2016_en.pdf (Accessed 15 September 2020).

Dewilde, F. (2016). *Mon Bataclan: Vivre encore*. Paris: French and European Publications.

Downing, J. (2019). Blurring European and Islamic values or brightening the good–bad Muslim dichotomy? A critical analysis of French Muslim victims of Jihadi terror online on twitter and in *Le Monde* newspaper. *Critical Studies on Terrorism*, 12(2), 250–272.

Erez, E. (2006). Protracted war, terrorism and mass victimization: Exploring victimo-logical/criminological concepts and theories to address victimization in Israel. In Ewald, U., & Turković, K. (Eds.). Large-Scale Victimisation as a Potential Source of Terrorist Activities (pp. 89–102). IOS Press.

Eyre, A. (2019). The value of peer support groups following disaster: From Aberfan to Manchester. *Bereavement Care*, 38, 2–3.

Fominaya, C. F. and Barberet, R. (2018). The right to commemoration and 'ideal victims': The puzzle of victim dissatisfaction with state-led commemoration after 9/11 and 3/11. *Critical Studies on Terrorism*, 11(2), 219–242.

Global Terrorism Database (2020). Causalities (fatalities) country by country data. https://start.umd.edu/gtd/ (Accessed 8 November 2022).

Green, S. and Pemberton, A. (2018). The impact of crime: Victimisation, harm and resilience. In S. Walklate (Ed.). *Handbook of Victims and Victimology* (pp. 77–102). London: Taylor and Francis.

Gregory, J., de Lepinau, J., de Buyer, A., Delanoy, N., Mir, O. and Gaillard, R. (2019). The impact of the Paris terrorist attacks on the mental health of resident physicians. *BMC Psychiatry*, 19(79). https://doi.org/10.1186/s12888-019-2058-y

Hersh, E. D. (2013). Long term effect of September 11 on the political behaviour of victims' families and neighbors. *PNAS*, 24 December, 110(52), 20959–20963.

Hoffman, B. and Kasupski, A. (2007). *The Victims of Terrorism: An Assessment of Their Influences and Growing Role in Policy*. Santa Monica, CA: Rand Corporation.

Janssen, H. J., Oberwittler, D. and Koeber, G. (2020). Victimisation and its consequences for well-being: A between and within person analysis. *Journal of Quantitative Criminology*. https://doi.org/10.1007/s10940-019-09445-6

Joyce, C., and Lynch, O. (2017). "Doing Peace": The role of ex-political prisoners in violence prevention initiatives in Northern Ireland. *Studies in Conflict & Terrorism*, 40(12), 1072–1090.

Jupp, J. (2019). Strengthening protection and support for victims of terrorism in crimi-nal proceedings in Afghanistan. *Studies in Conflict and Terrorism*. https://doi.org/10.1080/1057610X.2019.1657657

Knatchbull, T. (2010). *From a Clear Blue Sky: Surviving the Mountbatten Bomb*. London: Arrow.

Lawther, C. (2014). "The Construction and Politicization of Victimhood." In O. Lynch and J. Argomaniz (Eds.). *Victims of Terrorism: A Comparative and Interdisciplinary Study*, pp. 10–30. London: Routledge.

Le Vine, V. (2007). On the victims of terrorism and their innocence. *Terrorism and Political Violence*, 9(3), 55–62.

Levav, I. (2006). Terrorism and its effect on mental health. *World Psychiatry*, 5(1), 35–36.

Lynch, O. and Argomaniz, J. (2013). Supporting victims of terrorism, the role of Victim orientated organizations: The case of the UK and Spain. EU White Paper HOME/2012/ISEC/RAD/4000003818. http:// victimsofterrorism .co .uk/ project -summary-support-initiatives-for-victims-of-terrorism/ (Accessed 10 March 2016).

Lynch, O. and Argomaniz, J. (Eds) (2015). *Victims of Terrorism: A Comparative and Interdisciplinary Study*. London: Routledge.

Lynch, O. and Argomaniz, J. (2018). *Victims and Perpetrators of Terrorism: Exploring Identities, Roles and Narratives*. London: Routledge.

Madina, I. G., Bilbao, G. and Bermudez, A. (2020). Recognizing victims of political vio-lence: Basque literary narratives as an ethical tool. *Studies in Conflict and Terrorism*, 43(6), 548–564.

Moffett, L. (2016). A pension for injured victims of the Troubles: Reparations or reifying victim hierarchy? *Northern Ireland Legal Quarterly*, 66(4), 297–319.

Morrison, J. and Horgan, J. (2016). Reloading the armalite? Victims and targets of violent dissident Irish Republicanism 2007–2015. *Terrorism and Political Violence*, 28(3), 576–597.

Muldoon, O. T., Haslam, A. S., Haslam, C., Cruwys, T., Kearns, M. and Jetten, J. (2019). The social psychology of responses to trauma: Social identity pathways associated with divergent traumatic responses. *European Review of Social Psychology*, 30(1), 311–348.

Neria, Y. and Sullivan, G. M. (2011). Understanding the mental health effects of indirect exposure to mass trauma through the media. *JAMA*, 306(12), 1374–1375.

Neumann, P. (2020). Twitter post. https://mobile.twitter.com/peterrneumann/status/1321774988102434816?s=21 (Accessed 30 October 2020).

O'Carroll, S. (2013). Martin McGuinness: I don't expect people to forgive me for being in the IRA. *The Journal.ie*. www.thejournal.ie/martin-mcguinness-peace-lecture-1089901-Sep2013/ (Accessed 1 November 2020).

Parkin, W. S. (2017). Victimisation theories and terrorism. In G. LaFree and J. Frelich (Eds). *The Handbook of the Criminology of Terrorism*. Chichester: Wiley-Blackwell.

Parkin, W. S., Freilich, J. D. and Chermak, S. M. (2015). Ideological victimisation: Homicides perpetrated by far right extremists. *Homicide Studies*, 19(3), 211–236.

Peake, S. and Lynch, O. (2016). Victims of Irish Republican paramilitary violence: The case of 'The Disappeared'. *Terrorism and Political Violence*, 28(3), 452–472.

Pemberton, A. and Van Eck Aarten, P (2015). The perpetrator victim cycle. In O. Lynch and J. Argomaniz (Eds). *The Victimisation Experience and the Radicalisation Process*. Final Report to the EU. Funded by the European Commission through the Specific Programme 'Prevention of and Fight against Crime'. HOME/2012/ISEC/AG/RAD.

Pemberton, A., Mulder, E. and Van Eck Aarten, P. (2018). Stories of injustice, towards a narrative victimology. *European Journal of Victimology*, 16(4), 391–412.

Price, E. (2012). Literature on victims of terrorism: Monographs, edited volumes, non-conventional literature and prime articles and book chapters. *Perspectives on Terrorism*, 6(6). www.terrorismanalysts.com/pt/index.php/pot/article/view/236/html

Rew, N. E. J. (2021). Supporting the survivors: experiences and perceptions of peer support offered to UK terrorist survivors. *International review of victimology*, 27(1), 63–79.

Rock, P. (2008). The treatment of victims in England and Wales. *Policing: A Journal of Policy and Practice*, 2(1), 110–119.

Rubin, A. and Peltier, E. (2017). The Paris attacks, 2 years later: Quiet remembrance and lasting impact. *New York Times*, 13 November. www.nytimes.com/2017/11/13/world/europe/paris-november-2015.html/ (Accessed 6 August 2019).

Schmid, A. P. (2004). Frameworks for conceptualising terrorism. *Terrorism and Political Violence*, 16(2), 197–221.

Schmid, A. P. (2012). Strengthening the role of victims and incorporating victims in efforts to counter extremism and terrorism. www.icct.nl/download/file/ICCT-Schmid-Strengthening-the-Role-of-Victims-August-2012.pdf (Accessed 2 November 2020).

Schmid, A. P. and Jongman, A. (1988). *Political Terrorism*. New Brunswick, NJ: Transaction Books.

Schuster, M. A., Stein, B. D., Jaycox, L. H., Collins, R. L., Marshall, G. N., Elliott, M. N., Zhou, M. S., Kanouse, D. E., Morrison, J. L. and Berry, S. H. (2001). A national survey of stress reactions after the September 11, 2001, terrorist attacks. *New England Journal of Medicine*, 345, 1507–1512.

Shapland, J. and Hall, M. (2007). What do we know about the effect of crime on victims? *International Review of Victimology*, 14(2), 175–217.

Shaver, A. (2015). You're more likely to be fatally crushed by furniture than killed by a terrorist. *The Washington Post*, 23 November. www.washingtonpost.com/ news/ monkey-cage/wp/2015/11/23/youre-more-likely-to-be-fatally-crushed-by-furniture -than-killed-by-a-terrorist/ (Accessed 4 September 2020).

Silke, A. (2003). *Terrorists, Victims and Society*. Chichester: Wiley.

Staub, E. (2003). *The psychology of good and evil: Why children, adults, and groups help and harm others*. Cambridge University Press.

Tedeschi, R. G. and Calhoun, L. G. (1996). The post traumatic growth inventory: Measuring the positive legacy of trauma. *Journal of Traumatic Stress*, 9(3), 455–471.

Thomas, J. (1984). This time the IRA comes closer to Thatcher. *New York Times*, 14 October. www.nytimes.com/1984/10/14/weekinreview/this-time-the-ira-comes -close-to-thatcher.html (Accessed 14 September 2020).

Tulloch, J. (2006). *One day in July: experiencing 7/7*. Little, Brown.

Travers, S. (2007). *The Miami Showband Massacre: A Survivors Search for the Truth*. Dublin: Hodder.

UNODC (2018). The effects of terrorism. www.unodc.org/ e4j/ en/ terrorism/ module -14/key-issues/effects-of-terrorism.html (Accessed 28 October 2020).

Updegraff, J. A., Silver, R. C. and Holman, E. A. (2008). Searching for and finding meaning in collective trauma: Results from a national longitudinal study of the 9/11 terrorist attacks. *Journal of Personality and Social Psychology*, 95(3), 709–722.

Vollhardt, J. R. (2009). Altruism born of suffering and prosocial behavior following adverse life events: A review and conceptualization. *Social Justice Research*, 22(1), 53–97.

Walklate, S. (2018). *Handbook of Victims and Victimology*. London: Taylor and Francis.

Weinberg, L., Pedahzur, A. and Canette-Nisim, D. (2003). The social and religious characteristics of suicide bombers and their victims. *Terrorism and Political Violence*, 15(3), 139–153.

Wilson, C. (2020). Nostalgia, entitlement and victimhood: The synergy of white genocide and misogyny. *Terrorism and Political Violence*, 1–16.

4 Critical terrorism studies

Shirley Achieng', Samwel Oando and Richard Jackson

Introduction

The origins and impact of critical terrorism studies (CTS) has been discussed in detail elsewhere (see Jackson, 2015, 2016, 2019a; Stampnitzky, 2013). Intellectually, CTS can be genealogically linked to an earlier set of criticisms of the terrorism studies field in the 1980s and 1990s from scholars in political economy and anthropology (see, for example, George, 1991; Zulaika & Douglass, 1996). It also has roots in the Welsh school of critical security studies. Focusing on issues such as the state-centrism of terrorism studies, its problem-solving approach, its pro-Western bias, its tabooing of the terrorist subject, and its disproportionate focus on so-called 'Islamic terrorism', these earlier criticisms resonated with a group of critical scholars who observed similar dynamics occurring during the early days of the 'global war on terror'. In addition to concerns about the terrorism field's intellectual weaknesses (see Schuurman, this volume), these critical scholars were also motivated by the Abu Ghraib scandal in 2004, as well as the myriad other harms and costs caused by the invasion of Iraq and the global war on terror (Jackson, 2019b). As a consequence, they sought to distance themselves from a terrorism studies field they felt was organically tied to, and implicated in, the West's war on terror, and advocate for a more openly emancipatory approach to the study of terrorism and political violence. This led to a series of activities establishing the new field starting with a conference in 2006, soon followed by a series of books and articles outlining the core principles and approaches of CTS, a new journal, and a new scholarly network, among other activities (see Jackson, 2015).

Today, similar to the position of critical security studies within the broader security studies field, CTS is recognised as a distinct subfield and approach within the wider terrorism studies field. Rooted in different types of critical theory, including Frankfurt School-inspired critical theory, critical constructivism, post-structuralism, critical feminist security studies, historical materialism, and more recently decoloniality and critical race theory, CTS has carved out a distinctive perspective on terrorism research based largely upon a critical constructivist ontology and epistemology, interdisciplinarity and the pluralisation of methodologies, and a normative commitment to emancipatory ethics. Moreover, it has contributed an important body of research on terrorism and counterterrorism (see Jackson, 2016 for a summary), including powerful critiques of taken-for-granted understandings of terrorism, contemporary forms of counterterrorism, the global war on terror and the radicalisation field, as well as state terrorism, among many others. At the same time, CTS has not been immune to controversy and critique, not least the current claim that it remains trapped in the coloniality of the broader international relations (IR) and security studies fields.

This chapter will provide a brief overview of the main features of CTS, some of its important contributions, its controversies and criticisms, and its challenges, including the current challenge of decolonisation. It will attempt to argue that terrorism studies as a whole needs to acknowledge the colonial roots of the field, diversify its voices and approaches, and take concrete steps towards a more decolonised field of study. Adopting such an approach will go some way towards dealing with many of the broader weaknesses and problems with the field, including its continuing state-centrism, pro-Western bias, the terrorism taboo, Islamophobia, neglect of state terrorism, and so on.

Critical terrorism studies: contributions, controversies, and the decolonial challenge

The founders of CTS have argued that it can be characterised by an identifiable set of ontological, epistemological, methodological, and ethical-normative commitments which distinguish it from the broader terrorism field (Gunning, 2007; Jackson, 2007; Jackson et al., 2011). For example, CTS adopts the ontological position that terrorism is fundamentally a social fact rather than a brute fact, because deciding whether a particular act of violence constitutes an 'act of terrorism' relies on judgements about the context, circumstances, and intent of the violence, and a series of social, cultural, legal, and political processes of interpretation and labelling (Zulaika & Douglass, 1996). Importantly, the actors and actions understood as terrorism can change over time and place, as the current turn of focus to white supremacist terrorism arguably demonstrates.

Epistemologically, CTS takes the position that creating knowledge is ultimately a social process which depends on a range of contextual and process-related factors, such as the social position of the researcher, the institutional context within which they conduct research, and the kinds of methods they employ. From this perspective, it is argued that wholly objective or neutral knowledge – absolute or real 'truth' – about terrorism is impossible, and that there is always an ideological, ethical-political dimension to the research process.

The ontological and epistemological commitments of CTS have important consequences for methodology, where CTS is characterised by the embrace of methodological and disciplinary pluralism and a refusal to privilege social scientific methods and approaches to terrorism research based on rationalism, empiricism, and positivism (Dixit & Stump, 2016). This also implies a commitment to transparency in relation to the researcher's values and standpoints, which for Western-based scholars translates into a commitment to trying to overcome the Eurocentric, Orientalist, and patriarchal forms of knowledge which arguably dominate the terrorism studies and security studies fields (Gunning, 2007; Jackson et al., 2011). It also implies a commitment to taking subjectivity seriously, in terms of both the researcher and the often tabooed 'terrorist' research subject (Breen-Smyth, 2009), and more broadly, to engaging in primary research with militants when relevant (Zulaika & Douglass, 1996).

Lastly, CTS holds to a number of ethical-normative commitments, specifically a 'do no harm' research ethic which takes account of, and tries to avoid harming, the various end users of terrorism research. Such a position recognises the harmful, often violent consequences that can occur for individuals, groups, movements, or communities who come to be labelled as 'terrorist'. For some CTS scholars, such commitments further require the serious exploration of non-violence, conflict transformation, and reconciliation as practical alternatives to both terrorist and counterterrorist violence (Jackson, 2019b). Collectively, the ethical-normative commitments of CTS can best be described as a broad commitment to the notion of emancipation, understood as the process of trying to free individuals and communities from unnecessary structural constraints and the promotion of human security (Lindahl, 2018; McDonald, 2009).

It is relatively uncontroversial to suggest that since its founding, and despite still being in its infancy and its small size, CTS has had a genuine impact on the broader terrorism studies field, and to a lesser extent, other fields like security studies, area studies, history, literary studies, and IR, among others. More specifically, CTS has produced an impressive body of research on the language and discourses of terrorism, including analyses of the terrorism studies field itself, the social and cultural discourses of terrorism, the political uses and misuses of the terrorism threat narrative, the diverse impacts and harms of the global war on terror, the continuing relevance of state terrorism, and more recently an analytical and normative critique of counterterrorism, the radicalisation discourse, and countering violent extremism approaches (see Jackson, 2016 for a summary). Some CTS scholars have also had an important influence on human rights advocacy, such as Raphael and Blakeley's (2016) work on uncovering the global network of extraordinary rendition by the United States and its allies.

Despite its achievements, however, CTS has not been without its critics, both from within and outside its community. For example, there has at times been a robust reaction to the criticisms that CTS initially levelled at the orthodox field. Terrorism scholars responded by arguing that it offered little that was new, its criticism of the orthodox field was based on a straw man argument, it was misguided to include states in the study of terrorism, and there was little value in dividing the field into critical and traditional branches (see, among others, Horgan & Boyle, 2008). Other criticisms suggested that by focusing so much on the failures and abuses of Western counterterrorism, by arguing for deeper understanding of the context, motives, and perspectives of terrorist perpetrators, and by failing to ritually condemn the evil of terrorism, CTS implicitly sympathised with, and legitimised, the terrorist enemies of the West (Jones & Smith, 2009). Related to this, it has been argued that CTS has thus far failed to offer any real practical alternative approach for policymakers and practitioners who have to deal with the real-world threat of terrorist violence. In this sense, it is argued that in its continually 'critical' perspective, CTS lacks practical policy relevance. More broadly, it is fair to say that CTS has yet to have any noticeable impact on public policy, political activism, or the mainstream media.

On the other hand, criticisms from within the field include the argument that by retaining the term 'terrorism', CTS has risked reifying and reinforcing the dominant terrorism discourse which is unhelpful to the analysis of political violence and which so often results in violent and oppressive forms of counterterrorism (Mac Ginty, 2018). Others argued that CTS has been too focused on the discourses of terrorism and does not pay enough attention to the way in which terrorism and counterterrorism are an expression of the dominant political-economic structures and processes operating in the international system today, especially in relation to states, empires, and geopolitics (Herring & Stokes, 2011).

More recently, it has been argued that as much as CTS advocates for engagement with multiple perspectives and subjectivities in terrorism research, the multiplicity of knowledge production has rarely extended beyond the Western academic system and voices, thereby maintaining a Eurocentric focus. That is, the key scholars of CTS remain predominantly of Western origin, and thus the field continues to perpetuate the reproduction of Eurocentric research and the exclusion of non-Western voices (Ilyas, 2021a). Ultimately, this reflects broader 'hierarchical conceptions of subjectivity that place primacy of knowledge production with the liberal European self, as the authors and adjudicators of knowledge systems on populations' (Jabri, 2010, p. 55). Expressed differently, this critique concerns the challenge of 'the coloniality of knowledge, which the terrorism industry has tactfully avoided over time' (Ilyas, 2021a, p. 2). Such an unacknowledged condition results in both a contextual and temporal stagnation in terrorism studies.

In other words, CTS – and terrorism studies more broadly – has not yet adequately addressed the dual issues of positionality of knowledge production, and the need for an epistemic decolonisation in research methodology and approach. The issue of positionality in knowledge systems explores the inclusion of, and need to seriously engage with, divergent and subjugated voices in the geopolitics of knowledge production within the precincts of terrorism studies. The issue of epistemic coloniality calls for an analysis and acknowledgement of the role colonialism has played (and continues to play) in constructing the terrorism discourse itself, and explores whether (or how) CTS can 'enhance its future development in ways that are non-colonized' (Krishna, 2012, p. 1). The following sections explore these connected issues.

Positionality in the critical terrorism studies knowledge production system

According to Mwambari (2019), positionality deals with the divergent standpoints of different researchers within the complexity of the field of study, in this case, terrorism studies. Such differences relate to the micro-context, personal experience, language, culture, and of course the geographical diversity of researchers. The different perspectives of researchers in different societies (Haastrup & Hagen, 2021) create divergent 'categories, practices, and orders' of knowledge about terrorism (Toros, 2016, p. 71). At the same time, positionality in itself is never fixed, but evolves depending on the intellectual relationships between researchers, and the contexts within which the research is undertaken (Mwambari, 2019). While CTS, similar to security studies, is a 'derivative field of study' (Toros, 2016), where different societies, communities, and individuals bring their own ideas and perspectives to the table, it is nonetheless undisputable that 'little is known about the positionality, perspectives and experiences of local stakeholders in the production of knowledge' (Mwambari, 2019, p. 1) about terrorism, and there is still a dire need to account for the contextual and geopolitical milieu against which historical events unfold (Appadurai, 2021).

In part, this condition results because the dominant voices in CTS scholarship remain confined to the same relatively small set of (primarily Western or Western-based) scholars, and because CTS research is almost invariably linked to the analogous temporality around the global war on terror and the collective experience of the 9/11 spectacle. That is, despite its own appeals to broaden the focus of research, CTS scholarship remains trapped in the narrow scope based on 9/11 as *the* temporal marker of terrorism and counterterrorism. In other words, the voices of non-Western subjects in locations like Iraq, Syria, Afghanistan, and other parts of the Middle East or the Sahel region or the Horn of Africa, where the violence of the war on terror and terrorist insurgencies have produced severe forms of violence, challenge the experience of 9/11 as the fulcrum of terrorism studies and the universal marker for global knowledge on terrorism. As an example, it was not until 9/11 that Africa, for instance, gained global visibility in terms of terrorism and counterterrorism research. Despite the earlier bombings of the United States embassies in Kenya and Tanzania in 1998, only a small handful of studies have critically analysed their veracity as shaped by both regional and global contexts (Chacha & Marwa, 2016; Muhula, 2007). In short, local knowledge and contextual understanding – why and how different communities assign different meanings to events, ideas, and concepts based on their daily lived experiences – is yet to be adequately conceived and incorporated within the existing CTS literature.

To further illustrate, comparing Western and African scholarship on terrorism and counterterrorism demonstrates the conspicuous absence of CTS research, and compared to the Western situation, terrorism and counterterrorism in Africa remains highly underexplored. Furthermore, much of the terrorism research in Africa which does exist has been undertaken and presented primarily from a Western paradigm based on 'knowledge production, transfer and diffusion, including in the role of [Western] policy experts, think tanks and epistemic communities, in enabling, sustaining, or altering political processes and orders' (de Guevara & Kostić, 2019, p. 19). The specific and locally determined contextual dynamics in Africa have thus remained underexplored due to the (Eurocentric) premium placed on universality and generalisability in terrorism research, as opposed to the locality and specificity of knowledge.

It is on these terms that Ndhlovu (2008) argues that critical studies discourse, including CTS, remains incomplete unless it accounts for the role and place of contextual language, which occupies an important position in any meaningful dialogue on development and engagement within and between different geographical settings (Ndhlovu, 2008, p. 136; Solomon, 2015). The recognition of geopolitical diversity, therefore, has huge potential to overcome different constraints on the contextual understanding of terrorism, both as a global phenomenon and as a local problem (Meyer & Peukert, 2020).

For all these reasons, it can be argued that CTS, like the wider terrorism and security studies fields, has been complicit in reproducing knowledge that 'is not always grounded in a fair-minded appraisal of a complex, multi-context research, that often is either flawed or imperfect as a field of study' (Horgan & Boyle, 2008, p. 62). Shifting the research paradigm of CTS must be adopted as a priority, in the context of accommodating both the universality and specificity of knowledge in its analysis. There must be a shift away from looking at 'non-Western' contexts through the myopic lenses of 'Western knowledge and stereotypes', particularly those associated with the 'Western tourist gaze on Africa that often assumes to fix the local situations both in spatial and temporal sites' (Dunn, 2004, p. 384).

In short, there are several lessons for CTS research here. First, positionality in the CTS knowledge production system must embrace perspectives in theory and practice that appreciate the myriad ways of knowing with regard to how terrorism is 'perceived in reality' in non-Western contexts. Second, there is a need to overcome the concern that CTS research (Martini, 2020), just like peace research in its present form, still fails to meet its own standards and expectations of criticality (Gnoth, 2020), particularly in regards to how it engages with the non-Western 'other' and the emancipatory dimensions of research and practice. As argued by Martini (2020) about the centrality of normativity in CTS, it is evident that the expectations of pioneer CTS scholars to create an intellectual platform for challenging and reformulating the mainstream approaches to terrorism and counterterrorism remains for the most part unmet. Finally, and related to this, is the missing nexus between theory and practice that engages academics and policymakers, as 'CTS scholars have not always agreed on the practical aspects' of responding to terrorism (Martini, 2020, p. 47). Not only is CTS missing the voices and perspectives of non-Western others about the terrorism they face, but CTS is missing in the real-world debates about how to practically deal with the terrorism they face. This leads us to the related issue of a decolonial perspective in CTS research.

Epistemic decolonisation of critical terrorism studies

Even though the question of decolonisation in the social and natural sciences has been the subject of numerous debates, Western-centric scholarship has only recently begun to take it seriously (Ake, 1979; Blaut, 1993; wa Thiong'o, 1986). With each passing year, the issue of decolonisation has gained further traction. The pioneers of decolonial thinking, such as Anibal Quijano, Walter Mignolo, and Enrique Dussel, have called for a comprehensive epistemic reconstitution which demands a delinking from the coloniality of knowledge (Mignolo & Walsh, 2018). The call for epistemic decolonisation refers to the 'rejection of the continued and unexamined appeal to the western "canon"', and instead demands a 'knowledge re-centering by reclaiming the right to think and theorise from one's own geographic and socio-cultural location, and to choose for oneself the focus of one's epistemic endeavours' (Mitova, 2020, pp. 193–4). In part, this demand emerges simply because the Western paradigm's imported approaches are not working for the non-Western world, hence the need 'to reimagine the world anew' (Mpofu, 2018, p. 91). By rejecting this 'appeal' which Quijano (2007) refers to as 'cultural Europeanisation aspiration', epistemic decolonisation opens up space for alternative knowledges.

In other words, despite the commonly held belief that knowledge production is apolitical, in reality it is profoundly political (Sithole et al., 2017), with the global north exercising epistemic domination by dictating to the global south 'what counts as genuine knowledge, rational thought, and as real science' (Mitova, 2020, p. 191). As such, reflecting Edward Said's work, it can be argued that epistemic domination has its roots in Orientalist and 'othering' discourses which have historically dismissed the non-Western subject as intellectually inferior, hence the need for 'dealing with them by making statements about them, authorizing views about them, describing them, by teaching them, settling them and, ruling over them' (Said, 1978, p. 11). Similarly, Alatas (2000, p. 25), in his arguments about intellectual imperialism, draws a parallel between coloniality and knowledge production, positing that 'it was assumed that people there know less about practically all subjects than people in the West'. This argument resonates with the status quo currently witnessed in terrorism research, where despite terrorism claiming more lives in non-Western countries, 'the authorship of journal articles and by extension, knowledge production on terrorism is dominated by scholars with Western heritage and institutions based in Western countries' (Ilyas, 2021a, p. 12). Terrorism studies continues to function largely as a field where Western 'experts' produce knowledge and policy advice about non-Western people and societies, even when they don't speak the language of the cultures they are 'expert' in.

Consequently, the power dynamics that influence knowledge production reveal that actors from the global north shape knowledge while the rest are seen/taken/perceived as 'receivers' of knowledge. As Foucault explains, knowledge production is 'controlled, selected, organized and redistributed according to a certain number of procedures', hence making them systems of exclusion (Foucault, 1971, p. 8). Further, in his earlier work he describes the forces that construct and maintain how things are perceived, stating that 'there exists, below the level of its spontaneous orders, things that are in themselves capable of being ordered, that belong to a certain unspoken order; the fact in short, that order exists' (Foucault, 1970, pp. xx–xxi). Applying Foucault's observation, it can be argued that non-Western countries, and their scholars in terrorism research, are excluded as producers of knowledge because more often than not, they have been constructed as not only subjects to be ordered but also as 'victims and targets of counterterrorism intervention hence they remain located as mute objects or data points rather than serious interlocutors with an alternative standpoint or traditions of knowledge' (Sabaratnam, 2017, p. 17). Even though some may contest this argument, the fact still remains that the non-Western voice is marginalised not only in CTS but in the broader terrorism discourse (Feyyaz, 2016).

The ubiquity of coloniality of knowledge within CTS research is not surprising, given that, as Smith (1999, p. 65) argues, 'academic knowledges and most "traditional" disciplines are grounded in cultural world views which are either antagonistic to other belief systems or have no methodology for dealing with other knowledge systems'. Taking Smith's sentiments into consideration, as much as CTS is the most critical and reflective school of thought within terrorism research, its outlook can still amount to promoting epistemic homogeneity. To demonstrate this, Ilyas' findings on terrorism publications reveal that out of 194 articles published in the *Critical Studies on Terrorism* journal between 2015 and 2019, 157 (81 per cent) are authored by Western scholars based at institutions in the West. Only a paltry 32 (16 per cent) of these articles can be attributed to non-Western scholars (Ilyas, 2021a).

This kind of epistemic imbalance perhaps explains why Western knowledges on terrorism are falsely considered more authoritative than non-Western knowledges. Further, Ilyas' observation that 'a simple word search using the term decoloniality' could not be found in *Critical Studies on Terrorism* is not only disappointing but reveals a gaping blind spot that needs to be addressed (Ilyas, 2021b). While these analyses provide justification for the need for CTS to navigate towards a decolonial turn by 'detoxing method and methodology' (Zondi, 2018, p. 18), it also points to deeper problems of the wider coloniality of knowledge, as explained above. Considering that CTS has consistently exposed the pain and injustice that coloniality has engendered through its discourses of modernity, such as the global war on terror and counterterrorism discourses, CTS must now deal with the coloniality and imperialism embedded within terrorism knowledge production by first acknowledging that terrorism's entire epistemological debate occurs within a narrow Western-oriented and dominated space (Feyyaz, 2016). Consequently, CTS must distance itself from this coloniality by 'rethinking the world, the international, the themes, the key questions, the actions on the basis of listening effectively to voices outside Eurocentrism' (Zondi, 2018, p. 23).

Borrowing from Linda Smith's arguments about decolonisation and the need for a theoretical approach to assist in conceptualising history through the eyes of indigenous or rather marginalised people, we must recognise that critique does not necessarily offer alternative knowledge 'but at some point, there has to be dialogue across the boundaries of oppositions' (Smith, 1999, p. 39). Additionally, we must appreciate that 'to hold alternative histories is to hold alternative knowledges, hence alternative ways of doing things' (Smith, 1999, p. 34). Against this backdrop, we argue that CTS must continue the process of epistemic decolonisation by further delinking from the overall Western terrorism paradigm that continues to perpetuate intellectual imperialism (Mignolo, 2007, 2017) and engage actively with alternative knowledges through the incorporation of 'different points of view and their respective forms of criticisms' (Dylan & Knobloch, 2020, p. 5) in terrorism research. The decolonisation of the CTS agenda provides the opportunity for scholars to embrace epistemic humility by 'hearing the unheard and paying attention to the degraded and side-lined' (Zondi, 2018, p. 19), as opposed to the continuing 'acceptance of and continuity of coloniality, marginalization and silencing of scholars with non-Western heritage' (Ilyas, 2021b, p. 2). Importantly, CTS scholars should not perceive epistemic decolonisation as an event; rather, it is an ongoing process (wa Thiong'o, 1986). This is particularly crucial because epistemic power is still in the hands of the global north and to 'think of decolonisation as a once-off threatens to make us forget all this' (Mitova, 2020, p. 196).

Conclusion

In this chapter, we have provided a brief description of the rise of CTS, its intellectual antecedents, its primary commitments, its achievements, and its controversies and debates. Building on earlier criticisms of 'the terrorism industry', the newly inaugurated CTS field expressed concerns about the terrorism field's state-centrism, its pro-Western bias, its tabooing of terrorists, its complicity in violent forms of counterterrorism, and its rejection of the need to study state terrorism. Since the mid-2000s, CTS has produced a wealth of important research which exposes and illuminates the inner workings of the dominant terrorism discourse, the contradictions and harms of the global war on terror, the lack of scientific rigour in the radicalisation and countering of violent extremism discourse, the continuing problem of state terrorism, and many more. At the same time, CTS has been the subject of criticism from both within and without, although no substantive criticisms have fundamentally challenged the core ontological, epistemological, methodological, and ethical-normative commitments of the field.

However, as with other fields like security studies and IR more generally, CTS has not been immune to the criticism that much in social science is based on an ongoing coloniality of knowledge. In fact, a recent study has convincingly argued that the term 'terrorism', and particularly the term 'religious terrorism' which remains popular in the broader terrorism studies field, has its roots in racial ideology and colonial practice (see Khan, 2021). Certainly, there are identifiable continuities between historical processes of colonisation and the global war on terror as it has been enacted in Africa (Smith, 2010), among other places. In addition, as we have attempted to demonstrate in this chapter, knowledge production processes within terrorism studies remain dominated by Western-oriented and dominated paradigms and scholars, often with the events of 9/11 as the fulcrum through which knowledge is constructed and with non-Western scholars and perspectives noticeable by their absence.

In sum, the next phase of CTS, and indeed the next phase of terrorism research more broadly, must by necessity confront the structural reality of the coloniality of knowledge and its lingering effects. It will be challenging to undo and reconstruct hundreds of years of Western social science, but the good news is that it will, in the end, enrich and enliven the terrorism and security fields, and IR more generally. New voices, new perspectives, and new forms of knowledge can only be a positive addition to the complex and challenging phenomenon of terrorism and responses to it.

References

Ake, C. E. (1979). *Social Science as Imperialism: The Theory of Political Development*. Ibadan University Press.

Alatas, S. H. (2000). Intellectual imperialism: Definition, traits, and problems. *Southeast Asian Journal of Social Science, 28*(1), 23–45.

Appadurai, A. (2021). Beyond domination: The future and past of decolonization. *The Nation*.

Blaut, J. M. (1993). *The Colonizer's Model of the World: Geographical Diffusionism and Eurocentric History*. Guilford Press.

Breen-Smyth, M. (2009). Subjectivities, 'suspect communities', governments, and the ethics of research on terrorism, in R. Jackson, M. Breen-Smyth, & J. Gunning, eds. *Critical Terrorism Studies: A New Research Agenda* (pp. 194–215). Routledge.

Chacha, B. K., & Marwa, M. Z. (2016). Kenya's foreign policy and challenges of terrorism in the post-Cold War, in M. S. Smith, ed. *Securing Africa: Post-9/11 Discourses on Terrorism* (pp. 161–172). Routledge.

de Guevara, B. B., & Kostić, R. (2019). Knowledge, expertise and the politics of intervention and statebuilding, in N. Lemay-Hébert, ed. *Handbook on Intervention and Statebuilding* (pp. 19–29). Edward Elgar Publishing.

Dixit, P., & Stump, J., eds. (2016). *Critical Methods in Terrorism Studies*. Routledge.

Dunn, K. C. (2004). Fear of a black planet: Anarchy anxieties and postcolonial travel to Africa. *Third World Quarterly*, 25(3), 483–499.

Dylan, P., & Knobloch, T. (2020). Epistemological decolonization and education: International perspectives. *Foro de Educación*, 18(1), 1–10.

Feyyaz, M. (2016). The discourse and study of terrorism in decolonised states: The case of Pakistan. *Critical Studies on Terrorism*, 9(3), 455–477.

Foucault, M. (1970). *The Order of Things*. Vintage Books.

Foucault, M. (1971). Orders of discourse. *Social Science Information*, 10(2), 7–30.

George, A. (1991). The discipline of terrorology, in A. George, ed. *Western State Terrorism*. Polity Press.

Gnoth, A. M. (2020). *A Crisis of Criticality? Reimagining Academia in International Peacebuilding*. University of Otago.

Gunning, J. (2007). A case for critical terrorism studies? *Government and Opposition*, 42(3), 363–393.

Gunning, J. (2009). 'Social movement theory and the study of terrorism', in R. Jackson, M. B. Smyth, and J. Gunning, ed. *Critical Terrorism Studies: A New Research Agenda*, (pp. 170–191). London: Routledge.

Haastrup, T., & Hagen, J. J. (2021). Racial hierarchies of knowledge production in the women, peace and security agenda. *Critical Studies on Security*, 9(1), 27–30.

Herring, E., & Stokes, D. (2011). Editors' introduction: Bringing critical realism and historical materialism into critical terrorism studies. *Critical Studies on Terrorism*, 4(1), 1–3.

Horgan, J., & Boyle, M. J. (2008). A case against 'critical terrorism studies'. *Critical Studies on Terrorism*, 1(1), 51–64.

Ilyas, M. (2021a). Decolonising terrorism journals. *Societies*, 11(1), 1–18.

Ilyas, M. (2021b). Decolonising the terrorism industry: Indonesia. *Social Sciences*, 10(2), 1–16.

Jabri, V. (2010). War, government, politics: A critical response to the hegemony of the liberal peace, in O. P. Richmond, ed. *Palgrave Advances in Peacebuilding: Critical Developments and Approaches* (pp. 41–57). Palgrave Macmillan.

Jackson, R. (2007). The core commitments of critical terrorism studies. *European Political Science*, 6(3), 244–251.

Jackson, R. (2015). On how to be a collective intellectual – Critical terrorism studies (CTS) and the countering of hegemonic discourse, in C. Bueger & T. Villumsen Berling, eds. *Security Expertise: Concepts, Power, Practice* (pp. 186–203). Routledge.

Jackson, R., ed. (2016). *Routledge Handbook on Critical Terrorism Studies*. Routledge.

Jackson, R. (2019a). Revising the field of terrorism, in A. Gofas, R. English, S. Kalyvas, & E. Chenoweth, eds. *Oxford Handbook of Terrorism* (pp. 740–754). Oxford University Press.

Jackson, R. (2019b). CTS, counterterrorism and non-violence, in R. Jackson, H. Toros, L. Jarvis, & C. Heath-Kelly, eds. *Critical Terrorism Studies at Ten: Contributions, Cases and Future Challenges* (pp. 161–173). Routledge.

Jackson, R., Jarvis, L., Gunning, J., & Breen-Smyth, M. (2011). *Terrorism: A critical introduction.* Palgrave Macmillan.

Jones, D., & Smith, M. L. R. (2009). We are all terrorists now: Critical – or hypocritical – studies on terrorism? *Studies in Conflict and Terrorism, 32*(4), 292–302.

Khan, R. M. (2021). Race, coloniality and the post 9/11 counter-discourse: Critical Terrorism Studies and the reproduction of the Islam-Terrorism discourse. *Critical Studies on Terrorism, 14*(4), 498–501.

Krishna, S. (2012). Decolonizing international relations. *E-International Relations, October,* 1–3. www.e-ir.info/2012/10/08/decolonizing-international-relations/

Lindahl, S. (2018). *A Critical Theory of Counterterrorism: Ontology, Epistemology, Normativity.* Routledge.

Mac Ginty, R. (2018). No: Don't give it the oxygen of publicity, in R. Jackson & D. Pisiou, eds. *Contemporary Debates on Terrorism.* Routledge.

Martini, A. (2020). Rethinking terrorism and countering terrorism from a critical perspective: CTS and normativity. *Critical Studies on Terrorism, 13*(1), 47–55.

McDonald, M. (2009). Emancipation and critical terrorism studies, in R. Jackson, M. Breen-Smyth, & J. Gunning, eds. *Critical Terrorism Studies: A New Research Agenda* (pp. 109–123). Routledge.

Meyer, E., & Peukert, D. (2020). Designing a transformative epistemology of the problematic: A perspective for transdisciplinary sustainability research. *Social Epistemology, 34*(4), 346–356.

Mignolo, W. D. (2007). Delinking: The rhetoric of modernity, the logic of coloniality and the grammar of decoloniality. *Cultural Studies, 21*(2), 449–514.

Mignolo, W. D. (2017). Interview – Walter Mignolo, Part 2: Key concepts/interviewer: A. Hoffmann. *E-International Relations.*

Mignolo, W. D., & Walsh, C. E. (2018). *On Decoloniality: Concepts, Analytics, Praxis.* Duke University Press.

Mitova, V. (2020). Decolonising knowledge here and now. *Philosophical Papers, 49*(2), 191–212.

Mpofu, W. (2018). Decoloniality as a combative ontology in African development, in S. O. Oloruntoba & T. Falola, eds. *The Palgrave Handbook of African Politics: Governance and Development* (pp. 83–102). Palgrave Macmillan.

Muhula, R. (2007). Kenya and the global war on terrorism: Searching for a new role in a new war, in J. Davis, ed. *Africa and the War on Terrorism* (pp. 43–60). Ashgate Publishing.

Mwambari, D. (2019). Local positionality in the production of knowledge in northern Uganda. *International Journal of Qualitative Methods, 18,* 1–12.

Ndhlovu, F. (2008). Language and African development: Theoretical reflections on the place of languages in African states. *Nordic Journal of African Studies, 17*(2), 137–151.

Quijano, A. (2007). Coloniality and modernity/rationality. *Cultural Studies, 21*(2–3), 168–178.

Raphael, S., & Blakeley, R. (2016). Rendition in the 'war on terror', in R. Jackson, ed. *Routledge Handbook on Critical Terrorism Studies* (pp. 181–189). Routledge.

Sabaratnam, M. (2017). *Decolonising Intervention: International Statebuilding in Mozambique*. Rowman & Littlefield International.

Said, E. (1978). *Orientalism*. Routledge & Kegan Paul.

Sithole, T., Oloruntoba, S., & Nkenkana, A. (2017). Global politics of knowledge production and the African development trajectory: The imperative of epistemic disobedience, in S. Oloruntoba, M. Muchie, V. Gumede, & N. A. Check, eds. *Regenerating Africa: Bringing African Solutions to African Problems*. Africa Institute of South Africa.

Smith, L. T. (1999). *Decolonizing Methodologies: Research and Indigenous Peoples*. Zed Books.

Smith, M., ed. (2010). *Securing Africa: Post-9/11 Discourses on Terrorism*. Routledge.

Solomon, H. (2015). Terrorism and counter-terrorism in Africa: Fighting insurgency from Al Shabaab, Ansar Dine and Boko Haram, in S. Croft, ed. *New Security Challenges*. Palgrave Macmillan.

Stampnitzky, L. (2013). *Disciplining Terror: How Experts and Others Invented Terrorism*. Cambridge University Press.

Toros, H. (2016). Critical theory and terrorism studies: Ethics and emancipation, in R. Jackson, ed. *Routledge Handbook of Critical Studies on Terrorism* (pp. 70–79). Routledge.

wa Thiong'o, N. (1986). *Decolonising the Mind: The Politics of Language in African Literature*. University of Otago Press/St Martin's Press.

Zondi, S. (2018). Decolonising international relations and its theory: A critical conceptual meditation. *Politikon*, *45*(1), 16–31.

Zulaika, J., & Douglass, W. (1996). *Terror and Taboo: The Follies, Fables, and Faces of Terrorism*. Routledge.

PART II

Assessing theory, some methods and approaches

5   Applying theory to research

Daniela Pisoiu

Shortly after 9/11, John Mearsheimer was asked in an interview how he sees the problem of terrorism from the perspective of realist international relations (IR) theory. While acknowledging the increasing dimensions and gravity of the problem, Mearsheimer conceded that realist IR had little to say about it, since terrorists – and Al Qaeda in particular – are non-state actors. Thus, while realism might indeed be approached with regard to counter-terrorism policies, i.e. how and why states react to terrorism, it would not be suitable to address the *causes* of terrorism:

> So the terrorism problem has been with us for a while, and most IR theorists have spent some time thinking about it. But what has changed over the past year is the magnitude of the threat. We understand that we're up against a much more formidable and much more dangerous adversary than we thought was the case throughout the 1990s. So that's point number one. Point number two is the question of what does a Realist theory of international politics have to say about terrorists? The answer is not a whole heck of a lot. Realism, as I said before, is really all about the relations among states, especially among great powers. In fact, al Qaeda is not a state, it's a non-state actor, which is sometimes called a transnational actor. My theory and virtually all Realist theories don't have much to say about transnational actors. However, there is no question that terrorism is a phenomenon that will play itself out in the context of the international system. So it will be played out in the state arena, and, therefore, all of the realist logic about state behavior will have a significant effect on how the war on terrorism is fought. So realism and terrorism are inextricably linked, although I do think that realism does not have much to say about the causes of terrorism. (The Problem of Terrorism 2002)

The "handicap" of terrorist actors being non-state and "bad" non-state actors (as opposed to "good" civil society organizations) has largely put a blind spot on them in the context of major IR theories such as realism or institutionalism. This might appear strange considering the fact that technically and originally, the field of terrorism studies was placed within security studies and IR/politics more broadly. Reflecting this widespread fixation on the unit of analysis as not states but groups and individuals, the terrorism literature – in particular the one focusing on causes and processes – has thus reached out to other theoretical families in other disciplines, in particular sociology, psychology and criminology; or has proposed its own theories and concepts. The latter frequently in fact doubled existing ones in the aforementioned disciplines, however, this genealogy was not always explicitly acknowledged. Other bodies of work have concerned themselves rather with historical and empirical descriptions of terrorist organizations or terrorist phenomena. Largely under the effect of the war on terror and its implications for conflict and human rights worldwide, a critical scholarship on terrorism emerged, which concerned itself majorly with how discourse facilitates state behavior and followed post-structuralist and critical methodologies (for a brief overview see Jarvis 2016). A related field of investigation that pre-dated the war on terror period and continued after that focused on the role of states as perpetrators of terrorism (e.g. Stohl 2006; Blakeley 2010). This literature has equally followed critical principles, such as the assumed emancipatory mission of scholarship or the critical questioning of state actions or, in a more traditional manner, aimed to uncover the motivations and strategies behind state terrorism.

Discerning ways to understand the causes and processes of terrorism

Another way of thinking about how we might study terrorism and with what theoretical tools would be to focus not necessarily on the unit of analysis as such, but alternative aspects such as the underlying explanatory logic of our theoretical approach or the actorness of terrorism more broadly. For example, we might note that, even though they are not state actors, terrorist organizations also act strategically. In fact, a number of studies looking specifically at suicide terrorism – a phenomenon that might easily be explained away as religious fanaticism, outlined the strategic logic of suicide attacks (e.g. Pape 2003). Leading ideologues of jihadi terrorism have also pointed out the many tactical advantages of suicide terrorism, as they relate to costs, the damage inflicted to the enemy or the difficulty to identify and prosecute perpetrators (e.g. Ayman al Zawahiri in Hoffman 2003). Looking at the scholarship on the endurance of terrorist organizations in the face of the inability to achieve their objectives (Gaibulloev et al. 2020), we might conclude that terrorist organizations might harbor similar objectives of maintaining and increasing power, just like realist states. In fact, the recent ascension and expansion of the so-called Islamic State offers a number of parallels in this regard, such as the accumulation of military and economic power. In this particular example, the organization eventually proceeded to create state-like structures and was de facto governing over a territory. Had they been successful in their endeavor, a number of other historical organizations might have reached similar state-like dimensions.

Looking at terrorist organizations as *strategic* actors and the focus on actors as such constitutes the approach most similar to classic IR theories. But this is not the only direction in which terrorism research has developed. We can broadly differentiate four approaches in total: apart from strategic (or intentional), also deterministic, relational and critical approaches. All these approaches function on the basis of specific assumptions and follow broader paradigmatic divides in social science. Even more broadly, we can mention here the divide between "substantialism" (with three further categories) and "relationalism" (Emirbayer 1997). Substantialism assumes that "substances" of various kinds (things, beings, etc.) are the fundamental units of analysis, whereas relationism focuses on the process. Within substantialism, three approaches have been distinguished and they correspond to the three approaches in terrorism research. There is first of all the rational choice theory, which assumes that actors are rational and calculating, with given goals and interests. This is the *intentional or strategic* approach. Second, there is critical theory which conceives of individuals as driven by norms or social ideals. Following this, the importance of the normative perspective becomes apparent, and the preoccupation with "how things should be" rather than what and how they are. This obviously corresponds to the *critical approach* briefly mentioned earlier, with its emancipatory mission. A further category of substantialism looks at action among entities, "much like billiard balls or the particles in the Newtonian mechanics" (Emirbayer 1997: 286). This is the "variable-centered approach" whereby not the substances but the causation occurring among them is of interest. This is the *deterministic approach* which seeks to identify causes or chains of causation.

Looking at these approaches in terrorism studies more in detail: deterministic approaches, also known as the grievance paradigm, work with the assumption that terrorism is caused by identifiable and measurable factors which exist a priori of such terrorist behavior, and which "determine" it, i.e. cause it to happen. Depending on the disciplines involved, sociology and political science versus psychology, these factors can be of a broader social, political or cultural nature, such as poverty, regime type, ideology or religion, usually depicted as "root causes"; or they can be of an individual psychological nature, such as personality features (for some classic works on this topic see Bjorgo 2005 and Post 1990). The constellation structural causes–frustration is in fact the backbone of deterministic approaches. In spite of the prominence of large-N data, variables and correlations, terms that rather sound like research in natural sciences, the human element had to be captured in some way, and this is where frustration comes in. That is, one needs to experience some level of discomfort with the given circumstances in order for one to be willing to change them in a violent manner.

Intentional approaches prioritize agency over structure in explaining terrorism and generally explain individual and group involvement as a matter of gain. Studies in this tradition have been often labeled "rational choice" or "greed," as opposed to "grievance." Such labels are not entirely accurate though, as, first, the kinds of gains that individuals and groups are assumed to anticipate are only rarely of material nature; and second, the kind of rationality involved is not the classical economic one of profit maximization, but an "everyday" one, or "soft rationality" (for a broader discussion on terrorism and rational choice see Caplan 2006). This is the understanding under which "rational choice" theory in criminology for example works; the latter has been very influential on intentional approaches to individual involvement in terrorism.

Not unlike "regular" rational choice theories, the case of individual participation in violence poses a type of free rider dilemma. The free rider dilemma postulates that for goods that are public, i.e. which everyone would benefit from, such as, in this case, the gains of committing terrorism, there is no incentive to participate. This is because individual participation is not necessary in order for the individual to benefit from these gains. Participation in terrorism or the "doing" of terrorism is furthermore associated with high costs, which in this case can mean imprisonment or death. That is, at first sight, there is little if any incentive to participate in a highly risky activity and the gains from it could theoretically be enjoyed regardless of participation. Yet we see that both individuals and organizations regularly do resort to terrorism, so how can we explain this? There are two ways in which this dilemma can and has been resolved. One argues that individual participation might appear necessary to the person, from a subjective point of view. If we look at the testimonies of current or former terrorists, we get the distinctive impression that they believe that their own action will have an effect, that this action is absolutely necessary for the success of the overall undertaking and that there are no other alternatives. A second explanation which is more relevant for our discussion here is that there are immediate gains from participation, but gains of an emotional nature or non-material benefits, such as belonging or status, or for the case of organizations, the show of power or recruitment.

In the "transactional" or "relational" approach "the very terms or units involved in a transaction derive their meaning, significance, and identity from the (changing) functional roles they play within that transaction. The latter, seen as a dynamic, unfolding process, becomes the primary unit of analysis rather than the constituent elements themselves" (Emirbayer 1997: 287). In the relational approach, agency itself is defined by the relations in which it enters: "the relational point of view sees agency as inseparable from the unfolding dynamics of situations, especially from the problematic features of these situations ... Agency is always a dialogic process by which actors immersed in the dureé of lived experience engage with others in collectively organized action contexts, temporal as well as spatial" (Emirbayer 1997: 294). In fact, individual entities are not seen as given at all, but always defined by transactional contexts, such that their very being is given by the relations in which they are engaged (1997: 287). This *relational* approach therefore is less interested in the entities as such, but rather in their interaction and tries to establish or find out typical mechanisms and processes there. In practice, elements of the three are usually combined. For example, in relation to individual radicalization, models would ordinarily consider some type of motivation – whether of the intentional type or deterministic such as frustration for example, but also the impact of social networks.

Relational approaches in terrorism studies, as the name says, do not focus on individuals or structures, but on relations – between individuals/organizations, between individuals/organizations and the state. Since most of the scholarship in this approach stems from social movement research, it mostly deals with organizations, while some authors have attempted nevertheless to also include the individual level of analysis. As another consequence of this embedding in social movements research and their specific approach, studies here tend to be very much historical in nature and focus on specific cases which they describe in great detail. In terms of explanations, this approach prefers concepts such as "process" and "mechanism" to those of "cause" and "effect." Importantly, scholars in this category see terrorism as a form of political violence rather than something sui generis. Furthermore, and consequently, they see terrorism as emerging during various types of interactions between organizations and between those and the state. Typically, terrorism would occur towards the end of cycles of political violence and as a sign of failure of other, or less extreme, forms thereof. Again, here, agency is considered, yet the emphasis lays on these processes, mechanisms and on various elements of context that affect the nature of individual and organizational action. Similar to the determinist approaches, the ways in which these elements of context act are of a cause and effect nature (pioneering this approach were the works of della Porta 1995, 2013).

Approaches to terrorism studies in the context of social science research

These three approaches and the respective theories essentially apply existing concepts and hypotheses in the broader social sciences, although this genealogy is not always clearly identified. A classic explanation in the deterministic approach is the frustration–aggression hypothesis in combination with relative deprivation. The frustration–aggression hypothesis postulated that aggression is always a consequence of frustration, the latter occurring as a result of an interference with the pursuit of certain goals. Initially proposed in 1939 by John Dollard, Leonard William Doob, Neal Elgar Miller, Orval Hobart Mowrer and Robert Richardson Sears, it has remained extremely influential until today and is, explicitly or implicitly, at the basis of many root cause approaches to terrorism and political violence more broadly. For example, one of the major and often cited paradigmatic works on political violence is Ted Gurr's (1970) *Why Men Rebel*. Here, political violence is explained as the "perceived discrepancy between value expectations and value capabilities" (37), that is, between what people feel that they are entitled to and what they actually can achieve. In this case, Gurr also resorts to frustration and posits that the "primary source of the human capacity for violence" is indeed frustration (36). This conundrum can be found also in the criminological literature in the strain theory and later the subcultural theory of status frustration. The strain theory developed by sociologist Robert K. Merton posits that crime occurs as one of the possible responses to the discrepancy between culturally defined goals and the institutionalized means available to obtain them. To this, criminologist Albert Cohen (1955) added the psychological element of frustration to explain the emergence of deviant subcultures.

The conceptualization of the free rider dilemma and its solution goes back to the work of economic Mancur Olson, which was then used in social movement resource mobilization theory. Mancur Olson, Jr. presented his (revised) study *The Logic of Collective Action: Public Goods and the Theory of Groups* in 1971. In this influential but also criticized work he examines inter alia labor unions, trade associations and professional associations. He finds that in large groups there can be no collective action in the pursuit of a collective good (a non-excludable, public good) because rational, self-interested individuals seek to maximize their gains while minimizing their costs. As the contribution of each single member in large groups is small, their participation is not decisive for the overall outcome which provokes some group members to free ride, meaning that they enjoy the public good provided through the action of others. Olson states that this free rider dilemma can only be overcome in large groups by forcing the members to contribute to the achievement of the collective good or by offering them selective incentives like prestige or money. To the contrary, Olson assumes that this is somewhat different in small groups as there can be a group interest which makes coercion or selective incentives unnecessary to achieve the collective good. This is so because first, some group members might have such a high interest in achieving the goal, second, the return to each group member is much higher in small groups, third, the organizational costs are lower in small groups and finally, because it is easier to influence group members in smaller units.

Some authors have explicitly traced their approach to terrorism to such traditions. For example, Martha Crenshaw (1998) draws in her account of terrorism as strategic choice on the work of Harvey Waterman: "Reasons and Reason: Collective Political Activity in Comparative and Historical Perspective" (1981). As the title suggests, this did not deal at the time with terrorism in particular, but with collective political violence more broadly. Waterman situated his theory in the broader context of a debate between a pre-existing paradigm which emphasized external factors and psychological frustration on the one hand, and rational, "political" explanations on the other:

> The view that crowd behavior should be seen mainly in emotional terms has crumbled in the face of study after study of crowds that have acted in quite instrumental ways. Explanations of collective action in terms of social-psychological or socioeconomic variables have repeatedly been shown to be less apt than explanations employing the components of political decisions: calculations of cost, benefit, and risk, inspired by the provocations, inducements, and newly perceived weaknesses of political elites or by the challenges of newly mobilized competitors for status and power. The common thread running through these shifts in intellectual fashion has been a reaction against the dominant perspective of the 1960s, which turned to psychological, sociocultural, and socioeconomic explanations for political phenomena, especially in the literatures of "development," "revolution," "violence," and "political behavior." The corrective has been, in various ways, an assertion of the primacy of politics in explaining political phenomena, even those involving political action by large numbers of people not usually involved in political affairs. (Waterman 1981: 554–555)

Waterman made here a point out of the political nature of the phenomena that he studied, and that those political events were the outcome of conscious decisions, rather than the result of some external forces or broader variables. Instead, collective action here and, by extension, of the terrorists would follow a strategic logic whereby organizations would be looking to obtain a strategic advantage over their enemies, based on a calculation of costs and benefits and on the background of resources and opportunities. This strategic approach to explaining terrorism was presented at the time in contrast to a *deterministic*, psychological approach drawing on the concept of frustration. Crenshaw's and Post's chapters in the *Origins of Terrorism* (Reich 1990) dealt in fact with two units of analysis: organizations versus individuals, and although written in a somewhat contradictory manner, they reflected and still reflect a more general tendency in terrorism studies to consider organizations as strategic, rational actors, and individual action often as a result of some psychological or external force – essentially a deterministic take. At the same time, however, there are of course also intentional approaches focusing on individuals and their individual gains, as well as deterministic takes on terrorism, whereby variables of a higher order are considered behind the emergence of or spikes in terrorism, regardless of the activity or interests of specific organizations.

In some cases, terrorism theories build on related approaches in more than one discipline. For example, Max Taylor's framework for understanding individual motivation builds on the criminological rational choice theory and behaviorism in psychology. In his book *The Terrorist* (1988), Taylor builds on the basic assumption made in the criminological rational choice approach as formulated by Derek B. Cornish and Ronald V. Clarke in *The Reasoning Criminal* (1986), namely that "the offender benefits from his criminal choices, and that this benefit is the determining factor in his commission of crime" (181). As Taylor further points out, this benefit does not necessarily need to be of material nature as an individual "also gains excitement from his activity, status amongst his peer group, and confirms his membership of that marginalized group" (181). The key terms for the analysis of terrorist behavior are the "situation" and the anticipated feedback from the environment: "The factors contributing to both the 'involvement' and the 'event' processes can be conceptualized in environmental terms as various psychological stimuli that either 'set the occasion' for the terrorist act or terminate it" (183). In making this argument, Taylor draws on behaviorism and the work of Burrhus Frederic Skinner. The behavioral approach as explained by Taylor (1988: 201):

> is characterized by an emphasis on the relationship between the relevant conse-
> quences of behavior and events associated with those consequences. The important
> consequence to behavior is reward, or reinforcement. Behavior which is followed by
> reinforcement tends to have an increased probability of occurrence. Many things
> can act as reinforcers to us – social approval, gaining status, financial gain, food,
> and so forth. Specific reinforcers are mainly personal but there are broad classes of
> reinforcers (like those mentioned earlier) which are largely universal.

Going back to the parallels with theories and approaches explaining other types of phenomena, we can also see parallels in the *evolution* of approaches in time and as reflected in terrorism studies. In the field of social movements, for example, there was a determinist phase looking at higher-level variables and causes for mobilization, most prominently deprivation and other types of grievances and strain. Following this, two strands of theory focused on the instrumental or rational aspect of mobilization, specifically on resources and opportunities. The importance of language and discourse also penetrated the social movement literature with the framing theory and inquiries into how political messages can be formulated in a persuasive way for the intended audience. Similar developments can be observed in the political science literature on violent and political conflict, criminology or psychology, such as for example in relationship to (relative) deprivation or frustration. While in the classical disciplines we see a certain evolution in time of the various approaches and in particular a certain overhaul of the earlier deterministic explanations, for the case of terrorism we see similar evolutions and a coexistence of the different approaches at the same time. For example, the initial literature on individual radicalization processes focused on root causes (Veldhuis & Staun 2009), to then propose rational choice explanations (Pisoiu 2012) and later relational approaches (Malthaner 2014). At the same time, we still have more recent deterministic approaches, at times combined with additional elements such as social networks (Cherney et al. 2020).

Back to the future in international relations

As IR theory is discovering new avenues of research, there is an inevitable spill-over effect on the terrorism studies literature as well. One of these avenues is IR and pop culture conceptualized as a site where "power, ideology and identity are constituted, produced and materialized" (Grayson et al. 2009: 156). Following the approach of the aesthetic turn, representations are considered as sites of politics, political subjectivity and narratives, while the latter have an effect on material processes, too (2009: 157). Cultural artifacts such as video games (Robinson 2012), alien invasion films (Löfflmann 2013), war movies (Philpott 2010), television series (Wheeler 2014), novels (Shapiro 2010), celebrity politics (Street 2012), music (Baker 2013), photography (Bleiker & Kay 2007) or art (Danchev & Lisle 2009) have been in particular focus, as sites revealing underlying assumptions and understandings related to doing politics. Overall, it has been demonstrated how "popular culture and politics produce relations of power" and that "power relations engendered by popular culture must be taken seriously" (Grayson 2014: 223).

With regard to aesthetics and pop culture more broadly, terrorism works are mainly descriptive at this stage and without a systematic use of the IR and pop culture theoretical arsenal, yet this might change as authors increasingly notice the empirical presence of pop cultural material in radicalization processes and terrorist propaganda. Daesh's extensive use of Hollywood imagery and the general professionalization and increase in the use of audio-visual material by extremist and terrorist organizations have alerted researchers to the potential radicalizing effects of pop cultural elements as well as their strong presence in terrorist and extremist propaganda more broadly (see for example Kierke 2015; Russo & Giusti 2017; Robinson & Whittaker 2021).

Another emerging field of IR which might be relevant to apply to terrorism studies is the IR of the everyday. This line of research contests the exclusivity of states as the only locus of IR. The relevance of "ordinary people" for IR has been argued for example from the perspective of their role in preserving territorial states (Alvian 2019) or of a more general critique of classic IR being elitist, or by pointing out that the distinction between the global on the one side and the domestic/local/everyday on the other would be false (Björkdahl et al. 2019). Within this argumentation, as the relevance of the everyday for the global is being argued, the everyday remains everyday, remains local. In the context of terrorism, we have a somewhat more complex picture. In the last decades, terrorist organizations are increasing their IR and global scope, while counter-terrorism efforts in Europe, still led by national police, have been somewhat slow in recognizing this. There has been international cooperation such as between the Red Army Faction and the Popular Front for the Liberation of Palestine, the latter having hijacked a German plane in order to force the release of Red Army Faction prisoners. Engaging foreign governments and orchestrating terrorist operations has become standard with jihadi terrorism. Apart from this, contemporary terrorism in the West is manifesting in lone actor attacks and homegrown cells, some of which involve little indoctrinated individuals. These are everyday existences which do not remain as such but in fact do have a very visible and not only implicit effect on international politics.

This latter line of research brings us back to the original point of the chapter regarding the primacy of the unit of analysis in deciding on the theoretical approach to take in studying terrorism. We have seen how, given the lack of interest on the part of classic IR theories, most of the literature has developed drawing on other branches of political science, sociology, criminology and psychology. We then approached emerging IR research agendas and suggested their applicability, especially considering contemporary manifestations of terrorism. As IR is slowly changing and allowing for actors other than states and non-governmental organizations to populate the field, we can expect a more stable anchoring of terrorism studies within this discipline.

References

Alvian, R. A. (2019) *Locating "the Everyday" in "the International": An Exploration*, available at https:// www .e -ir .info/ 2019/ 10/ 03/ locating -the -everyday -in -the -international-an-exploration/

Baker, C. (2013) Music as a weapon of ethnopolitical violence and conflict: Processes of ethnic separation during and after the break-up of Yugoslavia, *Patterns of Prejudice*, 47, 409–429.

Bjorgo, T. (ed.) (2005) *Root Causes of Terrorism: Myths, Reality and Ways Forward*, London: Routledge.

Björkdahl, A., Hall, M., & Svensson, T. (2019) Everyday international relations: Editors' introduction, *Cooperation and Conflict*, 54(2), 123–130.

Blakeley, R. (2010) State terrorism in the social sciences: Theories, methods and concepts, in Jackson, R., Murphy, E., & Poynting, S. (eds), *Contemporary State Terrorism: Theory and Practice*, Abingdon: Routledge, 12–27.

Bleiker, R. (2001) The aesthetic turn in international political theory, *Millennium: Journal of International Studies*, 30(3), 509–533.

Bleiker, R., & Kay, A. (2007). Representing HIV/AIDS in Africa: Pluralist photography and local empowerment. *International Studies Quarterly*, 51(1), 139–163.

Caplan, B. (2006) Terrorism: The relevance of the rational choice model, *Public Choice*, 128, 91–107.

Cherney, A., Bolton, E., Norham, S. A. B., & Milts, J. (2020) Understanding youth radicalisation: An analysis of Australian data, *Behavioral Sciences of Terrorism and Political Aggression*. DOI: 10.1080/19434472.2020.1819372

Cohen, A. R. (1955). Social norms, arbitrariness of frustration, and status of the agent of frustration in the frustration-aggression hypothesis. *The Journal of Abnormal and Social Psychology*, 51(2), 222.

Cornish, D. B., & Clarke, R. V. (1986) *The Reasoning Criminal*, The Hague: Springer-Verlag.

Crenshaw, M. (1998) The logic of terrorism: Terrorist behavior as a product of strategic choice, in Reich, W. (ed.), *Origins of Terrorism: Psychologies, Ideologies, Theologies, States of Mind*, Washington, DC: Woodrow Wilson Center Press, 7–24.

Danchev, A., & Lisle, D. (2009) Introduction: Art, politics, purpose, *Review of International Studies*, 35(4), 775–779.

della Porta, D. (1995) *Social Movements, Political Violence and the State*, New York: Cambridge University Press.

della Porta, D. (2013) *Clandestine Political Violence*, Cambridge: Cambridge University Press.

Emirbayer, M. (1997) Manifesto for a relational sociology, *American Journal of Sociology*, 103(2), 281–317.

Gaibulloev, K., Hou, D., & Sandler, T. (2020) How do the factors determining terrorist groups' longevity differ from those affecting their success?, *European Journal of Political Economy*, 65(C).

Grayson, K. (2014) Special section: Editor's introduction, *Politics*, 34(3), 223–224.

Grayson, K., Davies, M., & Philpott, S. (2009) Pop goes IR? Researching the popular culture – world politics continuum, *Politics*, 29(3), 155–163.

Gurr, T. (1970) *Why Men Rebel*, Princeton, NJ: Princeton University Press.

Hoffman, B. (2003) The logic of suicide terrorism, *Atlantic Monthly*, June, 291(5).

Jarvis, L. (2016) Critical terrorism studies after 9/11, in Jackson, R. (ed.), *Routledge Handbook of Critical Terrorism Studies*, Abingdon: Routledge.

Kierke, X. (2015) Violence and political myth: Radicalizing believers in the pages of *Inspire Magazine*, *International Political Sociology*, 9, 283–298.

Löfflmann, G. (2013) Hollywood, the Pentagon, and the cinematic production of national security, *Critical Studies on Security*, 1(3), 280–294.

Malthaner, S. (2014) Contextualizing radicalization: The emergence of the "Sauerland-Group" from radical networks and the Salafist movement, *Studies in Conflict and Terrorism*, 37(8), 638–653.

Olson, M. (1971). *The Logic of Collective Action: Public Goods and the Theory of Groups* (2nd edition). Cambridge: Harvard University Press.

Pape, R. (2003) The strategic logic of suicide terrorism, *American Political Science Review*, 97(3), 343–361.

Philpott, S. (2010) Is anyone watching? War, cinema and bearing witness, *Cambridge Review of International Affairs*, 23(2), 325–348.

Pisoiu, D. (2012) *Islamist Radicalisation in Europe: An Occupational Change Process*, Abingdon: Routledge.

Post, J. M. (1990) Terrorist psycho-logic: Terrorist behavior as a product of psychological forces, in Reich, W. (ed.), *Origins of Terrorism: Psychologies, Ideologies, Theologies, States of Mind*, Cambridge: Cambridge University Press and Washington, DC: Woodrow Wilson International Center for Scholars, 25–40.

Reich, W. (1990) *Origins of Terrorism: Psychologies, Ideologies, Theologies, States of Mind*, Washington, DC: Woodrow Wilson Center Press with Johns Hopkins University Press.

Robinson, N. (2012). Videogames, persuasion and the War on Terror: Escaping or embedding the military—entertainment complex? *Political Studies*, 60(3), 504–522.

Robinson, N., & Whittaker, J. (2021) Playing for hate? Extremism, terrorism, and videogames, *Studies in Conflict and Terrorism*. DOI: 10.1080/1057610X.2020.1866740

Russo, A., & Giusti, S. (2017). Monuments under attack: From protection to securitisation. *Robert Schuman Centre for Advanced Studies Research Paper No. RSCAS*, 32.

Shapiro, M. J. (2010) *The Time of the City: Politics, Philosophy and Genre*, London: Routledge.

Stohl, M. (2006) The state as terrorist: Insights and implications, *Democracy and Security*, 2, 1–25.

Street, J. (2012) Do celebrity politics and celebrity politicians matter?, *British Journal of Politics and International Relations*, 14(3), 346–356.

Taylor, M. (1988) *The Terrorist*, London: Brassey's Defence Publishers.

The Problem of Terrorism (2002) Conversations with history, Berkeley, CA: Institute of International Studies, University of California. http://globetrotter.berkeley.edu/people2/Mearsheimer/mearsheimer-con5.html

Veldhuis, T., & Staun, J. (2009) *Islamist Radicalisation: A Root Cause Model*, The Hague: Netherlands Institute of International Relations Clingendael, October. www.diis.dk/files/media/publications/import/islamist_radicalisation.veldhuis_and_staun.pdf

Waterman, H. (1981) Reasons and reason: Collective political activity in comparative and historical perspective, *World Politics*, 33(4), 554–589.

Wheeler, M. (2014) "A city upon a hill": The wire and its distillation of the United States polity, *Politics*, 34(3), 237–247.

6 The interdisciplinarity challenge for terrorism studies

Asta Maskaliūnaitė

Introduction

The attacks of 9/11 transformed terrorism studies from a marginal endeavor of a few academics into a flourishing field of research. The amount of literature on the topic rose exponentially during the following 20 years and the understanding of (at least some) aspects of the phenomenon seems to have become more robust.

Terrorism attracted researchers from all the corners of social sciences and humanities.[1] While the "usual suspects" – criminologists, psychologists or political scientists, international relations scholars and sociologists – produced most works, researchers from other areas also came onto the wave of interest in the phenomenon. Historians, who dominated a large strand of the early research on terrorism by presenting broad overviews of its development, looked into some episodes of terrorism, presenting in-depth histories of some campaigns and attempts to defeat them (Burrough 2015; Irwin 2013; Jensen 2014; Webb 2014). Linguists and those taking the linguistic turn in social sciences explored the role and function of metaphors in the "war on terror" and the cultural studies scholars took on the culture and media role in our approach to terrorism (Hodges 2011; Jackson 2005; Lewis 2005; Steuter & Wills 2009). Scholars of literature looked into the "gothic connection" and rediscovered the works on terrorism in Victorian novels (Crawford 2013; Melchiori 2016). The list can go on.

---

[1]   There is a substantial amount of research on terrorism-related technical subjects, however, for the purposes of this chapter, I will focus only on the social science research into the phenomenon.

Thus, terrorism studies looks a truly interdisciplinary endeavor, where scientists from a variety of disciplines join together in order to advance understanding of the phenomenon. And yet, while there is much to celebrate, the field suffers from periodical bouts of doubt and scholars in it sometimes delve into "rhetoric of failure," identified by Lisa Stampnitzky, where the "actors perceive their field as having failed ... to become a bounded field of cultural production, a mature profession, or a fully institutionalized discipline" (Stampnitzky 2013, p.3).

The purpose of this chapter is to explore this (inter)disciplinary nature of terrorism studies and the potential for its move towards or away from disciplining itself properly. The principal argument here is that in order to be a truly successful interdisciplinary project, terrorism studies should actually become more robust as a discipline. For that, what is sorely needed is a more systematic theorizing on the phenomenon, which could truly integrate various disciplinary approaches. Given the already substantial amount of research on the subject, the researchers in the field should spend some time systematizing the existing knowledge and presenting, especially to newly arrived students or researchers, a common background on which new theories could be built upon or deepened.

This chapter is thus divided into four sections. The first section explores the woes of terrorism studies and the reasons for the rhetoric of failure. The second section will explore the ideal and reality of interdisciplinarity, and the third will evaluate terrorism research in light of these discussions. Finally, in place of conclusions, a way forward will be proposed.

Rhetoric of failure?

As psychological research is now an indispensable part of the study of the phenomenon of terrorism, so introspection seems to be a quality of the field of terrorism studies. In her widely acclaimed study of the state of the field, Lisa Stampnitzky forcefully showed that scholars deeply troubled by the perceived challenges in their area of research had produced the aforementioned "rhetoric of failure." She identified four clusters of sub-arguments to support this type of rhetoric: problems of the lack of commonly agreed definition; lack of boundaries; lack of methodological rigor; and lack of intellectual progress (Stampnitzky 2011, 2013).

The issue of definition is often mentioned by those arguing that the field has a fundamental problem. Proponents of revamping terrorism research gathered into the school of critical terrorism studies make the issue of definition (or rather, the failure of typical definitions to include the state as a perpetrator of terrorist violence) into one of the cornerstones of their objections to "mainstream" terrorism studies.[2] At the same time, there exist many proposals as to how to overcome this issue. For example, not using the term at all and focusing on certain groups/organizations/individuals as Marc Sageman does in his *Leaderless Jihad*, claiming that it is not necessary for him to search for an overarching definition of terrorism, is enough to define the subjects of the study (Sageman 2011, p.15). Or as Donatella della Porta (2013) does in *Clandestine Political Violence*, refusing the heavy negatively loaded term of terrorism and offering instead a seemingly neutral "clandestine political violence." In other works, particular definitions are offered and there still seems to be quite a wide consensus on the major ingredients in the definition of terrorism to be able to deal with the topic at a common level of understanding. Given that terrorism is quite a general term, it is hardly surprising that it does not have a precise definition. In this, it is in a venerable company of "democracy," "liberalism" or "revolution" – all terms with a certain normative load and as such difficult to "universally" define.

The second argument concerns the lack of boundaries for entry to the field, resulting in a proliferation of self-appointed experts and the prevalence of one-timers in the publications. Andrew Silke has dedicated considerable effort for the exploration of the quality of terrorism research and observed that "a huge proportion of the literature is the work of fleeting visitors" (Silke 2004b, p.1), as 80 percent of the publications on terrorism even before the 9/11 attacks were work of "transients," researchers who publish one or two articles in a decade and disappear from the radar (Silke 2001, 2004a). Similar findings are discussed in Avishag Gordon's bibliometric analysis (2007). More recent analysis by Bart Schuurman looking at the research trends from 2007 till 2016 found this aspect unchanged (2018).

The third issue regards the lack of methodological rigor. Stampnitzky couples lack of methodological rigor with two complaints: (1) a lack of statistical research and quantitative analysis; and (2) a lack of fieldwork. As regards the first two, Silke also emphasizes overreliance on the qualitative methods, little use of statistics and quantitative data, lack of depth of research and

---

[2]   See, for example, Jackson et al. (2009, 2011). Chapter 5 in the latter deals with the issue of definition.

consequently few achievements in prediction.[3] He indicates that the share of articles using statistics throughout the 1990s hovered at about 15 percent of all those published on the subject and only increased to 25–26 percent after the 9/11 attacks (Silke 2009, p.40). Schuurman's study indicates a "slow but steady upward trend" in the use of statistics, yet the majority of the articles are still written without any supportive quantitative data (Schuurman 2018, p.8). The other complaint is best expressed by an analogy of terrorist researchers as cartographers of Africa in the Victorian era: "Just as cartographers a century ago mapped from a distance a vast and impenetrable continent few of them had ever seen, most contemporary terrorism research is conducted far removed from, and therefore with little knowledge of actual terrorists themselves" (Hoffman 2004, p.xviii).

Often connected to these methodological concerns is the issue of a lack of data (Reid & Chen 2007, p.141; Schmid 2011, p.461). However, contrary to the widespread notion of the lack of empirics in this field, Ranstorp indicates a number of good sources that use first-tier data for the construction of their arguments and quotes the former head of the United Kingdom Joint Terrorism Analysis Centre that there is "an ocean of signals and open-source information" (Ranstorp 2009, p.126) that is available for researchers. Currently, there seems to be a move towards a consensus that there are enough data available for the scholars in terrorism studies. Indeed, admitting this, a major conference in the field organized by the Society for Terrorism Research in 2019 looked at how the increasing amounts of available data can be utilized.[4]

In contrast, looking for theoretical lenses that help make sense of these data, one would be hard pressed to find systematic assessments. Probably the best example here is a search of any online bookseller for the books with the title *Theories of Terrorism* which (at the time of writing) results in only one entry.[5]

---

[3] It could be argued that here terrorism studies is again in the venerable company of other social science approaches which may offer compelling explanations of events retrospectively but are unable to predict. Daniel Kofman, an analyst focusing on Russia, has jibed, for example, that "the science of predicting regime change seems to lag significantly behind astrology" (Kofman n.d.).

[4] The title for the 2019 conference of Society for Terrorism Research was *The Data Revolution in Terrorism Research: Implications for Theory and Practice.* www.societyforterrorismresearch.org/international-conference-2019

[5] See Pisoiu and Hain (2017). The books with the titles *Theory and Practice* (e.g. Bakker 2015) are not counted here as the term "theory" in their wording is clearly juxtaposed to "practice." This reflects everyday language use of terms where "practice" is rational and empirical and "theory" is groundless speculation which will collapse at the first encounter with the real world. The dictionaries provide

Typically, handbooks on terrorism deal with definitions, types of terrorism, its causes, tactics and the fight against it. The theories are implied and presented somewhere in between, but hardly ever in a systematic fashion.[6] Similarly, courses on terrorism often follow the historical development, typologies, case studies and sometimes go deeper into specific aspects of terrorism (such as tactics, targets and methods used). Theories here are also implied, but do not seem to be the driving force of the courses.[7]

As Magnus Ranstorp noted, "there is little self-conscious, sophisticated engagement with theoretical developments elsewhere and even less rigorous application of explicitly visible methodologies" in the field (2009, p.24). Ranstorp also emphasizes the "critical task of theory building and theory formation" (2007, p.10). This task is even more pressing given the general perception of terrorism studies as "theoretically barren" and "politically compromised" (Gunning 2007, p.381), a field in which observers are often hard pressed to find works which apply "any theoretical approach explicitly or robustly" (Ranstorp 2009, p.24).

The issue of theory can be clearly linked to the final cluster of complaints that centers on the lack of intellectual progress in the field. In 2001, Andrew Silke wrote damningly on the situation of terrorism studies:

> it is possible for a research community to remain active indefinitely without ever producing meaningful exploratory results (while tolerating very high levels of conceptual confusion and disagreement). It seems relatively clear that terrorism research exists in such a state and that after over 30 years of enquiry, the field shows little evidence that it is capable of making the leap to consistently producing research of genuinely exploratory and predictive value. (Silke 2001, p.58)

---

such examples of this juxtaposition as: "The precautionary principle sounds good in theory, but in practice it is a nightmare" or "although this sounds good in theory, in practice it never quite seems to work that way" (see *Oxford English Dictionary*, https://en.oxforddictionaries.com/definition/theory).

6   See, for example, Whittaker (2012) and Martin (2014). One exception is the recent book by Chenoweth and Moore, focusing exactly on the different approaches to the study of terrorism (Chenoweth & Moore 2019). The recently published *Oxford Handbook of Terrorism* contains a section on "approaches" to terrorism in different fields of social sciences. The *Routledge Handbook of Terrorism Research* edited by Alex Schmid (2011) did have a chapter on theories, but a later book in the series, the *Routledge Handbook of Terrorism and Counterterrorism* edited by Andrew Silke (2018) does not have such a separate section (Chenoweth et al. 2019; Schmid 2011; Silke 2018).

7   See, for example, the selection of exemplary syllabi at the American Political Science Association Task Force for Political Violence and Terrorism (APSA Task Force n.d.).

Twelve years later, in 2013, one of the grandees of the field, Marc Sageman, provoked an arduous debate on whether there was a "stagnation in terrorism research."[8] The debate around this issue resulted in an entire volume of *Terrorism and Political Violence* dedicated to the topic.[9] Sageman's own response to his critics goes back to data and suggests that without access to primary data, closely controlled by the government, the study of terrorism cannot progress (Sageman 2014, p.620). Yet, he also argued for the need of theoretical development in the spirit of the early RAND corporation, refining arguments in discussion, constructively criticizing colleagues' work and thus helping to improve theories. Contrary to this ideal, Sageman argues, theoretical discussion does not receive much attention and "publication of theoretical speculation is usually greeted with polite silence" (Sageman 2014, p.619).

These internal discussions, however, do not touch upon a more general question of how to demarcate the field as such or whether and for what such a demarcation would be needed. While it is noted that terrorism studies is a field torn between practitioners and academics (Stampnitzky 2013), and it is sometimes suggested that they are "conducted in the cracks and crevices which lie between the large academic disciplines" (Silke 2004a, p.1), the issue of interdisciplinarity is rarely explored. Interdisciplinarity, though, often offered up as an ideal to strive for, can work both to promote and hinder the development of robust bodies of knowledge. In the next section I will explore this ideal and its realities.

Interdisciplinarity

Renaissance humanists and Enlightenment *Encyclopédistes* were proudly generalists. Yet, already towards the end of the eighteenth century, the amount of knowledge available for humanity was becoming too much for a single person to successfully manage and improve on their own. In the nineteenth century the process of specialization moved at an increasingly fast pace and various disciplines took more distinct shapes. Almost at the same time that this process started, calls for the rediscovery of the unity of science were heard. With time, scholars focusing on ever narrower sets of issues were seen as factory workers tolling over tiny cogs and unable to see the big picture.

---

[8]   The original article was published as Sageman (2013). It has been reprinted elsewhere, including in *Terrorism and Political Violence*.

[9]   See, *Terrorism and Political Violence*, 2014, Volume 26, Issue 4.

To remedy this myopia, it was argued, a different way of researching and teaching was needed. It eventually came under the heading of "interdisciplinarity" and demanded the end of disciplinary divisions to focus on the existing issues using all the tools of science. These demands first had as their target university practices, but from the mid-1990s with the idea of the "mode 2 production of knowledge,"[10] the approach spread to the wider community of research as well.[11]

A two-pronged process seemed to be happening: on the one hand, disciplines were becoming entrenched and more of them were established throughout academic institutions. On the other hand, interdisciplinarity became an ideal to strive for and the yardstick by which to judge research. One of the most prominent researchers on interdisciplinarity, Peter Weingart, calls interdisciplinarity "a paradoxical discourse," "proclaimed, demanded, hailed and written into funding programs" while "at the same time specialization of science goes on unhampered, reflected in the continuous complaint about it" (Weingart 2000, p.26).

Weingart suggests this discourse persists because interdisciplinarity has become largely synonymous with innovation. For researchers (and by extension conferences and journals) to be interdisciplinary minded is to be forward looking and open. Simultaneously, they have to contend with the reality that their work will be judged by the standards of disciplines, thus limiting the appeal of a truly boundary-crossing work (Weingart 2000).

The difficulty of judging interdisciplinarity in research partly derives from the lack of tools for such judgment. It could also be partly linked to the variety of potential interdisciplinarities themselves. Julie Thompson Klein (2017) provides an extensive typology of interdisciplinarity, discussing the levels of integration achieved in these different ways of engagement between disciplines. For example, sometimes presented as "interdisciplinary," the take on a particular subject from different disciplinary perspectives would be considered

---

[10]   In 1994, Gibbons et al. argued that universities no longer had a monopoly on knowledge production. Rather, the loci of this production had multiplied. Additionally, it had taken on a more problem-solving character in contrast to a seemingly decontextualized search for universal truths that characterized the previous "mode 1" production of knowledge.

[11]   This section provides an extremely short version of the complex development of interdisciplinarity as a notion in science. For more detailed analysis and broader literature review, see, e.g. Chettiparamb (2007), Klein (1990) and Weingart (2000).

multidisciplinary in her typology. Interdisciplinarity proper requires a higher degree of integration. This can be done on a methodological or theoretical level. In the latter, "a more comprehensive general view and epistemological form embodied in creating conceptual frameworks for analyzing particular problems, integrating propositions across disciplines, and synthesizing continuities between models and analogies" (Klein 2017, p.25) is achieved.

"Interdisciplinarity" as a term has strongly positive connotations. Yet, it exists in the context of discipline-based institutions and in the context where the disciplines themselves interact in ways which are not necessarily linear and benign, leading to a discussion of "scientific imperialism" (Mäki et al. 2018).

The disciplines themselves at the most basic level are a combination of a subject matter and methodology. As such, they are sometimes reviled as parochial and xenophobic, trying to protect their turf from intrusion by others. Yet, they have additional uses that are more difficult to transplant. As Jerry Jacobs writes:

> disciplines exist because research and scholarship have an important social dimension. It is not enough for a lone scholar to come up with brilliant insights on her own. These insights need to be recognized, organized with other relevant theories and findings, and taught to the next generation. Disciplines are designed with these tasks in mind. They are forms of social organization that evaluate, organize, and disseminate research and scholarship. (Jacobs 2017, p.36)

As can be inferred from the above quote, disciplines not only serve to compartmentalize science, but they are also important social institutions. Research, though in itself a rational and logical activity, is done by fallible human scholars. Disciplines are thus not only organizing units for topics but also for the scholars who research them. They are institutions with "an *ethos*: a set of constructive goals, values, beliefs, standards, norms, practices, and/or traditions" (Salmela & Mäki 2018, p.33). Work in disciplines produces a "disciplinary culture" which, by extension, produces "disciplinary identity" (Salmela & Mäki 2018, p.34).

Consequently, disciplines and the scholars working within them can be analyzed as any other group and their relations with other disciplines as intergroup relations. For example, looking at the "disciplinary emotions," it is noted that scholars often express pride in one's own discipline and skepticism or envy about the achievement of others.

In this setting achievement of true interdisciplinarity is challenging. The issue is even further exacerbated by the differences in status between the various disciplines. For example, natural sciences is of a higher standing than social sciences. Within the social sciences economics is often considered as the highest-status science for its reliance on mathematical modeling that supposedly brings it closest to the ideal of natural sciences.

In this context, it is claimed, some forms of interdisciplinarity should be considered "scientific imperialism." Disciplines can encroach on others and impose their ontologies and methodologies on the subject matter(s) that originally were the preserve of other fields.[12] While sometimes this may result in the advancement of understanding the world, critics of "imperialist" scientific disciplines argue that by such expansion they may hamper the development of the "colonized" disciplines or ignore some important human values that these disciplines may be promoting.[13]

In addition, such encroachment produces what Kristina Rolin calls "epistemic injustice" or an "unfairness in distribution of credibility" (2018, p.55). When a discipline is considered superior to others, it suggests that scholars versed in this superior discipline are better experts in general and can thus authoritatively comment on issues that could potentially be assessed from a different disciplinary angle (2018, p.56). This aspect can have important repercussions for the field, particularly in a context of media fascination with its subject matter as in the case in terrorism studies, back to which we must now turn.

Interdisciplinarity of terrorism studies

As an (unlawful) activity of (usually) small groups of individuals with societal and political consequences, terrorism naturally needs to be understood from the perspective of various disciplines. Examples of its assessment from a variety of angles were offered in the introduction to this chapter. The question is whether the variety of assessments makes it into a truly interdisciplinary endeavor.

---

[12]   The initial work on this topic was presented by John Dupré (1994). It was later criticized and built upon by Clarke and Walsh (2009, 2013), Mäki (2013) and others (see Mäki et al. 2018).

[13]   An often cited example is the use of rational cost–benefit analysis from economics to analyze family life which is said to usurp the place of socio-cultural or psychological explanations, at the same time promoting a rather limited image of individuals as calculating emotionless machines. This is one of the starting points of Dupré's analysis (Dupré 1994).

According to the typology of Julie Thompson Klein, terrorism studies in its current state would probably belong to the "multidisciplinary" category. Here, while the subject is discussed from a variety of viewpoints, these disciplines remain separate and the topic is approached from the disciplinary angles without an attempt to integrate them into a more cohesive whole.

Interdisciplinarity itself requires a level of integration between the disciplines. This integration concerns all three pillars on which the disciplines operate: institutional/structural, methodological and subject matter/theoretical. The first pillar requires the establishment of departments and institutes dedicated to research of a topic, as well as continuous conferences and journals around which the community organizes itself. In this aspect, terrorism studies can be seen as an integrative field, already possessing a set of dedicated researchers, some research centers, numerous journals and a few continuous conferences bringing in scholars "originating" from different scientific areas of research.[14]

Methodological interdisciplinarity implies that the methods used in specific disciplines are integrated in others to make the results of inquiry more scientifically rigorous (Klein 2017, pp.24–25). In this area, terrorism studies follows the trajectory of social sciences in general.[15] Methodological pluralism and even eclecticism is becoming a norm in social sciences in general, making it a less useful yardstick by which to measure interdisciplinarity – as the methodological attachments of disciplines become weaker and more varied methodologies are used, methodology as such becomes less of an essential trait of identity.

In terrorism studies, the variety of methodologies used is quite extensive: fieldwork, historical case studies, quantitative analysis, discourse analysis, psychological research, etc. At the same time, not all methodologies are valued to the same degree. The calls for more quantitative research and for more data that would allow such research indicate that such research is considered more highly than qualitative research. In the qualitative sphere, fieldwork-based research is considered the most valuable, as is indicated by the complaints that not enough is happening in the field (see, e.g. Dolnik 2013, pp.2–5).

---

[14]   For extensive lists of centers and journals, see van Dongen (2018) and Tinnes (2013). Annual conferences of organizations such as the Society for Terrorism Research have already been mentioned.

[15]   Here, as later, while acknowledging that significant parts of research on terrorism remain descriptive literature reviews, without identifiable methodological approaches, there is a growing portion of research based on identifiable methodologies.

A more significant issue, however, is that of theoretical integration, and it is here that an impediment for the further development of terrorism studies can be seen. Interdisciplinary integration at the theoretical level does not really happen. With the potential exception of the social movements approach, an interdisciplinary area in itself, few theoretical investigations take into account the developments in other areas.

There are three aspects of this issue. First, disciplines involve the creation of common norms and language (Turner 2017, p.19). Coming from different disciplines sometimes makes it difficult to communicate in a theoretical setting as scholars do not know each others' theoretical language. As a result, given the differences in training that take researchers to different directions, the interdisciplinary discussion may turn around the lowest common denominator, thus being quite shallow and not conducive to the creation of integrative theories.

Second, it is not entirely clear to what extent commitment to terrorism studies could override commitments to the more general disciplines. As was discussed, disciplinary identities come with the baggage of disciplinary emotions and status questions. Thus, as some disciplines are more equal than others, so their contributions have different degrees of appreciation. For example, one of the complaints often voiced against researchers working in (or rather around) the field is that they do their work without having ever met a single "terrorist." While this statement conveys unease that many scholars have with the continuous proliferation of crackpot theories and "terrorists are evil madmen" type of statements, it also implies that disciplinary approaches that bring the researcher close to the perpetrators of violence (e.g. psychology, criminology or anthropological work in the conflict zones) are more valuable than, say, contributions of economists, political scientists or sociologists who use different kinds of data for their work, data which do not require them to "meet a terrorist." These latter can probably escape damnation by employing quantitative methods, but there is no such recourse for many historians or international relations scholars.

Third, disciplinary domination, linked to a practice focus of the studies, overvalues some questions at the expense of others, i.e. by focusing on the agent of violence at the expense of the impact of violence on society. The questions of who the perpetrators are and why they attack become paramount to the detriment of some potentially even more important issues, e.g. why terrorism, a minor threat statistically, especially in the West, has such a disproportionate effect on societies.

Examination of the question of impact in a truly interdisciplinary spirit is where terrorism studies could have a possibility to explain important factors of a social world. As it deals with the impact of small groups in country or even world politics, it is uniquely placed to explore the interaction between structure and agency (the latter in all its unintended consequences). Indeed, there are few other areas where single moments end up shaping the system of the world as terrorist acts did both at the beginning of the twentieth and at the beginning of the twenty-first centuries. There are also few areas where so much has been done and so many lives lost without achieving anything at all. In being able to look into this interaction of individual activities and their structural consequences, terrorism studies could carve out a clear niche for itself within the social sciences, thus becoming a genuinely interdisciplinary discipline.

The way forward?

Terrorism studies is mature enough to insulate itself from an events-driven approach to analysis. There exists a strong enough core of dedicated scholars to work on the topic in a more systematic manner. What is important in this respect is to try to overcome the hurdles that interdisciplinarity places in its stride.

Maybe paradoxically, disciplinarity is a precondition of true interdisciplinarity. In order to become a truly interdisciplinary endeavor, terrorism studies should become more like a discipline. The common ethos has to take shape here. One sub-set of terrorism studies – critical terrorism studies – has been much more effective in this endeavor, positing clearly its core principles and beliefs, while at the same time allowing a certain level of methodological and even theoretical eclecticism to exist under its umbrella. The "mainstream" terrorism studies could achieve the same degree of integration with some additional effort.

If we accept that we have enough data to go by, it is high time to devote attention to what we can do with that data and try to work out what theoretical strands are most promising for the development of our understanding of the phenomenon. There are two aspects of this endeavor.

First, it could help to create interdisciplinary teams that would work on integrative theoretical approaches to the study of terrorism. This requires openness to the ideas and approaches of others and a certain humility from the scientists involved, with the notion that not all the questions can be answered from a disciplinary perspective and that the disciplinary background may limit one's perspective on the questions that can be asked as well.

Second, we need to create a starting point for the discussion by agreeing on a kind of terrorism 101 course that would be based on theories rather than the disparate aspects of the phenomenon (definitions, typologies and methods used in the attacks) which have a great danger of becoming very descriptive and not allowing one to gauge the depth of the issue. Theories-based textbooks such as Pisoiu and Hain (2017) and Chenoweth and Moore (2019) are a good start for this endeavor.

Looking at terrorism studies as a kind of proto-disciplinary field, we should have a set of theories that create a common understanding of where we start. For example, as a psychologist working on the current issues with radicalization, one may not need to know much on the theories that explain the rise of terrorism in the nineteenth century, but this knowledge would allow them to find common talk with a historian of anarchist movements and maybe inspire some theoretical development that would span the two centuries. At the same time, such discussions could help us explain to one another the stances and underlying beliefs of our disciplines that shape the work we do, thus helping others to understand better the premises of the investigation and be more realistic about its potential achievements.

The amount of literature on terrorism is currently such that it is very difficult for a newcomer to wade through. It is thus important and helpful to create a common theoretical background from which to start the exploration of this field by pointing out clearly the theoretical basis for inquiry. This would not be something really unique but it is quite overdue.

We do not have to all agree with all the premises of the theories included in such a compendium, but we have to think about them as a kind of starting point for a discussion of theories that need refinement and the creation of new ones. As Marc Sageman suggested, it might be time to invoke the spirit of RAND to help forge terrorism studies into a proper discipline.

References

APSA Task Force, n.d. Exemplary Syllabi: Task Force on Political Violence and Terrorism. Available at: www.apsanet.org/politicalviolence-exemplarysyllabi

Bakker, E., 2015. *Terrorism and Counterterrorism Studies: Comparing Theory and Practice*, Leiden: Leiden University Press.

Burrough, B., 2015. *Days of Rage: America's Radical Underground, the FBI, and the Forgotten Age of Revolutionary Violence*, New York: Penguin Books.

Chenoweth, E. & Moore, P., 2019. *Politics of Terror*, Oxford: Oxford University Press.

Chenoweth, E., English, R., Gofas, A. & Kalyvas, S., Eds, 2019. *Oxford Handbook of Terrorism*, Oxford: Oxford University Press.

Chettiparamb, A., 2007. *Interdisciplinarity: A Literature Review*, Southampton: Interdisciplinary Teaching and Learning Group.

Clarke, S. & Walsh, A., 2009. Scientific Imperialism and the Proper Relations between the Sciences. *International Studies in the Philosophy of Science*, 23(2), pp.195–207.

Clarke, S. & Walsh, A., 2013. Imperialism, Progress, Developmental Teleology, and Interdisciplinary Unification. *International Studies in the Philosophy of Science*, 27(3), pp.341–351.

Crawford, J., 2013. *Gothic Fiction and the Invention of Terrorism: The Politics and Aesthetics of Fear in the Age of the Reign of Terror*, London: Bloomsbury.

della Porta, D., 2013. *Clandestine Political Violence*, Cambridge: Cambridge University Press.

Dolnik, A., 2013. Introduction: The Need for Field Research on Terrorism. In A. Dolnik, Ed. *Conducting Terrorism Field Research: A Guide*, London: Routledge.

Dupré, J., 1994. Against Scientific Imperialism. *Philosophy of Science Association Proceedings*, 2, pp.374–381.

Gibbons, M., Limoges, C., Schwartzman, S., Scott, P. & Trow, M., 1994. *The New Production of Knowledge: The Dynamics of Science and Research in Contemporary Societies*, New York: SAGE.

Gordon, A., 2007. Transient and Continuant Authors in a Research Field: The Case of Terrorism. *Scientometrics*, 72(2).

Gunning, J., 2007. Babies and Bathwaters: Reflecting on the Pitfalls of Critical Terrorism Studies. *European Political Science*, 6(3).

Hodges, A., 2011. *The "War on Terror" Narrative. Discourse and Intertextuality in the Construction and Contestation of Sociopolitical Reality*, Oxford: Oxford University Press.

Hoffman, B., 2004. Foreword. In A. Silke, Ed. *Research on Terrorism: Trends, Achievements, and Failures*, London: Frank Cass.

Irwin, L., 2013. *Deadly Times*, Guilford, CT: GLobe Pequot.

Jackson, R., 2005. *Writing the War on Terrorism: Language, Politics and Counterterrorism*, Manchester: Manchester University Press.

Jackson, R., Breen-Smyth, M. & Gunning, J., 2009. *Critical Terrorism Studies: A New Research Agenda*, London: Routledge.

Jackson, R., Jarvis, L., Gunning, J. & Breen-Smyth, M., 2011. *Terrorism: A Critical Introduction*, Houndmills: Palgrave Macmillan.

Jacobs, J., 2017. Sidebar: The Need for Disciplines in the Modern Research University. In R. Frodeman, J.T. Klein, & R.C. Dos Santos Pacheco, Eds. *Oxford Handbook of Interdisciplinarity*, Oxford: Oxford University Press.

Jensen, R.B., 2014. *The Battle against Anarchist Terrorism: An International History, 1878–1934*, Cambridge: Cambridge University Press.

Klein, J.T., 1990. *Interdisciplinarity: History, Theory and Practice*, Detroit, MI: Wayne State University Press.

Klein, J.T., 2017. Typologies of Interdisciplinarity: A Boundary Work of Definition. In R. Frodeman, J.T. Klein & R.C. Dos Santos Pacheco, Eds. *Oxford Handbook of Interdisciplinarity*, Oxford: Oxford University Press.

Kofman, M., n.d. Seven Deadly Sins of Russia Analysis. Available at: http://warontherocks.com/2015/12/the-seven-deadly-sins-of-russia-analysis/

Lewis, J., 2005. *Language Wars: The Role of Media and Culture in Global Terror and Political Violence*, London: Pluto Press.

Mäki, U., 2013. Scientific Imperialism: Difficulties in Definition, Identification, and Assessment. *International Studies in the Philosophy of Science*, 27(3), pp.325–339.

Mäki, U., Walsh, A. & Fernandez Pinto, M., 2018. *Scientific Imperialism: Exploring the Boundaries of Interdisciplinarity*, London: Routledge.

Martin, G., 2014. *Essentials of Terrorism: Concepts and Controversies*, London: SAGE.

Melchiori, B.A., 2016. *Terrorism in the Late Victorian Novel*, London: Routledge.

Pisoiu, D. & Hain, S., 2017. *Theories of Terrorism*, Abingdon: Routledge.

Ranstorp, M., 2007. *Mapping Terrorism Research: State of the Art, Gaps and Future Direction*, London: Routledge.

Ranstorp, M., 2009. Mapping Terrorism Studies after 9/11: An Academic Field of Old Problems and New Prospects. In R. Jackson, M.B. Smyth & J. Gunning, Eds. *Critical Terrorism Studies: A New Research Agenda*, London: Routledge.

Reid, E.F. & Chen, H., 2007. Mapping the Contemporary Terrorism Research Domain. *International Journal of Human Computer Studies*, 65(1), pp.42–56.

Rolin, K., 2018. Scientific Imperialism and Epistemic Injustice. In U. Mäki, A. Walsh & M. Fernandez Pinto, Eds. *Scientific Imperialism: Exploring the Boundaries of Interdisciplinarity*, London: Routledge.

Sageman, M., 2011. *Leaderless Jihad: Terror Networks in the Twenty-First Century*, Philadelphia, PA: University of Pennsylvania Press.

Sageman, M., 2013. The Stagnation of Research on Terrorism. *The Conversation*.

Sageman, M., 2014. Low Return on Investment. *Terrorism and Political Violence*, 26(4), pp.614–620.

Salmela, M. & Mäki, U., 2018. Disciplinary Emotions in Imperialistic Interdisciplinarity. In U. Mäki, A. Walsh & M. Fernandez Pinto, Eds. *Scientific Imperialism: Exploring the Boundaries of Interdisciplinarity*, London: Routledge.

Schmid, A., 2011. *The Routledge Handbook of Terrorism Research*, London: Routledge.

Schuurman, B., 2018. Research on Terrorism, 2007–2016: A Review of Data, Methods, and Authorship. *Terrorism and Political Violence*, 32(5), pp.1011–1026.

Silke, A., 2001. The Devil You Know: Continuing Problems with Research on Terrorism. *Terrorism and Political Violence*, 13(4), pp.1–14.

Silke, A., 2004a. An Introduction to Terrorism Research. In A. Silke, Ed. *Research on Terrorism: Trends, Achievements and Failures*, London: Frank Cass.

Silke, A., 2004b. The Road Less Travelled: Recent Trends in Terrorism Research. In A. Silke, Ed. *Research on Terrorism: Trends, Achievements and Failures*, London: Routledge.

Silke, A., 2009. Contemporary Terrorism Studies: Issues in Research. In R. Jackson, M.B. Smyth & J. Gunning, Eds. *Critical Terrorism Studies: A New Research Agenda*, London: Routledge.

Silke, A., Ed., 2018. *Routledge Handbook of Terrorism Research*, London: Routledge.

Stampnitzky, L., 2011. Disciplining an Unruly Field: Terrorism Expert and Theories of Scientific/Intellectual Production. *Qualitative Sociology*, 34.

Stampnitzky, L., 2013. *Disciplining Terror: How Experts Invented "Terrorism"*, Cambridge: Cambridge University Press.

Steuter, E. & Wills, D., 2009. *At War with Metaphor: Media, Propaganda, and Racism in the War on Terror*, Plymouth: L. Books.

Tinnes, J., 2013. 100 Core and Periphery Journals for Terrorism Research. *Perspectives on Terrorism*, 7(2).

Turner, S., 2017. Knowledge Formations: An Analytical Framework. In R. Frodeman, J.T. Klein & R. Dos Santos Pacheco, Eds. *The Oxford Handbook of Interdisciplinarity*, Oxford: Oxford University Press.

van Dongen, T., 2018. 130+ (Counter-)Terrorism Research Centres: An Inventory. *Perspectives on Terrorism*, 12(2).

Webb, S., 2014. *The Suffragette Bombers: Britain's Forgotten Terrorists*, Barnsley: Pen & Sword History.

Weingart, P., 2000. Interdisciplinarity: A Paradoxical Discourse. In N. Stehr & P. Weingart, Eds. *Practicing Interdisciplinarity*, Toronto: University of Toronto Press.

Whittaker, D.J., 2012. *The Terrorism Reader*, Abingdon: Routledge.

7 Ethnographic approaches in terrorism studies and research

Anastasia Filippidou

Introduction

In social science, research topics are neither neat nor clinical, rather they are characterised by overlaps and grey areas. This is strongly evident in ethnographic methodologies of protracted violent ethnically based conflicts. A variety of issues including but not limited to territory, history, economics, culture, religion, civil rights, and exclusivist identity, which on their own could constitute themes of research, become interlinked and interdependent in ethnographic methodologies. This multifaceted nature becomes a very satisfying challenge once the research is completed, and the process resembles more of a Van Gogh painting with the dramatic and overlapping brush strokes, which from up close gives a fragmented impression, but once completed and from a distance gives a unique result.

This chapter discusses the rationale behind the decision to adopt an ethnographic research method in terrorism studies, and it examines the strengths and challenges of the ethnographic approach. Ethnographic methodologies in terrorism studies focus on a breadth of topics and depth, as their emphasis is on the human element and the need to observe and actually interact with the research's key protagonists of the conflict in their real-life environment. However, for some this is equated to condoning the terrorists' acts. This chapter provides insights into the challenges, opportunities, and benefits of conducting primary research through the lens of ethnographic research methodologies and it is based on the author's personal fieldwork experiences on investigating violent ethnonational conflicts.

A key recommendation is the importance and utility of a pragmatic empathetic ethnographic approach in researching terrorism and political violence. With reference to case studies the chapter highlights the appropriateness of the specific research method when investigating predominantly ethnonational violent organisations. There is a plethora of historical and contemporary non-state terrorist organisations with deep nationalist roots. The ideas discussed in this chapter are the outcome of primary research predominantly from the cases of Spain/Basque Country, France/Corsica, United Kingdom/Northern Ireland, and Israel/Palestine. Although no two cases are identical, they share enough similarities to form a recognisable community of cases (Filippidou 2007; Poggioli 2015).

Ethnographic approach: the umbrella method

Social science researchers investigate concepts and events which can never be wholly explained and understood by trying to arrive to the best knowledge available at a certain point in time and within the specific conditions internal and external to the research. Researching terrorism and political violence entails much more than just identifying and measuring violent acts; rather it is a broad, complex, and ever changing phenomenon. In this sense, the broader the themes to be researched, the more the data and information that are collected, which in turn should render the researcher's endeavours fruitful.

Jackson et al. (2011) argue that terrorism is fundamentally a social rather than a brute fact, and although terrorism is experienced as the latter by its direct victims, its wider socio-political and cultural impact is interpreted and received differently within the same community. This is very prominent in ethnographic approaches, where political violence is decided by socially negotiated agreement and intersubjective practices involving most aspects of society (Jenkins 2003).

Admittedly, at times it is the very case study that selects the methodology. In violent ethnic conflicts the aim of the protagonist is to correct an injustice of the past, real or perceived, and they do not want to change the world order. Hence the conflict appears to be pervasive and lasting on the one hand, but also of limited and specific aim on the other, which emphasises the multifaceted nature of ethnographic research of these conflicts. 'It is here,' argues English (2019: 269), that there can be both 'the instrumental appeal of struggle, as a means of achieving worthwhile goals, as well as the attraction inherent in the struggle itself, with its psychological rewards.' From the above emanates that these conflicts entail more than just passive membership in a particular ethnonational community and that it requires social strife including individual and collective mobilisation, and an organised struggle for shared aims.

Through the use of ethnographic approaches the researcher can examine the phenomenon of terrorism and political violence at different levels and through different perspectives, including but not limited to the actors, the targets, and those involved in countering the phenomenon. The field of terrorism and political violence is submerged in subjectivities, and ethnographic methodologies reflect this very clearly. Ethnographic approaches entail tangible issues such as territory, but also intangible such as the affective element and identity. This can be a challenge, as it can easily lead the researcher down a rabbit hole, but it also gives this type of research its distinctiveness and provides an opportunity for a well-structured multitopic research. The breadth of the research categories in ethnographic methodologies provide investigative flexibility. Identity, for instance, is multifaceted and ethnographic approaches act as a thematic umbrella that encompasses a variety of topics including cultural, historical, ideological, and religious contexts. What adds to the research complexity is that homogeneity is non-existent, and the lack of uniformity is evident within a movement or even within the same organisation. In all case studies examined there are variations such as autonomists, independentists, regionalists, and actually the separatist movements themselves have been perpetually fraught with divisions, fractures, and competing claims to ethnic legitimacy. Although this becomes a challenge in research, this variation is not a weakness, as it is often portrayed by the opposing parties, but just a fact that a researcher has to take into consideration. What is important is that the common denominator between these variations is their starting point; that is, in some way, they are all unhappy with the status quo. In sum, the ethnonational idea of community is multilevel and multifaceted with deep roots in the past and strong commitment to a different future.

With reference to the tangible and intangible aspects of violent conflicts, ethnographic approaches become an umbrella research method that has to deal with a number of themes about the very strong feeling of belonging which is promoted by shared means and ends expressed either through 'a shared territorial attachment, shared economic interests, religion, history and values, or through an exclusivism which comfortingly separates us from an outgroup' (English 2019: 269). Although not all of the above features are present in every conflict, a number of them do need to be present, highlighting the complex and complicated nature of an ethnographic research methodology. Thus an ethnographic researcher cannot just deal with the measurable and practical aspects, but there has to be a particular focus on the affective and hence subjective element. This duality of the affective and the tangible aspect within each of the above elements helps explain the resilience and lasting appeal of ethnonational violent conflicts.

The beauty of and necessity for fieldwork

The chapter leaves out a discussion on the ethics approval process prior to conducting fieldwork. This is not because the topic is not important, but because most universities by now have internal review bodies in order to approve researches involving human subjects. Given the nature of terrorism and political violence, any researcher will have to go through a thorough ethics process, as it is unlikely that any ethnographic study in this field will fall into the category of low-risk research. These processes are well established by now in universities and are particular to every institution. Researchers just have to follow their organisation's procedure. These procedures have not been set up to put off the researcher. After all, as Silke (2004: 13) argues, 'the idea that terrorism research is inevitably highly dangerous and risky is mistaken'. The key to successful fieldwork is preparation, in-depth knowledge, awareness, realistic expectations by the researcher, and above all using common sense.

For studies that adopt an ethnographic approach fieldwork is vital. For conflicts that entail identity, and calls for territorial independence, the terrain provides historical and current contextualisation on many levels for both the subject of study but also for researchers. 'Quite simply,' Dolnik (2011: 7) argues, 'one can read all available books and sources on a particular terrorist campaign, but without field visits and exposure to the environment there is much tacit knowledge the researcher simply will not be aware of.' 'A fieldwork, as personal as it is political and theoretical, deepens the understanding of ethnographers, of the people with whom they associate, and of the violence they study', accurately state Robben and Nordstrom (1995: 14ff.). Even more, the combination of a number of issues such as territory, history, economics, culture, religion, civil rights, along with an exclusivist identity, and by the way each of these topics could constitute a theme of research on their own, becomes a unique interlink and interdependence in ethnographic methodologies.

Thus, the fieldtrips are not merely about geography, but about geopolitics. Geography becomes a point of reference, but it can also provide a distorted reflection of an environment. Human minds carry psychological maps, as they are inclined to reimagine their territory in ways that suit assumptions about their identity and their security interests (Filippidou 2020). Geopolitics is interactive and, as Hans Weigert (1942: 23) suggests, 'where the forces of the earth, where the spaces of state systems have become part of an ideology for which men are dying, we are no longer confronted with "facts" alone: geopolitics does argue. It argues against us.' In this sense, territory provides opportunities and constraints, which is also reflected in ethnographic methodologies.

Through fieldtrips, ethnographic researchers explore phenomena that are defined by local settings. A fieldtrip, through the actual geography and because of the human proximity, emphasises that in ethnonational and identity violent conflicts what takes place in reality is the clash of competing non-state and state nationalisms and identities, each resorting to some type and degree of violence. Indeed, empirically, state responses to ethnonational terrorism have been quite nationalistic. However, state nationalism is considered as legitimate, and non-state nationalism is illegitimate, or at the very least negative, and very often is categorised as the cause of the conflict. Yet, it is the mutually shaping relationship between these rival nationalisms that is crucial in researching such conflicts (English 2015). For instance, instead of merely focusing on the FLNC's violence (Corsican National Liberation Front) and elevating it from a symptom to a cause, the focal point should be the long-term relationship between competing French and Corsican nationalisms.

The relationship between researchers and interviewees

Primary research and especially interviewing those involved in violent ethnic conflicts requires that researchers in effect treat interviewees as co-participants. Interviewing people who are still active and participate or have participated in violent ethnic conflicts is not just limited to asking them questions about what they do. It is much more intrusive and it has more to do with talking with them about who they are, as well as about their day-to-day lives. It has to do also with the interviewees risking from their side getting arrested when participating in a research, as was the case in the French part of the Basque Country when I was interviewing the co-founder of ETA Iulen de Madariaga, or when meeting Arnaldo Otegi, the leader and spokesperson of Batasuna, the main independentist movement, when it had just been banned for being accused of having links to ETA.

In this context, the interviewees are not passive interlocutors but rather forceful personalities with strong narratives, even if subjective. Clifford (1988: 112) rightly states that 'ethnographic self-fashioning presupposes lies of omission and of rhetoric, [but] it also makes possible the telling of powerful truths. In point of fact if the researchers are not well prepared and confident they might end up being *talked to* by the interviewees instead of *talking with* them'. Even though Bourdieu argues that 'it is the investigator ultimately who starts the game and who sets up its rules ... without any preliminary negotiations, assigns to the interview its objectives and uses' (1996: 19), directly or indirectly the interviewees can set the tone and the agenda. Consequently, even though there may be an asymmetry in favour of the researcher, in reality there is often an element of varied dependency, as the interviewees have first-hand and insider's knowledge, which the researcher needs. This kind of dependency adds to the complexity of conducting primary research on contemporary violent ethnonational conflicts, which in turn renders impartiality urgent and challenging at the same time.

Dolnik (2011: 5) argues that given the highly emotional and subjective nature surrounding terrorism, available data tend to be heavily politically manipulated by all sides, requiring a higher standard of verification to ensure the reliability, validity, and accuracy of data and information collected from in-country sources. It is true that the interviewees provide their own narratives of the conflict, but still the researcher through a synthesis and analysis of these different narratives aims to untangle the complexities of the conflict and tries to make the conflict and its causes lucid and comprehensible. Within this context, an additional bias highlighted by Stern (2006: 184) emanates from the fact that the narrative of the interviewees takes place in a specific moment, which crucially informs the story told. Thus, it became evident that semi-structured interviews were the best fit for my ethnographic research, and they were used in all case studies. The 'semi' part gave freedom for the interviewees to talk freely enough, while the 'structured' part provided protection from the risk of ending up with just subjective narratives and rabbit holes from the interviewees.

Despite the fact that 'when people look back on something they often have a different construction of that than it was for them at the time' and can be 'now much more critical of the process than they would have been two–three years ago because it has not worked out quite the way they expected' (Alderdice 2005), the contribution of those directly involved in a conflict and its resolution is invaluable in a research. Even though hindsight may blur an argument there are no guarantees that other sources are more objective, as all humans can fall victim to retrospection and at least those interviewed were there in the conflict and during the efforts to resolve it.

Interviews are not useful just because a researcher managed to take them, they are useful if they are made relevant and if they bring the researcher closer to answering the research question at hand. When on the one hand, the component of identity is involved, as well as the affective element with all its interpretations and subjectivities, and on the other there are pragmatic targets and deadlines for the researcher, open-ended and unstructured interviews can create more difficulties rather than bring researchers closer to their aims. After all, the researcher wants to obtain specific information on the conflict from the interviewees who are talking about their lives past, present, and future. Thus, in order to be efficient and effective a kind of filter is needed, because as Said argues, 'facts get their importance from what is made of them in interpretation' (Said 1997: 162). Semi-structured interviews provide enough freedom for co-participants to open up and talk more broadly, as they might provide information that the researcher would not have thought to ask about. At the same time, semi-structured interviews offer enough guidance so that the information provided is useful and relevant. This protects the researcher from becoming overwhelmed by data and information on conflicts that may be centuries old with each conflicting side providing its own narrative and its own version of the truth. This is why the interviews and the fieldtrip have to be timed correctly. Too early in the research and a lot of the necessary and relevant information will be left out, too late and the interviews become of limited use as the findings would not reflect reality. It is not uncommon to come out from an interview with militants and realise that they did not provide any extraordinary and insightful information. There might be occasions for repeated interviews, but that is not always the case, which is why the researcher has to get it right the first time.

Given the nature of the phenomenon of terrorism, access to militants is limited which can put a question mark on the representativeness of the collected data. Often militants advocate that they talk for the organisation, which can be true as they are often designated by the organisation to talk. Interestingly, but at the same time quite frustratingly, in violent ethnic conflicts once a researcher talks to a member of a separatist organisation, any other member of that organisation will give the same answers. 'You talked to him, what different answers do you want from me' is a frequent comment.

Within the context of an academic research, the fact that the subjects of study become co-participants does not also elevate them and grant them a status of equality with the researcher. On the other hand, however, an aspect that is idiosyncratic to ethnographic studies, especially when the researcher is not of the same ethnographic community, is the matter of legitimacy. Interviewees' comments of 'why are you investigating this conflict, it is not as if you do not have similar conflicts in your country' are not uncommon, and it is not unusual for the interviewees to question the intentions and legitimacy of the researcher. The belief is that although anybody can be a member of a specific ideological or religious organisation irrespective of the ethnic background, not everybody can be a member of an ethnonational community.

From this legitimacy springs the issue of trust between the interviewee and the interviewer. An interview may be granted based on the perception of whose side the researcher is on. To an extent this is understandable as it links to a pragmatic need for self-preservation, since the participants are members of ethnonational violent organisations and are often under observation or being pursued by the authorities. Fieldwork ethnographic methodologies invite researchers to form a rapport with specific community members in order to create the necessary environment for the interviewees to want to share their stories, experiences, and analyses that are then transformed by the researcher into data and new knowledge. Furthermore, of particular importance is how the research is presented to potential interviewees. On a number of occasions during the initial contact requesting an interview the first reply has been 'who else have you interviewed', and depending on the answer the research would be considered legitimate and worth participating in. In fact, transparency and striving for impartiality through showing 'the same face to both militant and government interlocutors and be clear to both that you are not going behind the back of one to talk with the other' (Keppley Mahmood, 2001: 534) have facilitated significantly the interviewing process.

Interestingly, not being a member of either of the ethnic communities, be it the national or the regional, can help with trust building with the interviewees, as the researcher is perceived to be more prone to impartiality and not to have any personal or vested interests. During my own fieldtrips in different countries very often this fact appeared to reassure the interviewees and put them at ease. On the other, however, the elements of ethnicity and identity are accompanied by pride, and on a number of occasions there were efforts to downplay the conflicts and comments such as 'What conflict? Many countries have similar conflicts' were expressed. With the exception of the Israel/Palestine case, in France, Spain, and the United Kingdom, very often the interviewees would compare their own case with others and would almost always characterise their case as less severe than the others. Given the nature of the research, it was very useful to ask the interviewees if they could recommend anybody else who would be beneficial for the research and would be willing to participate. These recommendations were considered as a reference and this networking facilitated trust building. This proved to be valuable especially when interviewing in closed ethnic communities where individuals would be particularly protective of their security, and where external trust was very low. In point of fact, there were interviewees who expressed reservations to participate in the research unless the interview was face to face. This was experienced especially in the Basque Country.

On the issue of trust and rapport building with the interviewees, if the purpose of an interview is to bring the researcher as close to the truth as possible it is useful, although quite challenging, to apply what Rogers (2003) called accurate empathic understanding. That is, the ability to deeply understand the subjective world of the interviewees. This does not mean agreeing with what the interviewees are saying, but understanding their experiences, feelings, and 'where they are coming from' in an accurate way. The researcher recognises that the interviewees' experiences are subjective and therefore tries to see things from their unique perspective, without at the same time losing sight of impartiality. On a practical level, accurate empathic understanding allows the interviewees to see the researcher as a human who is genuinely interested in the conflict that is being examined rather than a researcher who is purely trans-actional and only interested in data. Given that fieldtrips are time constricted this approach can facilitate rapport building and lead to more fruitful conver-sations between the co-participants and the researcher. A 'how to' of accurate empathic understanding is for researchers to convey their understanding by reflecting the interviewees' experience back to them. This can help with confi-dence building and encourages the interviewees to become more relaxed, more reflective, and willing to share information.

To reiterate, empathy does not mean sympathy towards the armed actors, but rather this accurate empathic understanding becomes a channel through which collected data are filtered in order to become intelligible and also to bring the researcher closer to fulfilling the research aims. When taking the interview it is not the time to be antagonistic with the interviewees and to try and correct them or make them see the error of their ways. There is time and space for that at different stages of the research output. After all, in the age of social media and easy access to the public members of organisations and participants in violent ethnic conflict do not really have to grant any academic interview, which is usually lengthier than other interviews and it takes longer to see any outcome from it. As such, researchers are required to be willing to negotiate meanings with their co-participants, the interviewees, in order to create shared meanings (Toros 2016: 52).

In point of fact, ethnographic approaches in terrorism studies, because of their emphasis on the human element and the need to observe and actually interact in their real-life environment with the research's protagonists, who are the above-mentioned co-participants, have been questioned about their morality (O'Brien, 1995). In this sense, studies in terrorism appear to have the unique-ness of starting from the assumption that real and in-depth knowledge of the subject is not possible and for some not even desirable because to observe and talk to terrorists is seen as granting them legitimacy and approval for their actions. The challenge is to show accurate empathy without losing sight of objectivity, and to adopt what could be a subjective research approach for objective findings. These challenges and contradictions can lead to knowledge that may refute or verify established truths about terrorism and political violence and its resolution.

Language and cultural awareness

A great facilitator in interviews on a practical and accurate empathetic level has proven to be linguistic skills, as well as cultural and personal awareness. Empirically, the importance of knowing the language from the cases examined appears to be even more prominent in ethnonational and identity conflicts, as for instance demands for regional language rights always have a place on the socio-political agendas of independentists. On a practical level knowing the language eliminates the need for a translator with all the complexities this entails, and also helps build rapport as it is often perceived by the interviewee that the researcher has a genuine interest in the situation under investigation. After all, if a researcher aims to become an expert in the field, why not invest in learning the language?

As part of the accurate empathic understanding and language, if the end game is to gather data and information the lexicon has to be adapted, and in the same conflict certain words can be used with some conflicting parties but not with others. As Dolnik (2011: 27) argues, 'the purpose is to make the subject feel "heard" ... especially with people who see themselves as self-defending victims and who frame their involvement in terrorism as the "only way to be heard"'. It would be of limited or no benefit at all if researchers were not prepared to adjust the language in the interviews. Addressing the interviewees as terrorists, for instance, irrespective as to whether it is a fitting term or not, will not even get the researcher past the first hurdle of just talking to them to request an interview. From their perspective they speak for the regional nation, and they claim to be the authentic voice of the specific regional culture, from where they appear to obtain their legitimacy. Subsequently, they would never consider themselves as terrorists, and trying to persuade them otherwise would simply be pointless and counterproductive regarding the aim of the interview. If researchers want to investigate and comprehend the phenomenon of ethnonational terrorism, then they have to acknowledge that a great deal of political violence occurs from its practitioners' strong belief that they possess a moral high ground, what they often refer to as 'just cause'.

How terms are written in the final product will be up to the researcher. During every interview there will be a resounding statement that 'we are not the terrorists, the state is'. In the words of Fanon (1963: 1ff.), 'it is the colonist who fabricated and who continues to fabricate the colonised subject'. The members of violent political organisations would defend their *raison d'être* as that of correcting an injustice of the past, in this case the assimilation of the ethnic community and region by the central state. Consequently, those involved in ethnic political violence perceive their actions as justified by causes that have a higher moral imperative.

Conclusion

An ethnographic researcher in terrorist studies has the beauty and challenge of researching topics based on a concept that nobody really agrees on or no one can define lucidly, involving subjects of research that become co-participants but who nobody can access easily, focusing on life and death issues whose impact nobody can ignore.

Political violence is not something alien to human experience; it is part of it. As such, it needs to be studied and to be understood exactly in the same way as other political aspects of human experience are studied and become understood. It is not naivety but rather hard pragmatism that makes a researcher seek interviews and to interact with the research's key protagonists of violent ethnic conflicts. Ethnographic approaches encourage researchers to engage directly with their research subjects at a human level but not in the sense of condoning their actions. To this end, for ethnographic methodologies, fieldwork and interviews provide a pivotal source. This direct engagement in combination with the multifaceted nature of ethnographic approaches leads researchers to break the simplistic and therefore false dichotomy of us versus them. Through the use of pragmatic empathy researchers can obtain an understanding of the in-depth causes of the phenomenon of terrorism with the purpose of tackling it as effectively as possible.

References

Alderdice, J. (2005) Headed the Alliance Party of Northern Ireland at the all-party talks, Personal interview, London, 9 April.
Bourdieu, P. (1996) Understanding. *Theory, Culture and Society*, 13(2), 17–37.
Clifford, J. (1988) *Predicament of Culture: Twentieth-Century Ethnography, Literature, and Art*. Cambridge, MA: Harvard University Press.
Dolnik, A. (2011) Conducting field research on terrorism: A brief primer. *Perspectives on Terrorism*, 5(2), 3–35.

English, R. (ed.) (2015) *Illusions of Terrorism and Counter-Terrorism*. Oxford: Oxford University Press.

English, R. (2019) Nationalism and terrorism, in E. Chenoweth, R. English, A. Gofas and S. Kalyvas (eds), *The Oxford Handbook of Terrorism*. Oxford: Oxford University Press, 268–282.

Fanon, F. (1963). *The wretched of the earth*. New York: Grove press.

Filippidou, A. (2007) Negotiating tactics in low intensity conflicts: The cases of Northern Ireland, the Basque Country and Corsica. *Studies in Ethnicity and Nationalism*, 7(3), 94–108.

Filippidou, A. (2020) The impact of forced top-down nation building on conflict resolution: Lessons from the 1923 compulsory population exchange between Greece and Turkey. *Nationalities Papers*, 48(1), 144–157.

Jackson, R., Jarvis, L., Gunning, J. and Breen-Smyth, M. (2011) *Terrorism: A Critical Introduction*. Basingstoke: Palgrave Macmillan.

Jenkins, P. (2003) *Images of Terror: What We Can and Can't Know about Terrorism*. New York: Aldine de Gruyter.

Keppley Mahmood, C. (2001) Terrorism, myth, and the power of ethnographic praxis. *Journal of Contemporary Ethnography*, 30(5), 520–545.

O'Brien, C.C. (1995) *On the Eve of the Millennium: The Future of Democracy through the Age of Unreason*. New York: Free Press.

Poggioli, P. (2015) *Apres l'adieu aux armes Irlande, Pays Basque, Corse*. Ajaccio: Fiara Éditions.

Robben, A.C.G.M. and Nordstrom, C. (1995) The anthropology and ethnography of violence and sociopolitical conflict, in C. Nordstrom and A.C.G.M Robben (eds), *Fieldwork under Fire: Contemporary Studies of Violence and Survival*. Berkeley, CA: University of California Press, 1–23.

Rogers, C. (2003) *Client-Centered Therapy: Its Current Practice, Implications and Theory*. London: Constable & Robinson.

Said, E. (1997) *Covering Islam*. London: Vintage.

Silke, A. (2004) *Research on Terrorism*. London: Frank Cass.

Stern, M. (2006) Racism, sexism, classism and much more: Reading security-identity in marginalised sites, in B. Ackerly, M. Stern and J. True (eds), *Feminist Methodologies for International Relations*. Cambridge: Cambridge University Press.

Toros, H. (2016) Terrorists as co-participants?, in P. Dixit and J.L. Stump (eds), *Critical Methods in Terrorism Studies*. London: Routledge.

Weigert, H. (1942) *Generals and Geographers: The Twilight of Geopolitics*. London: Oxford University Press.

8 Guides, interviews, ethics: conducting fieldwork with Islamist extremists in Indonesia

Julie Chernov Hwang

In the summer of 2016 I visited "Anas," a former member of Jemaah Islamiyah and Mujahidin KOMPAK. I had interviewed him on three occasions by this time and had met him to *ngopi* (drink coffee and chat) another time. I had interviewed him in restaurants and in his home, always with a guide. However, on this occasion, he invited me to his home with his wife and kids. We had established sufficient rapport that, for the first time, I felt I didn't need to bring a guide. I asked him my questions, taking notes in a notebook rather than using the voice recorder. I chatted with his wife and kids. We all ate dinner together. Then, they left the front room and his demeanor changed. His eyes grew fiery and he looked very serious. Julie, I have to ask you a question. I felt a creeping sense of dread. Had I done something wrong? "Julie, WHY do Americans not sleep with their children?"[1] This launched into a long conversation about co-sleeping and cultural traditions. His wife joined us and we discussed breastfeeding. As they walked me to the train that evening, the two of them discretely holding hands, I realized that they truly trusted me. He had invited me into his home, introduced me to his family, fed me, and we were no longer just discussing his past history in the extremist movements. We had developed a solid rapport.

If one is going to interview successfully, it is imperative to build trust. This is no less true when interviewing jihadis. These relationships are difficult to build and important to maintain in order to gain a reasonably accurate representation of the individual's lived experiences in the movement and to learn more about the specifics of the movement on the whole. Moreover,

---

[1]   Interview with Anas, former member of Jemaah Islamiyah, July 2016, Bogor Indonesia.

sitting for an interview is not a comfortable experience. Very few people are truly an open book, irrespective of whether they are members of an extremist group or a bowling league. However, over time, as a person comes to trust an interviewer, they may share more openly and give a more accurate account of events. In short, interviewing Indonesian jihadis and most anyone else is entirely about relationship building and trust building. As a researcher, it is critical that it be done with empathy, patience, and a strong ethical compass.

Drawing on 10 years of experience conducting interviews in Indonesia with members of jihadist groups, this chapter will examine methods for interviewing members of these groups. In doing so, it will illustrate how one goes about identifying gatekeepers; securing permissions from the university's institutional review board (IRB), in-country sources and the jihadists themselves; sampling and maximizing variation within one's sample; conducting interviews; and follow-up. In so doing, it will highlight the importance of building relationships with interviewees over time, the importance of trust and rapport, and the benefits that come from doing so in terms of the quality of material gathered and the degree of understanding obtained.

It must be stated at the outset that one's experiences conducting such interviews may vary from country to country. The degree to which one can be systematic in sampling will also vary. In countries and cases, where participation in interviews is low risk and low cost, one may use a combination of purposive sampling, convenience sampling, and snowball sampling in order to identify respondents. In other cases where there may be higher risks associated with participation in interviews, an interviewer may rely more on convenience sampling (Bernard, 2011). As Indonesia is a democracy, the risks and costs to the interviewee for consenting to the interview are comparatively lower than in a more authoritarian country. Thus, it is possible to identify interviewees through research and contacts (purposive sampling) as well as asking guides and longtime interviewees to recommend other potential respondents (snowball sampling) (Kenney & Chernov Hwang, 2021). In the Indonesian context, it may not be possible to be as systematic when interviewing extremists as one might be in a mainstream social movement. For example, one typically cannot interview a certain number of individuals from each cell because extremist movements are reluctant to disclose membership lists, cells, and sub-organizational structure. One is reliant, therefore, on the access that can be gained from guides, gatekeepers, and current and former members.

Institutional review board

Once one has decided that he or she may want to conduct fieldwork interviewing current and former members of jihadist groups, the first step is to draft a proposal and to secure permission from your university's IRB. The *raison d'être* of an IRB is to minimize risk to the extent possible in human subject research. It pushes interviewers to assess risks and costs to both the interviewees and interviewer and to take whatever steps are possible to minimize those risks and costs. The IRB does not intend to eliminate risk; all research comes with an element of risk. However, the goal of an IRB is to ensure the researcher(s) are taking the steps to minimize negative consequences to the extent possible.

Second, the IRB takes steps to ensure that from start to finish, the potential interviewees/participants understand the following: their participation is strictly voluntary; what the goals of the project are; what the intended products are; what is *their* extent of possible exposure; and what, if any, adverse consequences could they suffer for participating. This enables the interviewee to have sufficient information to truly give what is termed "informed consent" to agree to participate in the interview, to be recorded for the interview, and to be quoted in the written products.

Third, the IRB requires that researchers consider how to protect the identity of the interviewee to the best of their ability. This may include using pseudonyms or general titles rather than a person's name or known alias and obfuscating any identifying information. Typically, when interviewing low-risk human subjects, the IRB might require an interviewer to obtain written consent. Among researchers who work in extremist communities, the tendency is to favor oral consent, for it is safer for both the researcher and the interviewee. Oral consent is safer for the interviewer because it removes concerns on the part of the interviewees about consent documents being handed over to the United States intelligence services. Thus, one is less likely to be questioned about being part of the CIA or subject to intimidation on the basis of such assumptions. It also can be safer for the interviewees should the researcher's bag be confiscated or rifled through by the authorities. In oral consent, the researcher would propose a script, and the IRB would revise the script, adding specific language to address points of concern. The researcher would then translate that script into the language in which the interviews were being done (in this case, Bahasa Indonesia). At the interview, the researcher would recite or paraphrase the script, being sure to address all the critical points raised by the IRB. For example, when I request oral consent, I adjust the language slightly to frame it in terms of "the ethics of research" and the interviewee's rights – to skip questions, to request off the record, to end the interview at any point.

The IRB also assists researchers in considering problems. What if prison officials wish to sit in on the interview? In that case, what would the guide and the researcher do? The researcher would map a plan of action, where they would request the official to leave and explain why that is necessary. However, should the official refuse to comply, the researcher should forgo the interview out of respect for the privacy of the interviewee and the ethics of conducting research among vulnerable populations.

The IRB may also seek to bring in an outside academic or human rights researcher to ensure that the claims you are making are accurate. The IRB may ask to correspond with your guides and fixers. I have been lucky in that many of my guides obtained masters degrees or PhDs through the British or Australian university systems. Thus, they were familiar with obtaining "ethics" permissions. As a result, it was easy for them to understand the demands of the IRB and our need to comply with them.

It is advantageous to volunteer to sit on an IRB to gain a sense of the composition of the IRB committee at a particular university and their primary considerations. A psychologist may problematize research proposals differently than a sociologist. An anthropologist with experience in ethnographic fieldwork may have different concerns than a political scientist. By evaluating the IRB cases of other scholars in the social sciences, one can gain a greater understanding of how risk and cost are evaluated across disciplines. Moreover, one can learn the common mistakes that faculty make when submitting proposals to the IRB in order to avoid it with one's own submission (when you would recuse yourself from the evaluation team).

It is important to remember that you, the researcher, know your country, the groups that you are studying, and the actual risks and costs more so than the committee members comprising the IRB. Moreover, interviewees are adults, capable of assessing risks and costs for themselves. This is something important to remind the IRB as part of the conversation. We want to be transparent with our interviewees with our intentions but not insult them by infantilizing them. Turning the IRB process into a conversation where all parties honestly assess risk is the best way to ensure a workable outcome.

Guides and gatekeepers

When conducting interviews with individuals from Indonesian Islamist extremist groups, the first order of measure is to identify the appropriate guides to facilitate interviews with members. These may be members of non-governmental organizations (NGOs) or civil society organizations working on terrorist rehabilitation initiatives; local academics researching on and in these communities; local journalists who cover extremism; former members of the group who are now disengaged and involved in terrorist rehabilitation; and/or local human rights activists. Each guide will have a network of persons involved in one or more extremist groups upon which to draw.

Guides and gatekeepers are necessary for several reasons. First, they bridge trust. Guides already have established and enduring bonds of trust with specific members of the jihadi group. Typically, the guide requests an interview on behalf of the scholar in question, especially in the initial interviews, before trust is established. The guide vouches for the scholar. The jihadi agrees to the meeting, in part, because they trust the guide. They may also feel more comfortable refusing the meeting because they trust the guide.

Second, the guide gives the researcher background on the individual beyond what he/she can find in the secondary literature. For example, he/she can inform the researcher about standards of dress for the interview. Should the researcher wear a headscarf or simply cover arms to the wrist and legs to the ankles with a large scarf wound around the neck? Moreover, he/she prepares the interviewer for any atypical aspects of the interview. For example, a strict Salafi may only agree to a meeting with a woman if they are separated by a divider, if they agree to the meeting at all. Thus, a female researcher would know, going in, that they would be physically separate from the interviewee and the guide and, as such, they would be unable to gauge body language.

Third, the guide or gatekeeper, particularly one from an academic, journalist, or NGO background, who has a prior relationship of trust with the interviewee, can ensure that the interviewee understands that their participation is strictly voluntary and that the request for an interview can be declined. By contrast, if one works through government, police, or military officials, one may not have the same degree of certainty. With government or security officials, there is an evident power differential, and it is possible that some coercion or pressure was used to secure the interview. Additionally, the guide maintains IRB standards by facilitating communication about the conditions under which the interview will occur. For example, where will the interview take place? If the interview is to be conducted in prison, the guide will take measures to ensure that the interview is arranged according to the terms stipulated in the scholar's IRB proposal (location of the interview, informed consent, etc.).

Fourth, should problems arise in the conduct of interviews, the guide will take steps to rectify them. For example, if one goes to interview in prison, and prison officials refuse to leave the room where the researcher plans to conduct the interview, the guide takes steps to address that problem. They can persuade the officials to leave the space, offer to conduct the interview themselves provided the officials leave the space, or seek the intervention of higher-ups within the prison.

Finally, if one is a female scholar/interviewer, the guide also functions as an intermediary. Having a male guide accompanying a female interviewer may make the interviewee more comfortable, as it would not be appropriate for male and female non-relatives to be alone together, according to Salafi and Salafi-jihadi norms of behavior. Moreover, it reduces the risk to the female researcher and reduces the likelihood of miscommunication between the researcher and interviewee, especially when the researcher is not a native speaker. Furthermore, if the researcher is female and the interviewee is male, the presence of the guide will likely reduce instances of sexual harassment and intimidation by unscrupulous interviewees.

Scholars engage with guides and gatekeepers differently. Some scholars will first identify the people s/he wants to interview. Then, s/he will see who could make that introduction. If s/he doesn't know someone in the movement who could facilitate that opening, s/he will then turn to a guide. By contrast, one can work more collaboratively with guides by sharing certain parameters for interviews, such as individuals who worked in social media for extremist websites or who could speak to recruitment in prisons. They may also give their guide names. Then, they would discuss what is possible and probable prior to departure and, when they arrive, confirm the schedule. It is often necessary to employ different guides and gatekeepers, especially when a researcher is working in different provinces and regions. Some guides may have closer relationships with specific extremists or extremist groups than others. Moreover, some guides may be otherwise committed during the time you are there to research. As a result, it is advantageous to work with more than one person.

Interviews

Whether one works collaboratively with guides or only works with guides when interpersonal connections fail, the goal for the researcher is to develop a rapport with their interviewees that exists independent of the guide or gate-keeper. One is building a personal relationship with the interviewee. These kinds of interviews are not easy conversations, especially if one is seeking personal information. As a result, it is important to develop that personal rapport with the interviewee. If the interviewee actually likes a researcher and enjoys conversing with them, and vice versa, the entire process of interviewing is much smoother.

Rapport building and trust building are best accomplished through iterated interviews. Interviewees may be reluctant to be fully open and forthcoming at the first meeting. It is far more likely that interviewees will be more cir-cumspect as they gauge their level of comfort with the researcher. Some may make provocative statements to see how the researcher reacts. Others may answer questions in a roundabout way, or conversely, give only superficial answers. In this first meeting they are doing a trust assessment. Can they trust the researcher with their story? Can they trust the researcher with their actual narrative and not a version of reality they practiced for researchers and reporters who may parachute in seeking to meet a jihadi? Does the researcher actually seek to learn about them or is he/she just seeking information? Does the researcher care? Will he/she empathize?

If a scholar can only visit the country where they do fieldwork once or twice per year, it may take more time to build that relationship of trust with interviewees. Communication via WhatsApp and Facebook can help, but it is no substitute for in-person conversation. One way of building that trust is to approach an individual not only for interviews but also for coffee and conversation. Over the course of that informal conversation, perhaps one can ask a clarifying question, if necessary. However, the purpose of the meeting is to touch base, to see how a person is doing, and how their family is doing. When the researcher returns a third time, then, perhaps one can do another interview, returning to those questions where you received only a surface answer and trying to peel back the layers to get deeper answers. People are like onions.

Repeat interviews enable the researcher to chart change, progress, and regres-sion in their interviewees. Over time, one can see an interviewee leave prison, get married, have children, start a business, fail at that business, and start another business. One can see an interviewee obtain a masters degree and a PhD, to not only disengage and reintegrate but also to deradicalize through their studies. One can see an interviewee take a second wife, adopt at least six cats, and in between the marriages and pet parenting, go to prison twice.[2]

In my experience, interviewees rarely lie to the researcher. More frequently, they obfuscate or leave out chunks of their narrative. Those missing pieces can only be found when trust is gained. For example, an interviewee may be hesitant to share that they were actually a member of an extremist group, rather than just a sympathizer. As one builds trust through iterated meetings, the interviewee may choose to share those more personal details. For example, "Amru" maintained he was simply a sympathizer of Jemaah Islamiyah, closer to one of its founders.[3] This was the narrative he shared with reporters and most scholars who would parachute in to meet him. At our fourth meeting, he shared the true story of his involvement in Jemaah Islamiyah; the extent of that involvement; how he joined; and the true extent of his disengagement. When asked why he was sharing this information at that juncture, some four years after our first meeting, he responded, "Because now, I trust you."[4] In later interviews, Amru would share specifics of how individuals joined Jemaah Islamiyah via study circles and how study circles functioned in building brotherhood. In order to learn that information, I first had to secure Amru's trust.

Through gaining trust, one can also learn personal details that round out an individual's narrative and enable the researcher to understand the diverse factors that lead to a person joining an extremist group or leaving one. For example, Nasir Abas, former commander of Jemaah Islamiyah's Mantiqi III training region, also has a narrative he shares with academics and journalists, which begins when his father drops him off at a mosque school in Johor, Malaysia. After knowing him for a decade, interviewing him on four separate occasions, and conversing with him on several others, he shared about his early life and the influence of his father on his path.[5] It enabled me to see that the core mechanism facilitating his entry into Darul Islam was not adventure; it was kinship.

---

2   Fieldwork notes from interviews with four members of Jemaah Islamiyah and Mujahidin KOMPAK, including Amru and Reza. Data on cats came from Reza's June 2021 Facebook page.
3   Interview with Amru, inactive member of Jemaah Islamiyah, January 2012, Semarang, Indonesia.
4   Interview with Amru, inactive member of Jemaah Islamiyah, July 2015, Surabaya, Indonesia.
5   Interview with Nasir Abas, former commander of Jemaah Islamiyah Mantiqi III, July 2017, Pekanbaru, Indonesia.

Building trust also helped in understanding "Reza's" tendency toward recidivism. Reza was a former member of Mujahidin KOMPAK, a gun runner, who, if he lived in the United States, would have been a member of the National Rifle Association in good standing. Reza liked teaching people to shoot guns; he liked selling guns. However, in the past, Reza had been careless about to whom he sold guns. After knowing Reza for about half a decade, interviewing him twice, and meeting him on two other occasions for conversation, Reza shared that the reason he kept returning to gun running, at that point in his life, was not only that he liked guns but also that selling guns and teaching shooting paid far better than being a driver.[6] This is useful information insofar as it highlighted that Reza might benefit from professional development programs that could help him tap into his existing transferable skills and diversify his skillset.

Language proficiency is also critical for trust and rapport building. While a scholar may choose to hire a native speaker to transcribe interviews to ensure that there is an accurate record of the interview, it is important to do the work of learning the language so that one can conduct the interview in the language and understand what is said to him/her in return. It is difficult to build trust when one is relying on another to communicate for them. How can a researcher build a relationship with an interviewee independent of a guide, if there is always someone speaking for them and they are incapable of having a simple conversation independently?

Additionally, empathy is a key component of successful trust building. It is important to develop the skill to understand the perspective that drove a person to commit acts of terrorism and to have the capacity to understand the emotions that undergirded that decision. This does not mean one sympathizes with them or supports the choices they made. However, for the purposes of the research, one must practice perspective taking. For example, many young men from the city of Poso became radicalized after the Walisongo massacre, when Christian militias killed over 100 mostly women and children at a mosque and Islamic boarding school in 2001. "Fauzan" and "Yuda" both profess to have lost dozens of relatives in the attack.[7] Others cited seeing headless bodies floating down the river as the catalyst for them to seek out

---

[6] Interview with Reza, former member of Mujahidin KOMPAK, July 2016, Jakarta, Indonesia.
[7] Interview with Fauzan and Yuda, former members of Tanah Runtuh, January 2012 in Palu and Ampana, Indonesia.

opportunities to take revenge.[8] Several years later, after these men felt the Malino Peace Accords failed to hold the perpetrators accountable, they sought revenge, launching a series of terrorist attacks between 2003 and 2007 against mostly Christian targets: bombings, assassinations, mutilations. Interviewing any of these young men from Tanah Runtuh and Mujahidin Kayamanya, the two primary jihadi militias operating in Poso at the time, necessitates empathy. One has to understand the role of Walisongo and empathize with how they must have felt to see those headless bodies floating down the river, the bodies of children and women, day after day, to make any headway in building trust.

In conclusion, interviewing jihadists in Indonesia, with its open society and lax prison system, will differ significantly from interviewing jihadists in more authoritarian countries. The risks and costs of consenting to an interview in Indonesia are far lower for the interviewee, which makes it easier to conduct such interviews. However, there are aspects that generalize from the Indonesian experience: the personal rapport, the role of the IRB, and the utility of guides.

Trust is paramount. In order to interview well, however, one must build a personal relationship. The interviewee must come to trust the interviewer with their narrative. For that to happen, the researcher must go back to the same people multiple times. Iterated interviews facilitate trust and help build a rapport between researcher and interviewee. It helps the researcher to chart progress and setbacks in the interviewee's personal narrative. Over time, when the interviewee comes to trust and genuinely like the researcher, what one can and does learn, what one can come to understand, increases exponentially.

Second, it is important to conduct this research with a strong ethical compass, assessing the degree of risk for one's person and the interviewees. Working with the IRB and keeping an open dialogue with the committee can help facilitate a plan of action for working in prison and outside prison, ensuring informed consent, protecting identities, and minimizing the risk to all parties. It also facilitates transparency between researcher and interviewer. The researcher must tell the interviewee what their purpose is, what the risks are, and through that, the interviewee can consent to the interviewer or refuse it with full knowledge.

---

[8] Fieldwork notes in Poso, July 2010, January 2012, and July 2015. Interviews with 23 former members of Tanah Runtuh and Mujahidin Kayamanya. All cited *dendam* (revenge) as their primary motivation.

Finally, working with guides and gatekeepers helps researchers because guides already have pre-existing bonds of trust within the communities that one seeks to enter. Thus, one can build upon their trust relationships initially until one can establish their own. Moreover, guides and gatekeepers can function as intermediaries between the researcher and the government or the researcher and prison authorities; they can protect the researcher and they can facilitate effective communication between interviewer and interviewee. In this work, trust is paramount.

References

Bernard, H. R. (2011). *Research methods in anthropology: Qualitative and quantitative approaches*. 5th edition. Lanham, MD: Altamira.
Kenney, M., & Chernov Hwang, J. (2021). Should I stay or should I go? Understanding how British and Indonesian extremists disengage and why they don't. *Political Psychology*, 42(4), 537–553.

9 Using social media to research terrorism and extremism

Ashton Kingdon and Emma Ylitalo-James

Introduction

The World Wide Web is a global information infrastructure, invented by Tim Berners-Lee in 1991 as a layer on the internet, and currently underpins and reflects the activity, digital economy, and societal interactions of the global population. The technology of the Web depends on a simple model of information exchange, utilising the Hypertext Transfer Protocol (HTTP) to access resources and documents that have been formatted in the Hypertext Mark-Up Language (HTML). This traditional Web architecture has evolved, with the development of innovative social opportunities and technologies, from the 'Web of documents' (Web 1.0), to the 'Web of the people' (Web 2.0), to the 'Web of linked data' (Web 3.0 – the Semantic Web). Significantly for this chapter, as the Web evolved, so did extremism, with many organisations utilising technological advancements and ever expanding virtual networks to increase recruitment and advance radicalisation on a global scale (Klausen, 2015; Conway, 2017; Wendling, 2018).

'Web 2.0' is the term assigned to the second generation of social media websites that emerged throughout the mid-2000s, such as Facebook, Twitter, and YouTube. The technological developments underlying these sites, in combination with the infrastructure that facilitated them, predominantly the expansion of broadband internet and the emergence of smartphones making video uploading and streaming possible, consequently enabled content to be generated by the users rather than the owners of the platforms. This subsequently shifted the balance of power on the Web from a technical few to the masses, resulting in the technology of 'Web 2.0' becoming ever more concerned with collaboration, participation, and the creation of social connections (Hendler et al., 2008). Social media research has a rich repertoire of methods through which to capture data to aid researchers in their understanding of extremists and terrorist activity. This chapter will outline the importance of the method-ological approaches of interviews, social network analysis, and open source intelligence (OSINT), and detail the affordances and limitations of each. The chapter will conclude by arguing that social media both necessitates and requires methodological innovation, specifically in relation to adapting tradi-tional methods and developing new ones tailored to examining extremism in the virtual environment.

Interviews

The challenges of interviewing primary source participants traverse the bound-aries of identification of participants and access to methodological approaches of analysis (Dawson, 2019). Extracting data from hard-to-reach communities, such as past active or current violent extremists, requires a process of introduc-tion, interaction, and building of trust, a process which has traditionally been conducted on a face-to-face basis (Bryman, 2012). Crucially, interviewing in the field, particularly subjects involved in terrorism, outside of a prison setting, presents its own unique issues. The process of engaging in interview settings on the ground and through online social media platforms becomes vitally important in the endeavour of understanding the causal factors, manifesta-tions, and interrelationships of moving into violent extremism (Dolnik, 2011). As areas of current combat can be difficult to access to gain primary source introductions and data, the use of online text, videotelephony, and social media has become more prevalent.

The practical side of face-to-face interaction allows for reassurance of confiden-tiality and an apparent degree of control on the part of the participant (Dolnik, 2013). It also provides access to interpret body language and the ability to assess and respond to physical cues during interaction to create fluidity within conversations that often involve difficult topics (Dawson & Amarasingam, 2016). Esteemed researchers in the field of terrorism studies have written com-prehensive guidelines on interview management with primary sources (White, 2000; Dolnik, 2011; Horgan, 2012; Nilsson, 2018; Khalil, 2019). However, the advantages and disadvantages of online interviews conducted through social media have been considerably less explored.

There are two approaches to interviewing using social media data and online communication platforms. The first is the transference of interview techniques onto a live online system, such as Skype, to conduct the equivalent of the commonplace face-to-face discourse. Structured, semi-structured, and organically developing interviews can take place on these platforms. The second is through social media text-based messaging through platforms such as Twitter and Facebook. These sites have little fluidity and thus give less opportunity to develop interpersonal connection (Dawson & Amarasingam, 2016). However, for recovering information from current violent extremists or terrorists in the field, where face-to-face interaction is limited, or impossible, even via platforms like Skype, this approach provides a valuable medium for interviews, even though there is greater possibility of misinterpretation and parochial evaluation (Dawson, 2019). It is important to note here that the transition to online platforms can be a complex adjustment for researchers. It can severely affect cultivation of contacts, cause practical and methodological changes in the process of the interview itself, and have an effect on the validity and reliability of the information gathered (Dawson, 2019).

For most researchers seeking primary source participants with past or current terrorist involvement, initial introductions are usually instigated through existing contacts, or 'gatekeepers' (Dolnik, 2011). Introductions conducted via social media significantly reduce the trust achieved by direct physical contact, particularly as the initial conversations in these formats require carefully recorded records allowing for replication of the research (Chenneville & Schwartz-Mette, 2020). It can also take more time to build trust with those contacts or 'gatekeepers' who are less known to the researcher. In the case of 'gatekeepers', the loss of a physical introduction and discussion may require additional validation and 'checks' of the researcher's intention and links to opposing groups or organisations. This often includes the preparation of more in-depth participant information sheets in an electronic format. Providing greater detail of the intent, use, and accessibility by authorities of the research conducted may be a greater consideration compared to face-to-face research, which usually serves as a better way for individuals to assess the legitimacy of the claims.

As most researchers rely on the snowball sampling technique, or referral, to gain participants, confidentiality within initial discussions to gain introductions is a paramount issue for researchers. As in the case of physical interviews, the aspect of anonymity brings the question of whether or not to record interviews. For online interviews, concerns about unwanted third parties accessing social media accounts or recordings, or the Internet Protocol (IP) addresses or account details of participants, raise security and trust considerations. This is not just an ethical concern, but also brings into play the basis of rapport and trust building with participants. The building of trust in these instances and addressing such factors can ease potential objections and suspicions at an early stage of the process as well as potential reluctance to refer further participants.

Within any confidentiality agreements in place, consideration has to be given to any recording of the IP address or account details of the participant and any identifying markers, especially if using any online software for the collection of questionnaires, data, or signed consent forms.

As mentioned previously, the building of trust between the researcher and participants becomes a longer process when interviews are conducted via social media, with the loss of being able to read full body language by both parties. There may also be concerns about confidentiality and content access. For example, an initial conversation after referral, or introduction, may take longer than in person. It takes longer to explain the research, reassure the subject, discuss confidentiality and anonymity, and generally build rapport. Two or three short sessions may be needed before the main interview takes place on the medium you plan to use to gain mutual trust. This may also help the interviewer note the responses and behaviours of the subject and adapt their interview style accordingly, as well as possible changes in question formation and approach. From the relative luxury of those initial short conversations online, there is opportunity to open up initial subject areas. This has been found to increase the length and detail of discussions through the interviews, from the initial conversations, which are not usually possible in physical interview scenarios (Nilsson, 2018).

As Khalil (2019) describes, the recording of interviews can be a stumbling block. Some participants are reluctant to have any audio recording, resulting in the researcher furiously taking notes, which invariably reduces the flow and natural evolution of the interview. Even through voice recording there is a possibility of identification, and the fear of being identified is particularly relevant for Skype or live video platforms as the participant can often be seen. Therefore, careful agreement of recording procedures, if any, needs to be maintained along with any encryption available to ensure no third parties can access the interview or recordings. This consideration has been extensively highlighted by the American Psychological Association in the advent of telepsychology in the mid-1990s, with ethical and code of conduct guidelines being produced (2013).

Within a structured or semi-structured interview, the planning of the questions may require reordering, or a deliberate period of 'pre-talk' to increase rapport and trust. As Nilsson (2018) discusses, the trustworthiness of information on any platform through interviews is always subject to the possibility of distortion, deletion, generalisation, and falsehood. Specifically, Nilsson attributes the likelihood of deliberate falsehood arguably to a lack of rapport between the interviewer and interviewee. This is a further incentive to spend extended time in rapport building with the subject where possible (as discussed above). Dawson (2019) also discusses the issues surrounding text-based online interviewing by messenger systems via social media and the likelihood of distorted information. In particular, Dawson cited criticism of results based on active foreign fighters who were interviewed over periods of days, weeks, and months. The criticism from an anonymous reviewer was that responses would be biased and were subject to religiosity, as frequently, jihadi fighters were only given their phones after religious training. Dawson and Amarasingam's (2016) view however was that it is 'implausible that most of the people who travelled to Syria and Iraq to wage jihad were not driven, at least partially, by their religious commitments'.

Nevertheless, even with all these drawbacks in mind, interaction and interviews with past and active combatants still provides a portal into the motivations, antecedent individual factors, and perceptions of those who take the pathway into violent extremism. Some information may be distorted, auto-propagandic, or ideologically biased. There may also be greater difficulties in the acquisition of interviewees, time considerations, loss of interpersonal fluidity, and greater possibility of inaccuracies. Even with these challenges, the need for the open discourse with terrorists and the understanding it brings is an essential part of the development of terrorism research. As John Horgan recounts:

> To understand the development of the terrorist, we must ask questions about how decisions emerged, the meaning of those decisions, and their consequences for the person concerned ... Interviews afford keen insight into how individuals involved in terrorism ... perceive themselves, their environments and their involvement pathways. Although survey data seemingly allows us to do the same thing, only through in-depth interviews ... are we able to understand the meaning associated with each individual's experience and how that meaning affects motivation to act. (Horgan, 2012, p.4)

Social network analysis

The activity of extremists on the internet is continuously growing with the increase of social media as a medium for communication. Social networking applications are built upon the foundation of participation; users of these platforms have the chance to share and create their own information, and consume and engage with the content created by others. All social research begins by scoping the population – defining the empirical subject. Frequently, researchers consider this in terms of particular people, their characteristics, values, and actions (Halford et al., 2017). In this respect, the appeal of social media lies in the fact that they offer insights into the everyday lives of their users – the subjects who post content online. Social network analysis is a research approach best suited to understanding, describing, and examining various types of structural and relational aspects. The benefit of this method lies in its ability to understand extremist communities by mapping the relationships that connect them as a network, and identifying key individuals and groups within the network and/or the associations between them (Knoke & Yang, 2019). Likewise, when researching extremism, it is beneficial to decipher who the most powerful people are operating within a network, and whether or not a matrix can be employed to predict and ultimately prevent nefarious activity. Social network analysis provides researchers with new ways of measuring power and influence, specifically by examining structure, propagation, and interaction – the conversations people are having, the number of interactions they are receiving, and the narratives that are being disseminated. This type of analysis on extremist social networks provides important information in terms of how to prevent the dissemination of propaganda, the propagation of ideologies, or recruitment of new members.

The precursor of social network analysis is graph theory, a branch of mathematics that represents nodes (Web pages) that are connected by vertices (links), and the relationships between them. Graph theory helps researchers understand the concept of 'centrality', which is a measure of the importance of different phenomena occurring within a social network (Borgatti & Everett, 2006). By incorporating the four different types of centrality, researchers can measure how influential or significant a certain individual is within the network overall. First, 'degree centrality' examines the number of edges a vertex in a graph has (the number of links coming in or out of an individual node). When applying this logic to an extremist network, it can be used to inform researchers of an individual's opportunity to directly influence others in the network, thus providing an indication of popularity. Second, 'betweenness centrality' attempts to capture each node's role as a connector between other groups by evaluating the number of shortest paths travelling through a node. This provides an indication of how vital someone is to communication within the overall network, producing evidence of a node's informal power through gatekeeping and brokering to detail who the key influencers are. Third, 'closeness centrality' captures how close a node is to any other nodes within the network – the average of the shortest distance – providing a measure of direct influence and evidence or how quickly a post, or a message, could travel from one individual to all members within the network. Fourth, 'eigenvector centrality' delivers a way of thinking about the most important nodes within the network. Instead of examining specific paths, or the number of links for one individual only, this particular type of centrality considers the idea that there is a way of ranking the importance of all nodes, the idea being that the most important people are connected to other important people.

Existing research utilising social network analysis to investigate extremism appears to focus on characterising power as a connection, employing the concept of 'centrality' to examine the ability or potential for an individual to influence others (Hopkins, 2010; Basu, 2014; Petrovskiy & Chikunov, 2019). More specifically, this approach has been used to predict the social impacts and connectivity of right-wing and jihadist networks (Benigni et al., 2017; Torregrosa et al., 2020). Significantly, this type of social network analysis enables assessment of the similarities and differences between isolated data points, in a visual format, so that researchers can establish patterns in the forces that connect extremist communities together. Graphical representations also reveal individuals in populations that bridge different social groups, thus providing evidence of the potential overlapping of extremist ideologies. Moreover, by analysing social networks through graph theory it is possible to learn which members of an extremist group can reach the largest audience, who is disseminating propaganda, who is connected to the most influential individuals, and who mediates important relationships.

In many ways the power of network theory lies in its high degree of abstraction and, when examining the impact of social media at scale, it is useful to view it as an entity that is more than a series of pages that link together. As with all research methods, there are strengths and limitations to this specific approach. A prominent advantage of social network analysis is that it enables researchers to explore the social interactions and personal relationships between specific people in a network, thus allowing for a more effective understanding of how individuals are connected and, more importantly, how information flows, which is crucial for advancing communication and mobilising knowledge (Burt et al., 2013). On the other hand, researchers using this approach have had a tendency to focus on the 'bigger picture', thus neglecting the smaller and more personalised factors that play a key role in the analysis of online extremist communication (Robbins, 2015). Additionally, scholars have often looked to network analysis to solidify their pre-conceived conclusions, consequently overlooking the significant numbers of people that do not participate in the chosen network, but may still be participating in or contributing to extremist discourse (Prell, 2012). Nevertheless, social network analysis is a robust methodological approach that enables scholars to examine all actors within a network – where they are located, how they are linked, and how communication changes over time – which is vital when examining extremism in a digital age.

Open source intelligence

Within the world of cybersecurity, there exists an influential body of knowledge and investigative techniques, collectively referred to as open source intelligence (OSINT), used directly to derive new insights from public data. In the midst of the data revolution, academic research has increasingly focused on the technological sophistication displayed by extremist and terrorist groups and organisations (Klausen, 2015; Conway, 2017; Gaudette et al., 2020). However, this emphasis could lead to a group attribution error, with the tech 'know-how' of some individuals being mistakenly assigned to the group as a whole. Specifically, group members remain as likely as any member of the public at large to overshare and leak data, thereby exposing their affiliations through a myriad of revealing and publicly accessible actions and interactions. Researchers should therefore explore the potential of structured and replicable OSINT techniques on such publicly available information to investigate and classify extremist groups, and connect them with their most influential members, many of whom are operating on multiple accounts across several platforms. OSINT approaches not only enable the identification of network boundaries, but also bring to light meaningful connections and key characteristics shared by extremist organisations relying on technology for recruitment.

Much research has been conducted into the Russian disinformation campaigns that came to light during the 2016 presidential election of Donald Trump (Berghel, 2017; Hellman & Wagnsson, 2017; Pacheco et al., 2020). These attacks exploited the anonymous nature of social media platforms like Twitter in an attempt to deepen political and social rifts in society by spreading false and misleading information designed to be polarising. To enable these campaigns, OSINT techniques were employed and online conversations meticulously studied to create information that would have maximum impact. Once powerful and persuasive narratives had been gathered, fake news was aggressively injected into public discussion by strategically placing bots – pieces of automated software designed by a human, programmed to complete tasks – targeting human users determined likely to share the content as legitimate. Social media companies have developed the ability to automatically categorise content by sentiment, using machine learning to identify patterns associated with positive or negative output. By exploiting sentiment analysis, the perpetrators of disinformation campaigns can amplify polarising discussions by triggering an army of bots (a troll factory) to retweet and share legitimate tweets about specific topics or people depending on whether they are saying positive or negative things. Essentially, an attacker can use sentiment analysis to sort polarising tweets to quickly overwhelm a discussion by amplifying fringe opinions. This prevents fair and open debate and allows the attacker to overcome dissenting views with content disseminated by real users. Due to the promise of open communication in real time, and in a scalable fashion, social media companies like Twitter have been used by journalists, activists, and others reporting critical information or coordinating events. This use has made the service a prime target for monitoring, interfering with, and suppressing online conversations by those with the resources to do so.

When examining the role played by social media on the propagation and impact of extremist beliefs, a key goal for researchers is to piece together as many disconnected clues as possible and build a coherent picture of extremists' operations online. During OSINT investigations, the discovery of a potential extremist's user name can lead to additional information, including multiple user accounts created by the same person, the accounts of friends or family members, and photographs, which lead to other avenues of collecting further information (Sinwindie, 2019). In particular, the Sherlock Project – a python-based OSINT tool – enables researchers to take a single piece of information, a unique user name, and expand it into as many disconnected accounts as it can locate, generating a list of further social media activity linked to that user name, thus allowing researchers to increase what they know about the target. The ability for Sherlock to locate user names across social networks not only drastically saves researcher time, but also provides unique insight into potential extremists' social media behaviour. Indeed, by utilising OSINT tools such as Sherlock, researchers can identify whether individuals are masquerading under pseudonyms, or if they are disseminating extremist content from multiple accounts across multiple fora. It also enables the identification of similar recruitment techniques among various extremist organisations and groups operating online.

The purpose of intelligence gathering is to refine raw data into insight. One of the main disadvantages of OSINT research is the potential for information overload. Indeed, filtering insight from 'noise' can be incredibly difficult and, without the right tools, extracting useful information can be a time-consuming activity for any researcher. As so much information exists online, it can be easy to get lost in data when researching, therefore, narrowing the question should be the first step in any OSINT investigation. Researchers of extremism might find it useful to utilise software like Maltego – an OSINT and graphical link analysis tool for gathering and connecting information for investigative tasks – to help refine initial data. Maltego allows for vast pools of data to be mined, analysed, and sorted, looking for relationships that would not be immediately obvious to the human eye. Essentially, Maltego acts as a canvas, onto which researchers can place data and then use algorithms called 'transforms' to mine related information. It takes care of the process of data importing, processing, analysis, and visualisation, pulling from vast application programming interfaces of data to be able to search for patterns and clearly display them. In particular, Maltego is an excellent tool for watching social media conversations unfold, offering the added advantage of importing targets directly to the software, enabling researchers to track content through key hashtags and users involved in the dissemination of information around a specific event, topic, or person. More specifically, researchers can track the social media accounts of known propagandists or extremists in real time and, because of Maltego's capabilities, it can be used as a 'snapshot' of longitudinal data. Significantly, OSINT investigation is not a matter of hacking, compromising, or manipulating any single electronic asset. Rather, much like the work conducted by security services, it is true trade craft, which involves the discovery and connection of multiple strands of disparate and seemingly unrelated pieces of publicly available information. Once collected, organised, and ultimately connected, this information provides new insights into the person of interest, which is extremely valuable for researchers looking at extremism.

Conclusion

The Web is the most powerful information construct developed by humanity and, as a technology, it enables users to connect globally, while abolishing the tyranny of distance and scale (Hendler et al., 2008). In the midst of the data revolution, academic research has increasingly focused on the technological sophistication displayed by terrorist and extremist groups and organisations. By the same token, the evolution of social media has generated new methodological approaches that draw upon computational resources and simulation and modelling techniques that had not been available until recently. Researchers frequently utilise rich sets of data sources, software tools, and computational infrastructures when investigating terrorism and extremism, often following a 'bottom-up' approach, building from the study of social interactions on a micro-level towards larger social trends. As this chapter has illustrated, social network analysis, in particular, has gained popularity, employing graph and network theory to measure, map, and visualise relationships and information flows between individuals embedded within extremist groups or organisations (Hopkins, 2010; Basu, 2014; Petrovskiy & Chikunov, 2019). Additionally, this chapter has drawn attention to the influential body of knowledge and investigative techniques of OSINT, used directly to derive new insights into extremism from publicly available data. More specifically, it has been highlighted that future researchers should explore the potential of structured and replicable OSINT on publicly available information to examine and classify extremist groups, and connect them with their most prominent members in an attempt to reduce their influence.

The advent of social media created a space for terrorism studies to evolve and unlocked new opportunities for researchers to prop up their methodological tool kit. It is undeniable that this technology has provided a global space for social, political, deviant, and extremist activity to flourish. To effectively study these phenomena, existing research methods need to be updated and reimagined to effectively respond to this powerful and globalised social structure. In relation to this chapter, it is feasible to ask when it comes to interviewing terrorists and extremists online, is this a new method? Or simply a case of old wine in new bottles? As has been illustrated above, it is difficult to transfer the traditional method of interviews to an online context, as the environment can severely impact the cultivation of contacts, cause methodological changes in the process of the interview itself, and have an effect on the validity and reliability of the information gathered. Additionally, there are more practical issues to consider, such as the acquisition of the interviewees, time constraints, loss of interpersonal fluidity, and the greater possibility of recorded inaccuracies. Hence the argument that traditional methods need to be modernised, particularly as the scale of social media, and ease by which people can be reached, make it the ideal technology for collecting evidence into how extremists are communicating online. Social media both necessitates and requires methodological innovation, specifically in relation to adapting traditional methods and developing new ones tailored to examining the virtual environment. Indeed, adequate methodologies and theoretical reflection will always be necessary to make sense of extremist and terrorist behaviour, whether the data are generated online or offline. Social media is in many ways modern society's Gutenberg Press, and research methods need to be technologically and ethically compatible if they are to aid the fight against online extremism.

References

American Psychological Association (2013). Guidelines for the Practice of Telepsychology. *America Psychologist*, 791–800.

Basu, A. (2014). Social Network Analysis: A Methodology for Studying Terrorism. In: Panda, M., Dehuri, S. & Wang, G.I. (Eds). *Social Networking: Mining, Visualization, and Security*. Cham: Springer, pp. 215–242.

Benigni, M.C., Joseph, K. & Carley, K. (2017). Online Extremism and the Communities That Sustain It: Detecting the ISIS Supporting Community on Twitter. *PloS One*, 12(12), e0181405.

Berghel, H. (2017). Oh, What a Tangled Web: Russian Hacking, Fake News, and the 2016 US Presidential Election. *Computer*, 9(1), 87–91.

Borgatti, S.P. & Everett, M.G. (2006). A Graph-Theoretic Perspective on Centrality. *Social Networks*, 28(4), 466–484.

Bryman, A. (2012). *Social Research Methods* (4th Ed.). Oxford: Oxford University Press.

Burt, R.S., Kilduff, M. & Tasselli, S. (2013). Social Network Analysis: Foundations and Frontiers on Advantage. *Annual Review of Psychology*, 64(1), 527–547.

Chenneville, T. & Schwartz-Mette, R. (2020). Ethical Considerations for Psychologists in the Time of COVID-19. *American Psychological Association*, 75(5), 644–654.

Conway, M. (2017). Determining the Role of the Internet in Violent Extremism and Terrorism: Six Suggestions for Progressing Research. *Studies in Conflict and Terrorism*, 40(1), 77–98.

Dawson, L. (2019). Taking Terrorist Accounts of Their Motivations Seriously: An Exploration of the Hermeneutics of Suspicion. *Perspectives on Terrorism*, 13(5), 74–89.

Dawson, L. & Amarasingam, A. (2016). Trying to Talk to Terrorists: Ethical and Methodological Challenges in Canada. *TSAS: The Canadian Network for Research on Terrorism, Security, and Society*, 1–23.

Dolnik, A. (2011). Conducting Field Research on Terrorism: A Brief Primer. *Perspectives on Terrorism*, 5(2), 3–35.

Dolnik, A. (2013). *Conducting Terrorism Field Research: A Guide*. London: Routledge.

Gaudette, T., Scrivens, R. & Venkatesh, V. (2020). The Role of the Internet in Facilitating Violent Extremism: Insights from Former Right-Wing Extremists. *Terrorism and Political Violence*, 34(7), 1339–1356.

Halford, S., Weal, M., Tinati, R., Carr, L. & Pope, C. (2017). Understanding the Production and Circulation of Social Media Data: Towards Methodological Principles and Praxis. *New Media and Society*, 1(1), 1–18.

Hellman, M. & Wagnsson, C. (2017). How Can European States Respond to Russian Information Warfare? An Analytic Framework. *European Security*, 26(2), 153–170.

Hendler, J., Shadbolt, N., Hall, W., Berners-Lee, T. & Weitzner, D. (2008). Web Science: An Interdisciplinary Approach to Understanding the Web. *Communications of the ACM*, 51(7), 60–69.

Hopkins, A. (2010). *Graph Theory, Social Networks and Counter Terrorism*. www.blog.republicofmath.com/wp-content/uploads/2010/09/ahopkins_report.pdf

Horgan, J. (2012). Interviewing the Terrorists: Reflections on Fieldwork and Implications for Psychological Research. *Behavioral Sciences of Terrorism and Political Aggression*, 4(3), 195–211.

Khalil, J. (2019). A Guide to Interviewing Terrorists and Violent Extremists. *Studies in Conflict and Terrorism*, 42(4), 429–443.

Klausen, J. (2015). Tweeting the Jihad: Social Media Networks of Western Foreign Fighters in Syria and Iraq. *Studies in Conflict and Terrorism*, 38(1), 1–22.

Knoke, D. & Yang, S. (2019). *Social Network Analysis*. London: Sage.

Nilsson, M. (2018). Interviewing Jihadists: On the Importance of Drinking Tea and Other Methodological Considerations. *Studies in Conflict and Terrorism*, 41(6), 419–432.

Pacheco, D., Flammini, A. & Menczer, F. (2020). Unveiling Coordinated Groups behind White Helmets Disinformation. *Companion Proceedings of the Web Conference 2020*, 1(1), 611–616.

Petrovskiy, M. & Chikunov, M. (2019). Online Extremism Discovering through Social Network Structure Analysis. *2019 IEEE 2nd International Conference on Information and Computer Technologies.* 243–249. https:// ieeexplore .ieee .org/ stamp/ stamp .jsp ?arnumber = 8711254 & casa _token = Qx0P09SGTTIAAAAA: FR -NlytJXr64 esvkLLyjmdN8ZETfqrBQwd1BbAlWMsRpFhv5g9LKPEXHAdAtZI6m9fDQ9YRN

Prell, C. (2012). *Social Network Analysis: History, Theory and Methodology.* London: Sage.

Robbins, G. (2015). *Doing Social Network Research: Network-Based Research Design for Social Scientists.* London: Sage.

Sinwindie (2019). *Gab OSINT Techniques.* www .secjuice .com/ investigate -gab -users -osint/

Torregrosa, J., Panizo-Lledot, Á., Bello-Orgaz, G. & Camacho, D. (2020). Analyzing the Relationship between Relevance and Extremist Discourse in an Alt-Right Network on Twitter. *Social Network Analysis and Mining,* 10(1), 1–17.

Wendling, M. (2018). *Alt-Right: From 4Chan to the White House.* London: Pluto Press.

White, R.W. (2000). Issues in the Study of Political Violence: Understanding the Motives of Participants in Small Group Political Violence. *Terrorism and Political Violence,* 12(1), 95–108.

10 Using online data in terrorism research

Stuart Macdonald, Elizabeth Pearson, Ryan Scrivens and Joe Whittaker

That terrorist groups exploit online fora, websites, social media sites and the dark web in order to carry out their core business of recruitment, propagandising, fundraising and planning is well documented (Gill et al. 2015; Macdonald & Mair 2015; Nacos 2014). So too is the fact that, while these online activities may facilitate the commission of attacks and act as a force multiplier, they are also a valuable source of information and intelligence for security agencies, in some instances enabling the detection and prevention of acts of terrorism (Benson 2014). Terrorists' online activities have proved significant for researchers, for historically one of the greatest challenges for the study of extreme or terrorist groups was access (Dolnik 2013; Horgan 2004, 2012; Silke 2003). Today, online spaces offer researchers a level of access to primary data that was previously unimaginable.

The variety of data available in the online realm lends itself to a number of different methodological approaches. In this chapter we examine three of these: machine learning; case studies; and netnography. Together, these offer a good indication of the variety of possible approaches that are available. Each approach is outlined, its strengths explained and its challenges and limitations considered. The aim is to introduce the reader to issues that should be considered at the design stage of a research project. With this aim in mind, the chapter concludes by highlighting the interplay between methodological considerations, research questions and research ethics.

Machine learning

It is becoming increasingly difficult to manually search for violent extremists, potentially violent extremists, or even users who post radical content online because the internet contains an overwhelming amount of information

145

(Scrivens 2021). This is a symptom of what some have described as the 'big data' phenomenon – i.e., a massive increase in the amount of data that is readily available, particularly online (Chen et al. 2014). These new conditions have necessitated guided data-filtering methods that can side-step the taxing manual methods that traditionally have been used to identify relevant information online (Cohen et al. 2014). Whether this work involves finding radical users of interest (e.g., Klausen et al. 2018), measuring digital pathways of radicalisation to violence (e.g., Hung et al. 2016) or detecting virtual indicators that may prevent future terrorist attacks (e.g., Johansson et al. 2016), the urgent need to pinpoint extremist content online is one of the most significant challenges faced by law enforcement agencies and security officials worldwide (Sageman 2014). In response, a number of researchers are shifting from manual identification of specific online content to machine-learning algorithms to do similar yet larger-scale tasks (Chen et al. 2014). But what is machine learning?

Machine learning is generally understood as what Mitchell (1997, p. 2) describes as the study of 'any computer algorithm that improves its performance at some tasks through experience'. Improvements in algorithm performance are guided by acquiring knowledge automatically rather than acquiring knowledge manually (Jordan & Mitchell 2015). Machine learning, in other words, involves the development of computer programs or the training of machines on how to learn automatically without human assistance. Two of the most widely adopted machine-learning methods in this regard are supervised or unsupervised learning, with the former using labelled training data to predict values of the label(s) on the unlabelled data and the latter identifying patterns in the data without the use of training data (see Chen & Chau 2005). Some advantages of machine learning include its ability to: (1) evaluate large volumes of data and identify patterns not easily identifiable to humans; (2) continuously improve and make more accurate predictions as it gains more experience with more data; and (3) analyse data that are multi-dimensional and multi-variety, and with a wide range of applications (Chen & Chau 2005). Machine learning, however, is not without its limitations. It is highly susceptible to error because it is automated. In addition, it can be a challenge to collect massive volumes of data that are needed to properly train a machine-learning algorithm. It can also be time-consuming for an algorithm to learn from and process the data, and it often requires substantial resources to function, including added computer power (Chen & Chau 2005; Riley 2019).

Nevertheless, various machine-learning techniques have been adopted by terrorism and extremism scholars in recent years, including – but not limited to – authorship analysis, sentiment analysis and affect analysis (see Chen 2012). One relatively novel machine-learning tool, sentiment analysis, has sparked the interest of many researchers in terrorism and extremism studies who are faced with new challenges in detecting extremist content online. Sentiment analysis software has become increasingly popular in this field because, as the amount of 'opinionated data' online grows exponentially, it offers a wide range of applications that can help address previously untapped and challenging research problems (see Liu 2012). Researchers, for example, have successfully used sentiment analysis to detect extreme language (e.g., Davidson et al. 2017), websites (e.g., Scrivens & Frank 2016) and users online (e.g., Scrivens et al. 2017), as well as to measure levels of online propaganda (e.g., Burnap et al. 2014) and cyberhate (e.g., Williams & Burnap 2015) following a terrorism incident, and to evaluate how radical discourse evolves over time online (e.g., Scrivens et al. 2018). Sentiment analysis has also been used to detect violent extremist language (e.g., Abbasi & Chen 2005) and users online (e.g., Kaati et al. 2016), as well as to measure levels of – or propensity towards – violent radicalisation online (e.g., Bermingham et al. 2009), all on a large scale.

Sentiment analysis, also known as 'opinion mining', is a category of computing science that specialises in evaluating the opinions found in a piece of text by organising data into distinct classes and sections, and assigning a piece of text with a positive, negative or neutral polarity value (Abbasi & Chen 2005). Typically, this process occurs through a two-step process that produces a polarity value: (1) a body of text is split into sections (sentences) to determine subjective and objective content; and (2) subjective content is classified by the software as being either positive, neutral or negative, where positive scores reflect positive attitudes and negative scores reflect negative attitudes. This is based on the notion that an author's opinion towards a particular topic is reflected in the choice and intensity of words he or she chooses to communicate (see Feldman 2013). Having said that, sentiment analysis is not without its limitations. It is estimated, for example, that 21 per cent of the time humans cannot agree among themselves about the sentiment within a given piece of text (Ogneva 2010), with some individuals unable to understand subtle context or irony. Understandably, sentiment analysis systems cannot be expected to have 100 per cent accuracy when compared to the opinions of humans. Researchers have in turn suggested that combining sentiment analysis with other methods and/or semantic-oriented approaches can improve accuracy rates in general and the detection of extremist content online in particular. This includes combining sentiment analysis with classification software (see Scrivens & Frank 2016), affect analysis (see Figea et al. 2016), social network analysis (Bermingham et al. 2009) or geolocation software (Mirani & Sasi 2016). Researchers also suggest that more work is needed to assess and potentially improve the classification accuracy and content identification offered by sentiment analysis software, which includes drawing comparisons between the performance of several sentiment methods and including a 'comparative human evaluation' component to validate a sentiment program's classifications (Figea et al. 2016).

Case studies

Case studies have long been an important part of academic inquiry. It is, in essence, 'an approach to research that facilitates exploration of a phenomenon within its context using a variety of data sources' (Baxter & Jack 2008, p. 544). In the study of terrorism, they have been used to analyse the lives of individual actors (Poppe 2018), specific attacks (Sageman 2019) or even interventions to dissuade individuals from engaging in extremism (Helmus & Klein 2018). For the purposes of this chapter, a case study involves collating information about a terrorist actor, group or event from a range of sources into a case file. Having been collected, data can be analysed singularly in a high level of detail for either an individual actor (e.g., Pearson 2017) or a cell (e.g., Schuurman & Horgan 2016). Similarly, researchers can conduct what Baxter and Jack (2008) call 'multiple case study' methodologies in which cases are compared against each other, for example, a small cohort in which cases can be analysed against each other (von Behr et al. 2013), or even as a large-n sample in which cases are quantitatively analysed as a database (Gill et al. 2017; Horgan et al. 2016; Klausen et al. 2018, Whittaker 2021).

Yin (2014) argues that case studies are particularly apt in a specific set of circumstances. He argues that they are suited to research questions which are focused around answering 'how' or 'why' a phenomenon occurs, when the researcher cannot control the environment they seek to analyse and when the focus of a study is contemporary. It is therefore easy to see why it has been adopted as a means of attempting to understand terrorism. Moreover, as the causes of terrorism are so ill understood (Schmid 2013; Sageman 2014), researchers must look at a wider set of contextual factors than a simple cause/effect observation. While it is possible for case studies to draw on primary data such as interviews (e.g., Schuurman 2017) or closed-source secondary data such as police files, psychological reports and interviews with law enforcement (Gill et al. 2019), these types of data are still scarce within the field of terrorism studies. Therefore, researchers have looked for ways to accumulate data from online sources.

There is a growing body of case study research that utilises data from open sources which has been substantially aided by the rapid growth of the internet.

For example, Whittaker's doctoral research (2019, 2021) built a database of case studies of Islamic State terrorist actors in the United States. This was facilitated by the availability of court documents via online repositories such as the George Washington University's Program on Extremism, which houses over 20,000 pages of criminal justice information on over 200 terrorists.[1] The growth of news aggregators such as Google News or the Lexisnexis News and Monitoring Service are also an invaluable asset, allowing researchers to comb through thousands of news articles in a short space of time and be kept abreast on developing cases. Moreover, there are online libraries of academic articles and grey literature – for example VOX-Pol's Library[2] – that can provide researchers with existing literature on their chosen topic which can help to triangulate data. This has led to a number of studies in which researchers have been able to develop in-depth case studies for a larger number of terrorist actors (Gill et al. 2017; Klausen et al. 2018; Schuurman et al. 2018; Whittaker 2021).

The primary benefit of this approach is the ability to analyse behaviours. Terrorists are a difficult research population to reach as a large number die as a result of their actions (for example when conducting an attack or travelling to foreign conflicts) and interacting with those that are incarcerated is fraught with practical impediments and ethical issues. As a result of this, recent research into terrorism has tended to focus on the content with which terrorists (could potentially) interact, such as magazines, videos or images (Conway 2017) or studies on terrorist *supporters* online on platforms such as Twitter (e.g., Berger & Morgan 2015; Berger & Perez 2016) or Telegram (e.g., Bloom et al. 2019; Clifford & Powell 2019). These types of studies add to the body of knowledge in important ways but fall short of investigating actual behaviours because one cannot be sure how (if at all) terrorists actually engage with this type of content, meaning that one must take a causal leap of faith to explain how it affected terrorists. In other words, 'they suggest a degree of causality between what is online and the influence on the person reading it, which cannot be proven' (von Behr et al. 2013, p. 9).

For an example of how this gap can be bridged using case studies, Whittaker's doctoral research is instructive. Many studies have focused on instructional material in jihadist magazines which aims to encourage and facilitate individuals to conduct acts of terror, including providing bomb-making instructions (e.g., Conway et al. 2017; Lemieux et al. 2014; Reed & Ingram 2017). While

---

[1]   The PoE ISIS Cases can be accessed via https://extremism.gwu.edu/cases.
[2]   The VOX-Pol Library can be accessed via www.voxpol.eu/library/.

these studies offer important insights, it is difficult to establish whether terrorists actually use this type of material. However, a case study can offer invaluable insight here for a number of reasons. First, they can be used to study terrorists' behaviours to establish whether such magazines are actually read. Whittaker's research suggested that this was indeed the case; jihadist magazines were the most popular type of propaganda collected and consumed within the sample. Second, a deeper dive can assess whether individuals are actually utilising this type of instructional material as part of their plots; in Whittaker's sample, only a small handful of individuals utilised this type of material to conduct an attack. Third, because case studies collect data on a wider set of contextual factors, they offer an opportunity to analyse the use of instructional material in relation to other factors. In Whittaker's research, not only did few utilise bomb-making instructions, but they were dwarfed by those that engaged in ideological behaviours such as actors taking to social media to mimic pictures or text from speeches, suggesting that instructional material may play a less important role than ideological content. Research that focuses purely on radical content cannot make the observations outlined above, yet taken together, a focus on content and behaviours can offer a clear picture in which hypotheses can be advanced and tested.

There are, however, important limitations to the use of case study data, particularly if the researcher is limited to secondary open sources available over the internet. Data are likely to include biases based on the intent of the original author. A prosecutor that is drafting a criminal affidavit is aiming to secure a conviction and a journalist is concerned with what is newsworthy. This means that certain terrorist actors or incidents may have a substantial amount of more coverage than others, for example, female actors or those that plotted attacks rather than travelled to Syria (Whittaker 2019). If the data are uneven then it can skew the results towards the demographics of the more newsworthy incidents. Relatedly, relying on secondary sources raises issues of missing data. It is difficult to establish whether a fact of a case is not reported because it did not happen or because it was merely not reported (Gill et al. 2015); it is unrealistic to expect either court documents or news articles to detail, for example, that an individual *did not* read jihadist magazines.

Despite these limitations, collecting open-source case study data via the internet can provide a fruitful way of advancing knowledge within the field of terrorism studies. Terrorism is, and will remain, a highly newsworthy event (Mitnik et al. 2018) and as such there will continue to be a large amount of data in the public domain that is not available for most other crimes. It is incumbent on researchers to make the most of online data collection sources such as news aggregators and academic journal libraries to gather these data and conduct robust research.

Netnography

Ethnographies of extreme groups, such as those by Wiktorowicz (2005), Kenney (2018), Weeks (2020) and Pilkington (2016), have contributed to increased understanding of how and why people radicalise. Such studies involve immersion in the cultures, rituals and practices of groups, becoming familiar with their members and developing empathetic researcher–participant relationships with them. In the fields of digital sociology and cultural studies there is a parallel seam of expertise on the function and practices of *digital* communities. Netnography – ethnographic study of internet communities – emerged as a market research tool, analysing consumer practices (Kozinets 2002). Subsequently it has enabled the study of communities of practice, considering questions of identity, friendship and affect, and exploring the ways in which online and offline spaces merge and intersect (Caliandro 2014). Such work has shed light on the interactions between social life, technology and knowledge (Marres 2017).

Following Conway's (2017) call for greater interdisciplinarity and a recognition of netnography, there are three important potential implications of applying netnography to studies of online extremism. The first is theoretical. Researchers of extremism have sought to understand the precise role of online spaces in relation to offline. Some academics, governments and the media have suggested that online radicalisation stands in a causal relation to offline violence. Although it is clear that what happens in online spaces impacts on aspects of terrorist behaviours, such as recruitment, propaganda or mobilisation, the reality is more complex (Hussain & Saltman 2014; von Behr et al. 2013). Netnographers and digital sociologists have studied online communities since the earliest days of the internet. Their work has long challenged the idea of the internet as a delimited space (Chen 2016; Lövheim 2005). Research instead suggests the 'embeddedness' of cyberspace in everyday life, meaning the dichotomous language of 'off' and 'on' does not do justice to the more fluid understandings of the interlinked relations within them. For instance, in her work on the virtual community 'Cybercity', Carter (2005) suggests online was 'just another place to meet'. It was also a trusted space. Despite the possibilities for deception online, she found residents of Cybercity presenting the same identity and personality offline as on, with friendships and behaviours ported, and indeed replicated, between domains. This is an important and relevant point for those seeking to understand the relationship between online and offline norms and identities in extreme groups. Gill et al. (2015, p. 35) indeed suggest there is 'no easy offline versus online radicalisation dichotomy to be drawn. It is a false dichotomy.' Actors tend to engage in the same activities online and off, and the spaces are not distinct, they note.

Second, digital sociology and netnography emphasise the emotional, affective and gendered aspects of online communities, 'extreme' or otherwise (see Kozinets 2019). Affect is often associated with bodies, but also understood as the emotion that is generated in community interactions. In radicalisation theory, the concept of affect is increasingly being applied to the understanding of 'processes' of joining a group. Authors have explored the ways in which recruitment is facilitated by the 'moral shock', for instance, of consuming distressing or brutal video or photo imagery, or of narratives aimed at mobilising engagement (Bartlett & Miller 2012; Cottee & Hayward 2011; Wiktorowicz 2005). What is less well explored is how relationships in extreme communities develop. Netnography offers some clues. Cybercity inhabitants for instance seek out meaningful friendships online and then pursue them offline. These relationships are, Carter (2005) suggests, often more intense, as participants regard the online space as one in which a 'pure friendship' is more easily achieved, given the initial absence of the encumbrance of prejudices based on appearance, weight, race or gender. This does not mean that there are not tensions between online and offline identity performances, and a degree of emotional labour can be required to sustain online roles (Gregg 2011; Lanier 2010). These findings may be particularly salient in communities with high stakes for membership, such as those committed to extreme ideology. For instance, Pearson (2020) found high levels of emotional work done by participants in an online Islamist community, where participants reported high personal risks of criminalisation and to mental health. Some of these risks came from outside their communities and some from within.

Finally, the application of findings from netnography would go some way to understanding the possibilities for deradicalisation of extreme actors. One of the key issues with the study of terrorism and extremism is that the terms and crimes associated with them are frequently exceptionalised as requiring both 'special' treatment and responses. The al-Qaeda attacks on 9/11 in particular heralded what some described as a 'new' era of terrorism (Hoffman 2002; Neumann 2009) which entailed exceptional responses. These have included indefinite detention at Guantanamo, or the imposition of a state of emergency in states grappling with al-Qaeda-inspired ideologies. The study of extremism as a specific and yet ill-defined category has to some degree exacerbated this tendency, assuming the extreme actor is fundamentally 'other'. Existing studies of everyday online communities emphasise the features shared with extreme groups. The problem of extremism becomes contextualised; it is a problem of societies and communities, a function of communities online, not simply a problem of extremists themselves. This fundamental insight enables a more nuanced approach to online behaviours observable in extreme communities but evident elsewhere.

Netnography as methodology of course poses some of the challenges of ethnography of extreme groups. Access to extreme communities online is no less challenging than offline (Bailey 2015). Researcher presence, even where possible, could alter interactions in communities or prompt deception. In practical terms, the best on offer might be 'ethnography by proxy' (Hegghammer, cited in Conway 2017, p. 86). Netnography as *theory*, however, already offers foundational insights into the key questions for those studying online extremism, questions about the relations between offline and on, and how communities work. As online extremism research does not look likely to abate, it should seek to build on pre-existing digital scholarship, and its lessons for extremism debates. Technology has made possible quantitative studies of large-n data associated with extreme groups. It is important, however, to use qualitative in-depth studies such as netnography to interrogate what these data mean.

Conclusion

The availability of online data opens up a number of different potential lines of academic enquiry, some of which we have explored in this chapter. Each methodological approach has its own particular benefits. Machine learning enables the evaluation of large volumes of data, the identification of patterns that might otherwise have gone unnoticed and the ability to analyse multi-dimensional and multi-variety data. Case studies investigate the behaviours of terrorists and thus shed light on the actual influence on terrorists of interaction with online terrorist content. Netnographic research has the potential to deepen understanding of online extremist communities by considering the ways in which movements coalesce online, and in particular how such communities are constituted. At the same time, however, each approach has its own limitations and challenges. Machine learning is susceptible to error and a significant amount of data, time and resource may be required to properly train a machine-learning algorithm. The use of secondary sources in case studies carries with it the risk of bias and the possibility of missing data. And netnography can present challenges in terms of access and the potential impact on participant behaviour.

When designing a research project, it is important to be mindful of the strengths and limitations of the various methodological approaches. The selection of methodological approach must be aligned with the research questions that your project will seek to answer. As this chapter has shown, different approaches are apt to answer different types of question. As you review the existing literature, identify the contribution your study will seek to make and refine your research questions accordingly. It may become necessary to adapt your methodology too. Conversely, refinements to your methodology may necessitate amendments to your research questions. The same point applies to research ethics, a topic that is covered in detail elsewhere in this volume. Different methodologies raise different ethical considerations and the way in which these ethics issues are addressed may require refinements to your methodology (Markham 2006). In short, your research questions, methods and ethics are inextricably connected and so designing a research project is inevitably an iterative process.

References

Abbasi, A. & Chen, H. (2005). Applying authorship analysis to extremist-group web forum messages. *Intelligent Systems*, *20*(5), 67–75.

Bailey, G. (2015). Extremism, community and stigma: Researching the far right and radical Islam in their context. In K. Bhopal & R. Deuchar (Eds), Researching Marginalized Groups. Routledge.

Bartlett, J. & Miller, C. (2012). The edge of violence: Towards telling the difference between violent and non-violent radicalization. *Terrorism and Political Violence*, *24*(1), 1–21.

Benson, D. (2014). Why the internet is not increasing terrorism. *Security Studies*, *23*(2), 293–328.

Baxter, P. & Jack, S. (2008). 'Qualitative Case Study Methodology: Study Design and Implementation for Novice Researchers', *The Qualitative Report*, *13*(4), 544–559.

Berger, J.M. & Morgan, J. (2015). 'The ISIS Twitter Census: Defining and Describing the Population of ISIS Supporters on Twitter', *The Brookings Project on U.S. Relations with the Islamic World: Analysis Paper*, March (20).

Berger, J.M. & Perez, H. (2016). *The Islamic State's diminishing returns on Twitter: How suspensions are limiting the social networks of English-speaking ISIS supporters.* George Washington University: Program on Extremism.

Bermingham, A., Conway, M., McInerney, L., O'Hare, N. & Smeaton, A.F. (2009). Combining social network analysis and sentiment analysis to explore the potential for online radicalisation. *2009 International Conference on Advances in Social Network Analysis Mining*, Athens.

Bloom, M., Tiflati, H., & Horgan, J. (2019). Navigating ISIS's preferred platform: Telegram1. *Terrorism and Political Violence*, *31*(6), 1242–1254.

Burnap, P., Williams, M.L., Sloan, L. ... & Voss, A. (2014). Tweeting the terror: Modelling the social media reaction to the Woolwich terrorist attack. *Social Network Analysis and Mining*, 4, 1–14.

Caliandro, A. (2014). Ethnography in digital spaces: Ethnography of virtual worlds, net-nography, and digital ethnography. In P. Sunderland & R. Denny (Eds), *Handbook of Business Anthropology* (pp. 738–761). Left Coast Press.

Carter, D. (2005). Living in virtual communities: An ethnography of human relation-ships in cyberspace. *Information, Communication and Society*, 8(2), 148–167.

Chen, C.-P. (2016). Playing with digital gender identity and cultural value. *Gender, Place and Culture*, 23(4), 521–536.

Chen, H. (2012). *Dark Web: Exploring and Data Mining the Dark Side of the Web.* Springer.

Chen, H. & Chau, M. (2005). Web mining: Machine learning for web applications. *Information Science and Technology*, 38(1), 289–329.

Chen, M., Mao, S., Zhang, Y. & Leung, V.C.M. (2014). *Big Data: Related Technologies, Challenges and Future Prospects*. Springer.

Clifford, B. & Powell, H. (2019). 'Encrypted Extremism: Inside the English-Speaking Islamic State Ecosystem on Telegram', Program on Extremism.

Cohen, K., Johansson, F., Kaati, L. & Mork, J.C. (2014). Detecting linguistic markers for radical violence in social media. *Terrorism and Political Violence*, 26(1), 246–256.

Conway, M. (2017). Determining the role of the internet in violent extremism and ter-rorism: Six suggestions for progressing research. *Studies in Conflict and Terrorism*, 40(1), 77–98.

Cottee, S. & Hayward, K. (2011). Terrorist (e)motives: The existential attractions of terrorism. *Studies in Conflict and Terrorism*, 34(12), 963–986.

Davidson, T., Warmsley, D., Macy, M. & Weber, I. (2017). Automated hate speech detection and the problem of offensive language. *11th International AAAI Conference on Web and Social Media*, Palo Alto, CA.

Dolnik, A. (Ed.) (2013). *Conducting Terrorism Field Research: A Guide.* Routledge.

Feldman, R. (2013). Techniques and applications for sentiment analysis. *Communications of the ACM*, 56(4), 82–89.

Figea, L., Kaati, L. & Scrivens, R. (2016). Measuring online affects in a white supremacy forum. *2016 IEEE International Conference on Intelligence and Security Informatics*, Tucson, AZ.

Gill, P., Conway, M., Corner, E. & Thornton, A. (2015). What are the roles of the internet in terrorism? VOX-Pol. http:// voxpol .eu/ wp -content/ uploads/ 2015/ 11/ DCUJ3518_VOX_Lone_Actors_report_02.11.15_WEB.pdf

Gill, P., Corner, E., Conway, M., Thornton, A., Bloom, M., & Horgan, J. (2017). 'Terrorist Use of the Internet by the Numbers: Quantifying Behaviors, Patterns, and Processes', *Criminology and Public Policy*, 16(1), 99–117.

Gregg, D.M. (2011). *Work's Intimacy*. Polity.

Helmus, T.C. & Klein, K. (2018). 'Assessing Outcomes of Online Campaigns Countering Violent Extremism: A Case Study of the Redirect Method', RAND Research Report [Preprint].

Hoffman, B. (2002). Rethinking terrorism and counterterrorism since 9/11. *Studies in Conflict and Terrorism*, 25(5), 303–316.

Horgan, J. (2004). The case for first hand research. In A. Silke (Ed.), *Research on Terrorism: Trends, Achievements and Failures* (pp. 30–57). Routledge.

Horgan, J. (2012). Interviewing the terrorists: Reflections on fieldwork and implications for psychological research. *Behavioral Sciences of Terrorism and Political Aggression,* 4(3), 195–211.

Horgan, J., Shortland, N., Abbasciano, S., & Walsh, S. (2016). 'Actions Speak Louder than Words: A Behavioral Analysis of 183 Individuals Convicted for Terrorist Offenses in the United States from 1995 to 2012', *Journal of Forensic Sciences,* 61(5), 1228–1237.

Hung, B.W.K., Jayasumana, A.P. & Bandara, V.W. (2016). Detecting radicalization trajectories using graph pattern matching algorithms. *2016 IEEE International Conference on Intelligence and Security Informatics,* Tucson, AZ.

Hussain, G. & Saltman, E.M. (2014). *Jihad Trending: A Comprehensive Analysis of Online Extremism and How to Counter it.* The Quilliam Foundation. www.quilliamfoundation.org/wp/wp-content/uploads/publications/free/jihad-trending-quilliam-report.pdf

Johansson, F., Kaati, L. & Sahlgren, M. (2016). Detecting linguistic markers of violent extremism in online environments. In M. Khader, L.S. Neo, G. Ong, E.T. Mingyi & J. Chin (Eds), *Combating Violent Extremism and Radicalization in the Digital Era* (pp. 374–390). Information Science Reference.

Jordan, M.I. & Mitchell, T.M. (2015). Machine learning: Trends, perspectives, and prospects. *Science,* 349(6245), 255–260.

Kaati, L., Shrestha, A. & Sardella, T. (2016). Identifying warning behaviors of violent lone offenders in written communications. *2016 IEEE International Conference on Data Mining Workshops,* Barcelona.

Kenney, M. (2018). *The Islamic State in Britain: Radicalization and Resilience in an Activist Network.* Cambridge University Press.

Klausen, J., Marks, C.E. & Zaman, T. (2018). Finding extremists in online social networks. *Operations Research,* 66(4), 957–976.

Kozinets, R.V. (2002). The field behind the screen: Using netnography for marketing research in online communities. *Journal of Marketing Research,* 39(1), 61–72.

Kozinets, R.V. (2019). *Netnography: The Essential Guide to Qualitative Social Media Research* (Third Edition). Sage.

Lanier, J. (2010). *You Are Not a Gadget: A Manifesto.* Penguin Books.

Lemieux, A. F., Brachman, J. M., Levitt, J., & Wood, J. (2014). 'Inspire Magazine: A Critical Analysis of its Significance and Potential Impact Through the Lens of the Information, Motivation, and Behavioral Skills Model', *Terrorism and Political Violence,* 26(2), 354–371.

Liu, B. (2012). *Sentiment Analysis and Opinion Mining.* Morgan and Claypool.

Lövheim, M. (2005). *Young People and the Use of the Internet as Transitional Space.* https://doi.org/DOI:10.11588/heidok.00005826

Macdonald, S. & Mair, D. (2015). Terrorism online: A new strategic environment. In T. Chen, L. Jarvis & S. Macdonald (Eds), *Terrorism Online: Politics, Law and Technology* (pp. 10–34). Routledge.

Markham, A. (2006). Method as ethic, ethic as method. *Journal of Information Ethics,* 15(2), 37–54.

Marres, N. (2017). *Digital Sociology: The Reinvention of Social Research.* Polity.

Mirani, T.B. & Sasi, S. (2016). Sentiment analysis of ISIS related tweets using absolute location. *2016 International Conference on Computational Science and Computational Intelligence,* Las Vegas, NV.

Mitchell, T. (1997). *Machine Learning.* McGraw-Hill.

Mitnik, Z.S., Freilich, J.D. & Chermak, S. (2018). 'Post-9/11 Coverage of Terrorism in the New York Times', *Justice Quarterly*, 1–25.

Nacos, B.L. (2014). Tactics of terrorism. In E. Mahmoud (Ed.), *Exchanging Terrorism Oxygen for Media Airwaves: The Age of Terroredia* (pp. 110–123). IGI Global.

Neumann, P. (2009). *Old and New Terrorism*. Polity Press.

Ogneva, M. (2010). How companies can use sentiment analysis to improve their business. http://mashable.com/2010/04/19/sentiment-analysis

Pearson, E. (2017). Online as the new frontline: Affect, gender, and ISIS-take-down on social media. *Studies in Conflict and Terrorism, 41*(11), 850–874.

Pearson, E. (2020, September 14). An insider perspective: What the internet means to UK jihadists – GNET. *GNet Insights*. https://gnet-research.org/2020/09/14/an-insider-perspective-what-the-internet-means-to-uk-jihadists/

Pilkington, H. (2016). *Loud and Proud: Passion and Politics in the English Defence League*. Manchester University Press.

Poppe, K. (2018). *Nidal Hasan: A Case Study in Lone-Actor Terrorism*. Washington, DC.

Program on Extremism (n.d.). The cases. George Washington University. https://extremism.gwu.edu/cases

Reed, A. & Ingram, H. (2017). 'Exploring the Role of Instructional Material in AQAP's Inspire and ISIS' Rumiyah', *1st European Counter Terrorism Centre (ECTC) conference on online terrorist propaganda*.

Riley, P. (2019). Three pitfalls to avoid in machine learning. *Nature, 572*, 27–29.

Sageman, M. (2014). The stagnation in terrorism research. *Terrorism and Political Violence, 26*(4), 565–580.

Sageman, M. (2019). *The London Bombings*. Philadelphia, PA: University of Pennsylvania Press.

Schmid, A.P. (2013). *Radicalisation, De-Radicalisation, Counter-Radicalisation: A Conceptual Discussion and Literature Review*. The Hague.

Schuurman, B. (2017). *Becoming a European homegrown Jihadist: A multilevel analysis of involvement in the Dutch Hofstadgroup, 2002-2005*, Doctoral Thesis. Leiden University.

Schuurman, B. and Horgan, J. (2016). 'Rationales for terrorist violence in homegrown jihadist groups: A case study from the Netherlands', *Aggression and Violent Behavior, 27*, 55–63.

Scrivens, R. (2021). Exploring radical right-wing posting behaviors online. *Deviant Behavior, 42*(11), 1470–1484.

Scrivens, R. & Frank, R. (2016). Sentiment-based classification of radical text on the web. *2016 European Intelligence and Security Informatics Conference*, Uppsala.

Scrivens, R., Davies, G. & Frank, R. (2017). Searching for signs of extremism on the web: An introduction to sentiment-based identification of radical authors. *Behavioral Sciences of Terrorism and Political Aggression, 10*(1), 39–59.

Scrivens, R., Davies, G. & Frank, R. (2018). Measuring the evolution of radical right-wing posting behaviors online. *Deviant Behavior, 41*(2), 216–232.

Silke, A. (Ed.) (2003). *Research on Terrorism: Trends, Achievements and Failures*. Routledge.

von Behr, I., Reding, A., Edwards, C. & Gribbon, L. (2013). Radicalisation in the digital era. www.rand.org/pubs/research_reports/RR453.html

Weeks, D. (2020). *Al Muhajiroun: A Case Study in Contemporary Islamic Activism*. Palgrave Macmillan.

Whittaker, J. (2019). *Building Secondary Source Databases on Violent Extremism: Reflections and Suggestions.* Resolve Network.
Whittaker, J. (2021). The online behaviors of Islamic state terrorists in the United States. *Criminology and Public Policy, 20,* 177–203.
Wiktorowicz, Q. (2005). *Radical Islam Rising: Muslim Extremism in the West.* Rowman & Littlefield.
Williams, M.L. & Burnap, P. (2015). Cyberhate on social media in the aftermath of Woolwich: A case study in computational criminology and big data. *British Journal of Criminology, 56*(2), 211–238.
Yin, R.K. (2014). *Case Study Research Design and Methods.* Sage.

11   Terrorism databases: problems and solutions

Stephen Johnson and Gary A. Ackerman

Introduction

Terrorism is a highly complex and multi-faceted phenomenon and, as such, many observations about terrorism will be distinct to a particular actor with a particular ideology, in a particular time and place. This does not mean, however, that we should dismiss the possibility of underlying patterns that might exist across groups and settings. Indeed, if terrorism research is to move beyond the merely descriptive to the more prescriptive and thus policy-relevant, it arguably needs to look for generalizable dynamics that can be applied to new contexts. Identifying these patterns requires the analysis of data that can be usefully compared across cases of terrorism, which in turn requires the collection and curation of these data in databases.

By databases, we are referring to organized collections of empirical data, usually systematically recorded in the form of consistently formatted and characterized items. When it comes to terrorism databases, although these often take the form of quantitative representations of information in the form of numerical "codes," it is important to realize that they can be made up of a vast array of additional types of data, ranging from qualitative descriptions of cases and symbols to archives of terrorist manifestos and video recordings of interviews with terrorists.

Data on terrorism have been collected almost from the beginning of the era of modern terrorism. For example, the Pinkerton security services company collected accounts of terrorist incidents from 1970, while the RAND Corporation think tank began assembling its chronology of terrorist attacks in 1972, following the Munich Olympics attacks (RAND n.d.). However, before the twenty-first century, the bulk of research on terrorism was either comprised of stand-alone case studies of specific groups or was largely theoretical and informed by a handful of well-known cases. This made it difficult to discern general patterns of terrorism, especially when it came to research that could guide counterterrorism policy. Indeed, in 2006, a Campbell systematic review found that out of 20,000 pieces of literature on terrorism, there were only seven that rigorously evaluated the effectiveness of counterterrorism programs (Lum, Kennedy and Sherley 2006).

This has changed in the past two decades, with the introduction of a wide variety of databases capturing different aspects of terrorism beyond terrorist attacks, including organizational-level data on terrorist groups, counterterrorist operations, terrorist ideological artifacts and pre-attack activities. Today, terrorism researchers have access to a rich catalogue of terrorism databases that can be mined for new insights into the phenomenon. However, the mere existence of a plethora of databases is not a panacea for terrorism research. Not all databases are of equal quality and uninformed or careless usage of these databases can lead to the drawing of incorrect inferences and thereby to poor policy guidance and specious contributions to our understanding of terrorism. This chapter seeks to describe the current range of terrorism-related databases, providing practical guidance on how best to make use of them, while remaining cognizant of their limitations and potential pitfalls for analysis. An example is given which considers terrorism research in the United Kingdom (UK) and how a researcher might choose a source.

Key databases

The number of terrorism data resources can be bewildering. Many have been created by processing and transforming other existing databases, making their selection and use complex. The Global Terrorism Database (GTD) (UoM 2021b) has incorporated many other sources in its history, e.g., the Worldwide Incidents Tracking System (WITS) (NCTC 2021). The International Terrorism: Attributes of Terrorist Events (ITERATE) (Duke 2021) dataset was based heavily on the now defunct RAND Terrorism Chronologies, which itself transformed into the RAND Database of Worldwide Terrorism Incidents (RDWTI) (RAND 2021). This section will introduce some of the major datasets.

Table 11.1 summarizes the most used datasets. The GTD has dominated due to its breadth, currency and availability. Previously ITERATE, RDWTI and WITS were very popular but this declined as their collection activities stopped. Private databases such as Terrorism Tracker (Aon 2021) and Jane's (2021) tend to be more current reflecting their subscribers' need. But currency is often the enemy of accuracy and comprehensiveness.

Table 11.1   Overview of a selection of major terrorism databases

Name	Maintained by	Availability	Qualitative/ quantitative	Active
Global Terrorism Database (GTD)	University of Maryland	Academic	Quantitative	1970– present
Europol Terrorism Situation and trend report	Europol	Full	Quantitative	2007– present
Worldwide Incidents Tracking System (WITS)	National Counter Terrorism Center	Now part of GTD	Quantitative	2004–2012
RAND Database of Worldwide Terrorism Incidents (RDWTI)	RAND	Full	Quantitative	1968–2009
International Terrorism: Attributes of Terrorist Events (ITERATE)	Duke University	Restricted	Quantitative	1968–2018
Major Episodes of Political Violence, 1946–2018	Integrated Network for Societal Conflict Research (INSCR)	Full	Quantitative	1946–2018
High Casualty Terrorist Bombings, 1989–2020	Integrated Network for Societal Conflict Research (INSCR)	Full	Quantitative	1989–2020
Suicide Attack Database	Chicago Project on Security and Terrorism (CPOST)	Offline	Quantitative	1982–2018
Armed Conflict Dataset	Uppsala University and the Peace Research Institute, Oslo	Academic	Quantitative	1989– present

Name	Maintained by	Availability	Qualitative/ quantitative	Active
Terrorism and Extremist Violence in the United States Database (TEVUS)	University of Maryland	Academic	Quantitative	1970–2015
Armed Conflict Location and Event Data (ACLED)	ACLED Project	Academic	Quantitative	1997– present
Big Allied and Dangerous Database (BAAD)	University at Albany	Academic	Quantitative	1998–2015?
Radiological and Nuclear Non-State Adversaries Database (RANNSAD)	University of Maryland	Academic	Quantitative/ qualitative	1974–2008
Nuclear Facilities Attack Database (NuFAD)	University of Maryland	Academic	Quantitative/ qualitative	1961–2016
Profiles of Incidents Involving CBRN and Non-State Actors Database (POICN)	University of Maryland	By request	Quantitative/ qualitative	1990–2017
Chemical and Biological Non-State Adversaries Database (CABNSAD)	University of Maryland	By request	Quantitative/ qualitative	1946–2016
Profiles of Individual Radicalization in the United States Dataset (PIRUS)	University of Maryland	Academic	Quantitative	1948–2018
The Prosecution Project	Prosecution Project (Non-Profit)	By request	Quantitative	1990– present

Name	Maintained by	Availability	Qualitative/ quantitative	Active
Leadership of the Extreme and Dangerous for Innovative Results Dataset (LEADIR)	University of Oklahoma	By request	Quantitative	2008–2017
Salafi Jihadist Inspired Profiles and Radicalization Clusters (SPARC)	University of Southern California	By request	Qualitative	2011–2017
Country Reports on Terrorism	United States State Department	Full	Quantitative	1989–present
Militant Ideology Atlas	West Point	Full	Qualitative	1950–present
Terrorism Tracker	Aon/Risk Advisory	Payment	Quantitative	2007–present
Triton	Optima	Payment	Quantitative/ qualitative	Not known
Terrorism Threat	Jane's	Payment	Quantitative/ qualitative	Not known

Note: CBRN = chemical, biological, radiological and nuclear.

Databases can be structured, like the GTD, with a very rigorous taxonomy and codebook describing the methodology for processing incidents, or unstructured like the Europol Terrorism Situation and Trend Report (Europol 2021), which has excellent quantitative data but reports them within a written report. Many of the best resources combine both quantitative data on incidents with qualitative details, but there are resources that focus on qualitative data only, e.g., the Military Ideology Atlas (USMA 2021).

Use of terrorism data in research

Researchers can utilize terrorism databases for several purposes. The first is to simply derive discrete facts from the qualitative or quantitative data, usually citing particular cases or using descriptive measures of particular variables to support or inform a broader argument. Examples of this "journalistic" approach to using databases are when a researcher might search the American Terrorism Study's Court Record Repository (UoA Terrorism Research Center 2021) for all cases linked to the Earth Liberation Front for use in a qualitative analysis, or when a researcher studying the phenomenon of mass casualty terrorism queries the GTD's online browsing tool to determine that out of 191,464 incidents, only 798 (0.42 percent) resulted in more than 100 casualties.

The most common use by academic researchers of quantitative databases is to conduct inferential statistical analyses. To cite some of the more commonly used datasets, a basic search by database name of Google Scholar reveals 950 scholarly works using the ITERATE database, 550 using WITS data, 43 using the LEADIR database and a whopping 8,530 using the GTD. Most of these studies utilize elements drawn from the quantitative data as either dependent or independent variables and apply standard statistical methods and models, such as hypothesis tests or regression analyses, to test theoretical arguments about association or causation related to terrorism. This often takes the form of testing the hypothesized relationship between various factors such as demographic, environmental or organizational attributes and different terrorism outcomes (types of attack, number of casualties, weapon used, etc.). For recent examples, see Asal, Linebarger, Jadoon and Greig (2021), Demir and Guler (2021), Fleming, Manning, Pham and Vorsina (2020) and Windisch, Logan and Ligon (2018). Some databases contain data that allow for additional analytical approaches, such as social network connections (Asal and Rethemeyer 2008; Barber 2015; Zech and Gabbay 2016) or geospatial analysis (Behlendorf, LaFree and Legault 2012). In addition to deriving inferences directly, the data drawn from terrorism databases sometimes provide an empirical baseline that is used to parameterize a host of models, primarily those oriented towards risk assessment. These can include game-theory models (Zhang and Zhuang 2019), Bayes nets (Whitney, White, Walsh, Dalton and Brothers 2011) and machine-learning algorithms (Curia 2020).

Yet, for those not well versed in statistical techniques, deriving value from quantitative data can sometimes be difficult. Therefore, an increasingly common practice is to facilitate the understanding of terrorism-related datasets by representing them in visualizations designed to allow for quick comprehension of large quantities of data (Bhatia, Chhabra and Kumar 2020; Chhatwal and Rose 2008). Examples include the Keshif representation of the Profiles of Individual Radicalization in the United States (UoM 2021c), the use of tools like Tableau to visualize terrorism data (Lam 2019) as well as more dynamic visualizations (Google 2020).

While most users of terrorism databases are researchers in academia, this is not exclusively the case. Of course, government agencies maintain classified databases of terrorist individuals and activities for use by law enforcement and intelligence analysts, but even open-source databases collected by scholars are at times utilized directly by government agencies to guide counterterrorism policy and practice. An example in the United States is the *Country Reports on Terrorism* (NCTC 2021), produced annually by the State Department, which contains a statistical annex drawn from terrorism databases.[1] The fact that data drawn from terrorism databases are often used – whether through direct analysis or by leveraging data-derived findings from the scholarly literature – to inform government policies to address terrorism means that it is critical that these data are of the highest quality and are used appropriately by researchers.

Metrics of a "good database"

It should be possible to determine the characteristics of a good database from the discussions in research papers. Desmarais and Cranmer (2013, pp. 1–12) and Hoffman, Shelton and Cleven (2013, pp. 896–909) are some of the better examples who explicitly acknowledge the limitations on the conclusions they can draw from the data, and Nesser (2014, pp. 440–456) recognizes the challenge of bias. Others record challenges in the processing but proceed to the analysis anyway. Gao, Guo, Liao, Webb and Cutter (2013, pp. 676–691) acknowledge that a lot of data is lost when they geocode the GTD but see it as unavoidable. White, Porter and Mazerolle (2013, pp. 295–320) are open about removing data where no date or responsible group is found with limited discussion of the impact. But there are examples like Gries, Krieger and Meierrieks (2011, pp. 493–508) and Caruso and Schneider (2011, pp. 37–49) where there is even less discussion of the data source. For many scholars it is enough, for example, to simply say they used the GTD because so many others choose to use it. Barker (2011, pp. 600–620) uses a commercial resource, the Triton database (Optima 2021), made available to the author for free but not available for others to scrutinize without payment.

---

[1]   From 2012 to 2017, this statistical annex was produced by the National Consortium for the Study of Terrorism and Responses to Terrorism, based on the Global Terrorism Database, while since 2018, it has been produced by the Global Terrorism Trends and Analysis Center. The 2019 edition can be found at the Development Services Group (2020).

Figure 11.1 proposes five major categories to use in the evaluation of a terrorism database and suggests sub-categories within them. It includes some categories proposed by Sheehan (2012, pp. 13–40), who produced one of the first examinations of terrorism databases. It also includes the analysis of Behlendorf, Belur and Kumar (2016, pp. 641–667), who found that media sources gave a reasonable geographic spread of a problem but lacked accuracy in the frequency of incidents. This chapter's authors found similar results in an analysis of UK incidents, discussed later in this section.

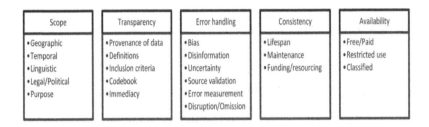

Figure 11.1   Factors for the analysis of a terrorism database

It is not possible to fully discuss every factor in detail here, but the intent of each is introduced:

- *Scope.* This relates directly to the applicability of the dataset to the question being asked. If the scope is well understood and characterized it can increase confidence in conclusions and can assist in comparing one study with another.
- *Transparency.* A thorough codebook can help the researcher understand what the curators of the database mean and intend in their coding. The sources included in the database must be scrutinized and placed in context with the database entry.
- *Error handling.* Subjectivity infects all aspects of terrorism research. A good database is unlikely to solve these problems, but it will honestly address them and recognize the potential impact.
- *Consistency.* Databases will see fluctuation in quality due to staff turnover and resource variation. The GTD is an excellent example of this, and its codebook is very honest about patchy periods of collection or lost data.
- *Availability.* Access can be controlled directly behind pay walls (e.g., Triton) or in classified repositories or there can be indirect constraints on usage through terms and conditions (e.g., GTD).

Table 11.2   Comparison of databases for United Kingdom terrorism
incidents

Database	Europol	WITS	GTD	RDWTI
Scope	Covers the UK Covers period Situation report	Covers UK Covers period Research	Covers UK Covers period Research	Covers UK Covers period Research
Transparency	No codebook Discrepancies in definitions between countries and inclusion acknowledged	No codebook	Codebook Definitions and inclusion discussed	Partial codebook Some definitions and inclusions discussed
Error handling	Countries are accepted as presenting accurate data, no error handling	Not possible to verify	Discussed in the methodology of collection	Not possible to verify
Consistency	Government funded and produced by Europol Collected from 2001 to present	Government funded Collected from 2004 to 2012	Academic, private and government funding across its life Collected from 1970 to present	Public and private sources Gaps acknowledged 1968 to 2009
Availability	Open, online and unstructured	Not available	Open, online for academic use	Open, online

Applying these tools to a real-world example

Table 11.2 shows an example where four resources are compared for suitability
in analyzing the frequency of terrorist attacks in the UK and if they increased
or decreased between 2007 and 2010. The resources are discussed in detail in
the preceding sections, so they should be familiar.

A simple table is used here as ultimately judgment is needed and scoring the
database may be too simplistic. Table 11.2 helps structure the analysis and
taken with Figure 11.2, a bar chart of the incidents in the databases, allows the
researcher to make an informed choice. It may be that no resource fits per-
fectly, in which case the process helps the researcher manage risks and temper
their conclusions.

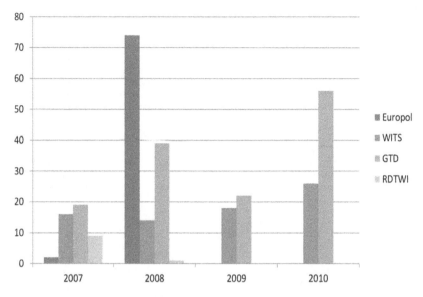

Figure 11.2   Terrorism incidents in the United Kingdom as recorded in four major databases, 2007–2010

GTD stands out as being the better resource across all categories, but it differs from Europol reporting in 2008 hugely. Examining the Europol report for that year would find that in 2008 Europol reported failed, foiled and successful attacks as one number (74 for the UK). GTD has the higher number in the other years, which is likely to be due to its collection resources but may be associated with inclusion criteria. The researcher would be advised to select the GTD, with careful consideration of filtering the attacks to ensure the incidents meet the researcher's definitions. They would be able to defend variations from official sources (Europol) by the knowledge they acquired from carrying out this analysis.

Good practice in utilizing terrorism data

Assuming that one has a high-quality terrorism database in hand, there is still the matter of using it correctly. While there is probably no such thing as an unequivocal "best practice," there are some good practices that should be adopted by any serious researcher seeking to utilize terrorism data. The following is not comprehensive but includes some basic approaches to improve the outputs of research involving terrorism databases.

Study previous research conducted by others

In many cases, other researchers using the dataset that you plan on employing have had to deal with the same questions and data issues that you might face. If the products of their research have managed to make their way through the scholarly peer-review process, their solutions to these issues have undergone at least some outside scrutiny and therefore can provide credible guidance as to how to navigate the use of a particular dataset. Conducting a basic literature review for prior papers and other published studies that have employed the particular dataset (paying attention to the methodological aspects of those publications) can be helpful to researchers who are considering using a data-base for the first time. It should be noted, however, that prior researchers might have utilized the same database in a very different way to the manner in which you intend to use it and so the applicability of previous approaches will vary from case to case, depending on how close your research design is to ones used previously. Reviewing prior research also helps to obtain a sense for the reputation of the database, since if there is no published research using the database and it is not fairly new, one might want to explore further before utilizing the database.

Scrutinize the codebook

We have discussed how crucial a well-designed and well-documented code-book is to the overall quality of terrorism databases (Sheehan 2012). A good codebook can also provide invaluable guidance for conducting research on the database that it describes. By their nature, codebooks can sometimes be rather dense, running to hundreds of pages outlining myriad variables, so it is easy to overlook nuances about how the data were collected and coded. For instance, the GTD has been collected by several different entities utilizing slightly differ-ent methodologies, the most consequential being that several years' worth of data was collected retrospectively rather than as incidents were reported (UoM 2021a). Yet, many researchers overlook such nuances and simply use all of the data that they find in a database, even if their particular research question would prescribe the use of a more limited subset (see the discussion in Enders, Sandler and Gaibulloev 2011, p. 320). Moreover, not paying attention to such issues can lead to the misinterpretation of results, for example, perceiving a change in the nature of terrorist attacks where the apparent change is merely an artifact of different collection or coding methods. The managers of some databases (e.g., the GTD and POICN database) have taken great pains to note these differences in collection approaches, but not all terrorism databases are as explicit, so researchers need to pay close attention to codebooks.

Conduct sensitivity analyses

Terrorism is an inherently problematic phenomenon to record accurately, given the uncertainties, politicization and other potential obfuscating factors that attend reports of terrorism (Sheehan 2012; Behlendorf et al. 2016). This makes it critical for researchers to pay close attention to how these aspects are handled by those who create and manage terrorism databases and take these into account in their analyses. The better databases contain metadata that reflect the uncertainties that more often than not are presented when trying to codify terrorism-related data. For example, several terrorism databases (including the GTD and RANNSAD) have separate codes that denote cases that might not meet the definition of terrorism or where there is considerable uncertainty as to the value of a particular variable. Some databases, e.g., POICN, even provide metadata on the reliability of the sources that the database draws from (Ackerman and Pinson 2016). It is good practice in these cases to conduct multiple analyses (whether quantitative or qualitative) to see how robust initial results are to different levels of uncertainty or different inclusion criteria. It is also often a good idea to identify outliers in the data and to run analyses with and without those outliers to investigate the extent to which the outliers might drive the conclusions one draws from the data (Nussbaum 2010).

Perform independent verification

No database is perfect and even high-quality terrorism databases can include errors, whether these result from measurement biases beyond the control of the data collectors or whether these occur during the collection or coding process. Wherever possible, it is thus good practice for researchers to verify the data that are presented in terrorism databases. Obviously, this verification cannot be comprehensive, because that would require recreating the database and thus render its use moot. However, at least for the variables in which the researcher is interested, a random sample of cases can be extracted and then the researcher can attempt to verify the data in those cases from the original sources of information, or even better, independent alternative sources. How large the independently verified sample needs to be will depend on a number of factors, including how extensively the database has been scrutinized by previous researchers and how much time and access to sources the researcher has. Moreover, if there is more than one database that purports to independently capture the same data (e.g., terrorist attacks or terrorist group leaders), the variables under consideration can be extracted from each database and compared in an effort to either confirm the coding across databases or at the very least to identify the strengths and weaknesses of each dataset with respect to those variables or cases overall (Behlendorf et al. 2016; Vergani, Navarro, Freilich and Chermak 2020).

Be explicit about errors and uncertainties

Above all, it is critical that researchers carry forward any caveats from the databases into their findings and conclusions and hence into any products (publications, reports, briefings) of their analysis. Even if after following the steps above they cannot resolve the error or uncertainty themselves, they must be explicit about any limitations or uncertainties in their findings that result from using a particular database. In the ideal situation, any systematic source of error (or at least its direction) would be reported in the database (Chermak, Freilich, Parkin and Lynch 2012), which would then, for example, allow the researcher to describe whether any observed associations are likely to be under- or over-represented by using the database. Failing to acknowledge any potential distortions introduced by issues in the databases used could mislead other scholars or policymakers and thereby substantially set back terrorism scholarship.

Creating a new terrorism database

Although it is not the goal of this chapter to provide detailed instructions on database construction, the preceding discussion provides some general guidance for those researchers who intend not only to use existing terrorism databases, but also create and populate their own.

Scope

The most important initial decision is establishing the objectives and scope of your database. What questions about terrorism is your database intended to answer? Why are existing databases or other resources not sufficient for answering these questions? How does the database conceptualize terrorism or counterterrorism? Who do you envisage the users of your database to be and what are their needs? The answers to these questions will help to determine the database's inclusion criteria and its geographic, temporal and functional scope. As we have mentioned, terrorism is a controversial and conceptually slippery phenomenon and it is essential that these central issues are resolved and documented explicitly before proceeding.

Data collection and coding process

The key to all successful databases is consistency in collecting, organizing and recording information as part of a systematic process. Before any data are collected, rules and procedures for these activities must be developed and then codified in a codebook. In addition to guiding future users of the database, many databases are populated by more than one person, so codebooks are essential for ensuring consistency across multiple collectors and coders.

Reflecting uncertainties explicitly

One glaring deficit that has been noted regarding many terrorism-related databases is a failure to explicitly incorporate measures of uncertainty, whether this is about the reliability of sources or the actual variable itself (e.g., the number of casualties caused by an attack) (Sheehan 2012). Particularly in the domain of terrorism and related activities, it is important to capture and record these uncertainties, which form metadata that are attached to cases and even individual variables. This has successfully been accomplished with respect to more recently developed event-based databases (Binder and Ackerman 2019). Another valuable suggestion is for database creators, who are probably the most knowledgeable about the data they are collecting, to develop "error profiles" (Chermak et al. 2012; Sheehan 2012) that explain any systematic biases that might have been incorporated into the database through measurement or selection bias, either from sources or constraints on collection.

Quality control

There are a number of standard data collection and coding quality control measures that are especially useful in preventing errors in terrorism databases and should be employed wherever possible. These include having multiple independent individuals separately code each case and then calculating measures of inter-rater reliability; incorporating a robust review process to catch errors; having more senior, experienced personnel recode a sample of cases; having a process for incorporating feedback from users and subsequent revision when errors are detected; updating the codebook whenever it is found to be lacking in providing sufficient guidance to coders; and periodically reassessing sources and search procedures to check whether additional, previously unaddressed biases have arisen that must be dealt with.

If these guidelines are broadly followed, the prospects for a newly created terrorism database being able to yield relevant analysis and advance understanding in the field of terrorist studies will increase markedly. In contrast, failure to adhere to the core aspects of having a well-defined scope, well-documented procedures and robust quality control can result in data that are either not accepted by researchers or, even worse, a widely utilized database that masks defects and thereby results in inaccurate findings that lead to poor policy decisions and flawed government responses to terrorism.

Conclusion

There has been an huge increase of terrorism databases since 2000, providing researchers with a wealth of empirical data on various aspects of the terrorism phenomenon. In order to prevent the classic "garbage in, garbage out" problem, the development and use of both existing and future terrorism databases should follow several quality criteria broadly outlined in this chapter. This is especially true as researchers and officials devise ever more applications for terrorism data in their analyses.

However, the richness of current data on terrorism hides a burgeoning crisis. Consistent funding to enable databases to meet the necessary quality criteria is not only absent, but multiple database initiatives often compete for the same resources. As a result, some databases have paused (e.g., the Suicide Attack Database) others have had to charge commercial users (e.g., the GTD) and some have stopped completely (e.g., RDWTI). The erratic maintenance and availability of terrorism databases place even more pressure on researchers to exercise caution in their database use. Yet, provided that these databases are used judiciously, they can contribute much to terrorism research and counter-terrorism policy.

References

Ackerman, G.A. and Pinson, L. (2016). Speaking truth to sources: Introducing a method for the quantitative evaluation of open sources in event data, *Studies in Conflict and Terrorism*, 39(8), pp. 617–640.

Aon (2021). *Terrorism Tracker*, accessed January 10, 2021 at www.terrorismtracker.com/

Asal, V. and Rethemeyer, R.K. (2008). The nature of the beast: Organizational structures and the lethality of terrorist attacks, *Journal of Politics*, 70(2), pp. 437–449.

Asal, V., Linebarger, C., Jadoon, A. and Greig, J.M. (2021). Why some rebel organizations attack Americans, *Defence and Peace Economics*, DOI: 10.1080/10242694.2021.1878320

Barber, V. (2015). The evolution of Al Qaeda's global network and Al Qaeda core's position within it: A network analysis, *Perspectives on Terrorism, 9(6)*.

Barker, A.D. (2011). Improvised explosive devices in southern Afghanistan and western Pakistan, 2002–2009, *Studies in Conflict and Terrorism, 34(8)*, pp. 600–620.

Behlendorf, B., Belur, J. and Kumar, S. (2016). Peering through the kaleidoscope: Variation and validity in data collection on terrorist attacks. *Studies in Conflict and Terrorism, 39(7–8)*, pp. 641–667.

Behlendorf, B., LaFree, G. and Legault, R. (2012). Microcycles of violence: Evidence from terrorist attacks by ETA and the FMLN, *Journal of Quantitative Criminology, 28(1)*, pp. 49–75.

Bhatia, K., Chhabra, B. and Kumar, M. (2020). Data analysis of various terrorism activities using big data approaches on Global Terrorism Database, *Sixth International Conference on Parallel, Distributed and Grid Computing*, Waknaghat, India.

Binder, M.K. and Ackerman, G.A. (2019). Pick your POICN: Introducing the Profiles of Incidents involving CBRN and Non-State Actors (POICN) database, *Studies in Conflict and Terrorism*, DOI: 10.1080/1057610X.2019.1577541

Caruso, R. and Schneider, F. (2011). The socio-economic determinants of terrorism and political violence in western Europe (1994–2007). *European Journal of Political Economy, 27*, pp. 37–49.

Chermak, S.M., Freilich, J.D., Parkin, W.S. and Lynch, J.P. (2012). American terrorism and extremist crime data sources and selectivity bias: An investigation focusing on homicide events committed by far-right extremists, *Journal of Quantitative Criminology, 28*, pp. 191–218.

Chhatwal, S.D. and Rose, S.J. (2008). Visually exploring worldwide incidents tracking system data, *Visualization and Data Analysis, SPIE Proceedings, 6809*.

Curia, F. (2020). Unsupervised hybrid algorithm to detect anomalies for predicting terrorist attacks, *International Journal of Computer Applications, 176(35)*, pp. 1–8.

Demir, M. and Guler, A. (2021). The effects of the 9/11 terrorist attacks on suicide terrorism, *Behavioral Sciences of Terrorism and Political Aggression*, DOI: 10.1080/19434472.2020.1866052

Desmarais, B.A. and Cranmer, S.J. (2013). Forecasting the locational dynamics of transnational terrorism: A network analytic approach. *Security Informatics, 2(1)*, pp. 1–12.

Development Services Group (2020). *Annex of Statistical Information: Country Reports on Terrorism 2019*, accessed March 3, 2021 at https://dsgonline.com/GTTAC/2020/2019Annex-of-Statistical-Information.pdf

Duke (2021). *International Terrorism Attributes of Terrorist Events (ITERATE)*, accessed January 10, 2021 at http:// library .duke .edu/ data/ duke -only/ iterate/ ITERATE%20COMMON%20FILE%20(Y)1968%20-%202018.xls

Enders, W., Sandler, T. and Gaibulloev, K. (2011). Domestic versus transnational terrorism: Data, decomposition and dynamics, *Journal of Conflict Resolution, 48*, pp. 319–337.

Europol (2021). *Europol Terrorism Situation and Trend Report*, accessed January 10, 2021 at www.europol.europa.eu/sites/default/files/documents/european_union_terrorism_situation_and_trend_report_te-sat_2020_0.pdf

Fleming, C.M., Manning, M., Pham, H.-T. and Vorsina, M. (2020). Ethnic economic inequality and fatalities from terrorism, *Journal of Interpersonal Violence*, December, accessed March 3, 2021 at https:// journals .sagepub .com/ doi/ abs/ 10 .1177/0886260520976226

Gao, P., Guo, D., Liao, K., Webb, J.J. and Cutter, S.L. (2013). Early detection of terrorism outbreaks using prospective space–time scan statistics. *The Professional Geographer, 65(4)*, pp. 676–691.

Google (2020). *Hate by the Numbers*, accessed March 3, 2021 at https://jigsaw.google .com/the-current/white-supremacy/data-visualization/

Gries, T., Krieger, T. and Meierrieks, D. (2011). Causal linkages between domestic terrorism and economic growth, *Defence and Peace Economics, 22(5)*, pp. 493–508.

Hoffman, A.M., Shelton, C. and Cleven, E. (2013). Press freedom, publicity, and the cross-national incidence of transnational terrorism. *Political Research Quarterly, 66(4)*, pp. 896–909.

Jane's (2021). *Terrorism Threat Database*, accessed January 10, 2021 at www.janes.com/ military-threat-intelligence/terrorism-and-insurgency

Lam, P. (2019). *Terrorism Activity by Region*, accessed March 3, 2021 at https://public .tableau.com/ profile/ pris.lam4751 #!/ vizhome/ TerrorismActivityByRegion/ Terro rismActivityByRegionDashboard2

Lum, C., Kennedy, L. and Sherley, A. (2006). Are counter-terrorism strategies effective? The results of the Campbell Systematic Review on counter-terrorism evaluation research, *Journal of Experimental Criminology, 2*, pp. 489–516.

NCTC (2021). *Worldwide Incident Tracker System*, accessed January 10, 2021 at https:// en.wikipedia.org/wiki/Worldwide_Incidents_Tracking_System

Nesser, P. (2014). Toward an increasingly heterogeneous threat: A chronology of jihadist terrorism in Europe 2008–2013. *Studies in Conflict and Terrorism, 37(5)*, pp. 440–456.

Nussbaum, B. (2010). Including extremists in the political process: "Irreconcilables," constraints on violence, and the social scientific analysis of terrorism, in Frost, N.A., Freilich, J.D. and Clear, T.R. (eds), *Contemporary Issues in Criminal Justice Policy: Policy Proposals from the Society of Criminology Conference*, Wadsworth: Belmont, CA.

Optima (2021). *Triton*, accessed January 10, 2021 at https://tritonintel.com/reports

RAND (2021). *Worldwide Terrorism Incidents*, accessed January 10, 2021 at www.rand .org/nsrd/projects/terrorism-incidents/about.html

RAND (n.d.). *About the RAND Database of Worldwide Terrorism Incidents*, accessed March 3, 2021 at www.rand.org/nsrd/projects/terrorism-incidents/about.html

Sheehan, I.S. (2012). Assessing and comparing data sources for terrorism research, in Lum, C. and Kennedy, L. (eds), *Evidence-Based Counterterrorism Policy*, New York: Springer, pp. 13–40.

UoA (University of Arkansas) Terrorism Research Center (2021). *Investigative and Prosecutorial Tools for Mitigating Pathways to Radicalization: Creation of a Federal Terrorism Court Record Repository*, accessed March 6, 2021 at https:// terrorismresearch.uark.edu/research/corr/

UoM (University of Maryland) (2021a). *About the GTD*, accessed January 10, 2021 at www.start.umd.edu/gtd/about/

UoM (University of Maryland) (2021b). *Global Terrorism Database*, accessed January 10, 2021 at https://start.umd.edu/gtd/

UoM (University of Maryland) (2021c). *Profiles of Individual Radicalization in the United States (PIRUS) dataset*, accessed January 10, 2021 at www.start.umd.edu/ profiles-individual-radicalization-united-states-pirus-keshif

USMA (2021). *Militant Ideology Atlas*, accessed January 10, 2021 at https://ctc.usma .edu/militant-ideology-atlas/

Vergani, M., Navarro, C., Freilich, J.D. and Chermak, S.M. (2020). Comparing different sources of data to examine trends of hate crime in absence of official registers, *American Journal of Criminal Justice*, DOI: 10.1007/s12103-020-09567-9

White, G., Porter, M.D. and Mazerolle, L. (2013). Terrorism risk, resilience and volatility: A comparison of terrorism patterns in three Southeast Asian countries. *Journal of Quantitative Criminology*, *29*(2), pp. 295–320.

Whitney, P., White, A., Walsh, S., Dalton, A. and Brothers, A. (2011). Bayesian networks for social modeling, in Salerno, J., Yang, S.J., Nau, D. and Chai, S.K. (eds), *Social Computing, Behavioral-Cultural Modeling and Prediction*, Cham: Springer.

Windisch, S., Logan, M.K. and Ligon, G.S. (2018). Headhunting among extremist organizations: An empirical assessment of talent spotting. *Perspectives on Terrorism*, *12(2)*, pp. 44–62.

Zech, S.T. and Gabbay, M. (2016). Social network analysis in the study of terrorism and insurgency: From organization to politics, *International Studies Review*, *18(2)*, pp. 214–243.

Zhang, J. and Zhuang, J. (2019). Modeling a multi-target attacker-defender game with multiple attack types, *Reliability Engineering and System Safety*, *185*, pp. 465–475.

PART III

Controversies and debates

12 Debating the health of terrorism studies: methodological issues, research biases and cautious optimism

Bart Schuurman

Introduction

Terrorist violence has had a marked influence on twenty-first-century politics and society. Deadly and dramatic attacks such as those in New York, Mumbai, Paris and Christchurch have punctuated a more continuous form of terrorist violence in countries like Iraq, Syria and Nigeria, where terrorism has been part of long-running insurgencies. The United States and its allies have been waging an international war on terrorism that is moving into its third decade, and which has included the extremely costly and ultimately futile invasions of Afghanistan and Iraq. At home, efforts to prevent terrorism and the radicalization trajectories thought to precede it have led to legislative changes and increased powers for intelligence agencies and police forces that have sparked debate about their proportionality and effectiveness (Howell and Lind, 2010; Roach, 2011; Kowalski, 2014).

This high level of attention for (counter)terrorism from governments, citizens and the media has been mirrored by the research community. Terrorism began to attract scholarly interest decades ago, but initially remained something of a niche subject. This changed dramatically after 9/11, as interest in the subject soared and new sources of funding became available (Kennedy-Pipe, 2018; Silke, 2019b; Phillips, 2021). Research on terrorism seemed to become one of the most easily marketized academic commodities, able to offer both in-depth analysis of movements and groups foreign to most Western policymakers and practitioners, as well as applied research with the promise of increasing the effectiveness of counterterrorism policies and programs. Conditions in the early 2000s seemed set to allow terrorism studies to flourish. But in the years that followed, the field was consistently subjected to harsh criticism from within its own ranks. While the quantity of output had risen dramatically, the quality of much of that work was cast in doubt (Silke, 2001, 2009; Lum, Kennedy and Sherley, 2006; Sageman, 2014).

This chapter revisits some of the key debates about the health of terrorism studies. It addresses the disparity between the field's outwards signs of good health and the often notably pessimistic assessments of some of its most influential scholars. Starting with a brief look at how research on terrorism developed in the latter half of the twentieth century, the main discussion assesses how the field developed in the two decades after the 9/11 attacks. Alongside longstanding concerns over research methods and sources, attention is given to the discussion about whether terrorism researchers too closely align their research agendas with those of states. Somewhat unusually for a contribution on terrorism, the chapter ends on a note of careful optimism by drawing attention to those areas where the field has shown signs of steady improvement.

A tradition of self-criticism

There is no single discipline of terrorism studies, with work on the subject done by researchers with a diverse range of academic backgrounds such as political science, psychology and criminology (Gordon, 2010; Phillips, 2021). The roots of this broad field of research can be traced back to the 1960s and 1970s when the subject of terrorism first began to attract notable academic attention (Schmid, 2011b). While it remained initially on the fringes of larger debates about the Cold War and (counter)insurgency, one element that was quite quickly apparent was a penchant for self-reflection and self-criticism. These early debates foreshadowed more current ones in drawing attention to methodological issues and concerns over biases that might result from the often close relationships between researchers and state institutions, which frequently fund research and in so doing also influence research agendas.

Most of this self-reflective criticism has taken aim at methodological issues. In a trend that started in the late 1970s, terrorism researchers have criticized an overreliance on secondary sources and a limited set of research designs other than the literature review. Early reviews of the field reached damning verdicts, noting the lack of an 'effective academic approach' (Bell, 1977, p. 488), output high in quantity but marred by impressionistic and anecdotal conclusions (Schmid, 1982) and a 'disturbing lack of good empirically-grounded research' (Gurr, 1988, p. 115). Other scholars criticized work on terrorism for being frequently ahistorical and alarmist (Crenshaw, 1986), simplistic in its conclusions (Reich, 1990) or 'superficial and ideological' (Wieviorka, 1995, p. 597). In the decades prior to 9/11, the number of academic pieces on terrorism published annually could be measured in the hundreds. As output soared to thousands of books and articles per year in the twenty-first century, the field's problems suddenly impacted a much larger body of work (Silke, 2019b; Phillips, 2021).

That little had changed on the eve of the 9/11 attacks was made clear by Silke's landmark 2001 study on the state of the field. Taking stock of articles published in two leading journals on terrorism between 1995 and 1999, Silke reached several worrying conclusions. More than 80 percent of the work surveyed relied exclusively on secondary data, using material found in other articles, books and media sources. A majority of 62 percent of articles surveyed relied on the literature review method, with other types of data collection and analysis, such as interviews (10 percent) or databases (7 percent), trailing far behind. Underlining the emphasis on qualitative research designs, over 70 percent of pieces did not use any form of statistical analysis. Silke's 2001 conclusion that the field had struggled to make significant headway despite 30 years of research set the tone for what was to become a widespread sense of pessimism.

Silke's work described a field of study hesitant to engage directly with the subjects it sought to explain. In practice, the overreliance on secondary sources meant that most scholars' analyses, and the theories they developed or tested, were built on empirical observations done by others. Certainly, it is part and parcel of academic writing on terrorism to incorporate secondary sources such as journalists' accounts of terrorist attacks, annual government reports on the terrorist-threat level and other researchers' publications. There are also plenty of pieces that do not require any particular first-hand data to be of high quality, such as those exploring key concepts. But issues arise when a field as a whole prefers to rely on information gathered by others, as this risks adopting the biases and potential inaccuracies of those sources.

Journalists have written numerous high-quality pieces on terrorism, and their ability to be 'first providers' of information on terrorist attacks is often a boon to scholars (e.g. Wright, 2011; Wood, 2018; Chaussy 2020). The downside to relying on media-based information is that it is also prone to several potential issues. The demands of real-time reporting and the constraints imposed by limited space in newspapers and websites can lead to issues of factual inaccuracy and limited detail (Silke, 2001; Schulze, 2004; Quiggin, 2013). Editorial bias, for instance by prioritizing news on jihadist terrorism while underemphasizing right-wing attacks, can lead to tunnel vision on what is subsequently researched as terrorism and disparities in terms of the journalistic information available (Franzosi, 1987; Kearns, Betus and Lemieux, 2019). There is also a tendency to underreport failed or foiled terrorist attacks, problematizing the degree to which media sources can be relied upon to provide an accurate overview of terrorist activities (Schmid, 2011b).

Of course, secondary sources also include academic books and articles and the 'gray' literature comprised of government reports, think tank studies and the like. Academic writing's emphasis on factual accuracy, objectivity and referencing of sources is an important bulwark of reliability. But with so little first-hand data making their way into terrorism research in the 1980s and 1990s, the field was largely talking amongst itself (Reid, 1997; Ranstorp, 2010). Without the in-depth detail offered by primary sources such as interviews with (former) extremists, access to government archives or fieldwork among those people directly involved in or impacted by terrorism, how could the veracity of explanations for terrorism be tested? One of the most detrimental consequences of the scarcity of primary sources has been the inability to thoroughly test the dozens of assumptions about subjects, such as how and why people become involved in terrorism (King and Taylor, 2011; McAllister and Schmid, 2011; Pisoiu and Ahmed, 2016; Desmarais et al., 2017). Just as demand for objective and high-quality research on terrorism was skyrocketing in the post-9/11 period, Schmid and Jongman's damning 1988 (p. 179) indictment of the field as a place where 'so much is written on the basis of so little research' seemed truer than ever.

The stagnation debate

Silke's 2001 assessment not only functioned as a wake-up call, but it also offered a template against which the further development of the field could be charted. Unfortunately, research on terrorism showed few signs of improvement during the 2000s, despite the soaring numbers of publications on the subject. In 2004, Silke pointed to additional problems, namely the limited number of researchers who studied terrorism over a longer period of their careers, and the fact that over 90 percent of authors worked alone (Silke, 2004a, 2004b). The large number of one-time contributors reflects the popularity of the subject, but also limits progress on key issues as, generally speaking, such short-term engagement hampers the ability to develop concerted research agendas or to participate in discussions as they evolve over time. The clear preference for working alone also limits the scope of projects that can be undertaken, as teams of researchers will by and large be able to mobilize more financial and intellectual resources than any individual can.

In 2006, Lum and colleagues reviewed over 6000 peer-reviewed articles on terrorism that were published between 1971 and 2003. They found that only 3 percent of their sample had used any kind of empirical data, which the authors defined as being based on 'terrorism data' as opposed to pure 'thought pieces' (Lum et al., 2006, p. 8). Moreover, most of the work continued to be published by one-time contributors (Gordon, 2007). As Silke revisited the topic several more times in the mid- to late 2000s, pessimism about the field's ability to find and utilize primary data solidified further. Although the use of statistical analyses was gaining ground, and while scholars were beginning to work together slightly more often, the general impression was one of an area of study that had been unable to make significant progress on the methodological issues that had plagued it – and had been known – for decades (Silke, 2007, 2008, 2009).

With the 2010s approaching, there seemed few grounds for optimism about the state of research on terrorism. Authors continued to note the field's various methodological issues (Jacques and Taylor, 2009; Young and Findley, 2011), the detrimental influence of pseudo-experts (Stampnitzky, 2014) as well as a tendency to use data because they are available, rather than because they suit the research design (Mahoney, 2018). Particularly noteworthy was Sageman's (2014) claim that so little progress had been made on understanding key issues, that research on terrorism had become stagnant. In his view, the academic community continued to lack sufficient access to the high-quality primary data needed to make progress on theory development. While the intelligence community did have such access, it missed, in Sageman's assessment, the methodological rigor to use this material to its fullest potential.

Interestingly, however, whereas previously such criticisms had been broadly accepted, by the mid-2010s contrarian views were beginning to emerge. In 2013, a survey of research on radicalization found 'clusters of excellence that meet the highest scholarly standards' (Neumann and Kleinmann, 2013, p. 360). Other authors noted an uptick in quantitative approaches (LaFree and Freilich, 2012) as well as more opportunities to gather primary data (Loadenthal, 2015). In the special issue devoted to Sageman's claim that the field had stagnated, well-established authors voiced their disagreement (Schmid, 2014; Stern, 2014). In the broader debate, several scholars highlighted areas where considerable progress had indeed been made (Crenshaw, 2014; Sandler, 2014). While none of these authors claimed that there was not still significant need for further improvement, the widespread sense of pessimism about the study of terrorism was beginning to show signs of abating.

This sense of progress, albeit slow and subject to various qualifications, was strengthened by empirical work carried out by Schuurman. Looking at all publications that had appeared between 2007 and 2016 in nine of the field's leading journals, Schuurman concluded that the scarcity of primary-data use finally seemed to have dissipated. By 2016, just under 60 percent of the articles surveyed used some form of first-hand information. Similarly, the use of statistical analyses had increased from circa 17 percent in 2007 to 28 percent in 2016. Papers relying solely on the literature review method were still the most common at 39 percent, but this was down significantly from the figures reported by Silke in 2001. At the same time, most authors continued to work alone and one-time contributors were still responsible for the majority of publications. While there remained plenty of room for further improvements, the field did appear to have made significant progress on addressing some of the methodological problems that had plagued it for decades (Schuurman, 2020).

This shift towards a more positive outlook on research on terrorism has been supported by other assessments as well. Silke and Schmidt-Petersen's (2017) study of the 100 most cited articles in research on terrorism revealed that the top performers were more likely to be the result of collaborative efforts, to include new data and to have been published after 9/11. These findings suggest that papers with higher methodological rigor stand a better chance of attaining prominence, and that more such high-quality papers have appeared (relatively) recently. Silke and Schmidt-Petersen conclude that, far from having stagnated, the field is in fact enjoying a golden age. Deriving its insights from interviews with dozens of terrorism researchers, Morrison's (2020) work lends further credence to the notion that the pessimistic assessments of the early 2000s no longer reflect contemporary research on terrorism. At least in terms of methodological rigor, there is good cause for an optimistic outlook on how the field has developed.

A state-centric research agenda?

Criticism of research on terrorism has not been limited to pointing out an overreliance on secondary sources or little variety in research methods. Already in 1988, Schmid and Jongman argued that much of the work on terrorism was not primarily focused on the objective pursuit of knowledge but more interested in helping governments overcome their non-state opponents. A respondent quoted in their book aptly summarized the field at the time as resembling 'counterinsurgency masquerading as political science' (Schmid and Jongman, 1988, p. 182). Some three decades later, Silke (2019b) found that most researchers continue to see themselves as waging counterterrorism by other means. As states are also among the principal funders of research on terrorism (Silke, 2004a), what does this close working relationship mean for the subjects being investigated?

For proponents of the critical terrorism studies (CTS) school of thought that arose in the mid- to late 2000s, the field's state-centrism represents a funda-mental flaw (Blakeley, 2007; Gunning, 2007a; Jarvis, 2009; Heath-Kelly, 2010). By deriving research questions from governments' terrorism-related concerns and priorities, scholars risk a biased approach to the subject. One area where this is argued to be apparent is in what is understood and studied as terrorism. The relative absence of work on state terrorism has helped propel a biased per-spective in which terrorism has become virtually synonymous with non-state terrorism (George, 1991; Blakeley, 2007; Gunning, 2007a; Jackson, 2008; Silke, 2019a). CTS scholars further argue that, by taking a problem-solving approach, the field of terrorism research essentially seeks to help state actors with solving their terrorism-related challenges, uncritically supporting the status quo rather than challenging its assumptions and practices (Gunning, 2007b).

While CTS-oriented academics have been right to warn against biases that can and have followed state-centrism, their presentation of these and other issues has been criticized as disregarding the critical tradition within decades of estab-lished scholarship (Horgan and Boyle, 2008; Hegghammer, 2013). Indeed, the influential 1988 book by Schmid and Jongman already critically discussed whether scholars should be counterterrorists by other means. Neither was it the advent of critical theory-infused scholarship that first brought terrorism scholars to look critically at states. Sharp appraisals have been plentiful, dealing not just with specific counterterrorism campaigns or policies (Mueller, 2005; Art and Richardson, 2007; Horgan and Braddock, 2010), but also with how states (mis)use core concepts such as 'radicalization' (Coolsaet, 2019) or fail to recognize a shifting terrorist-threat landscape (Koehler, 2019).

Arguably, the larger issue here is one of balance. Has the academic community been able to sufficiently balance work that takes its cue from states' views on and concerns about terrorism with what could be called a bottom-up research agenda? The pursuit of policy-relevant research that aims to help minimize political violence represents a laudable ambition to combine aca-demic research with positive societal impact. It does mean that the field tends to tunnel vision on those groups or threats that present the most immediate threat, and it has also led to continuously evolving 'trending topics', such as weapons of mass destruction or suicide terrorism, that rise to prominence only to disappear again in a relatively short period of time (Ranstorp, 2007; Silke, 2007; Jackson, 2012). But this is not necessarily a significant problem, as long as outside of these core topics there is also vibrant academic debate on a much broader range of subjects and perspectives.

As is to be expected of any field of academic research, there is a clear sense of which topics have been unstudied and understudied (Schmid, 2011a; Schmid and Forest, 2018). Particular subjects included the aforementioned state terrorism, historical approaches to the subject, evaluations of counterterrorism measures and terrorism as it takes place outside of a Western geographical context (Duyvesteyn, 2007). Yet, as Schuurman's (2019) review of 10 years of research on terrorism found, the field has a poor track record when it comes to actually broadening its focus or resisting the urge to jump on the latest hot topic. Some 75 percent of all research published in the field's core journals between 2007 and 2016 focused on jihadist terrorism by groups like al-Qaeda or Islamic State, while not even 2 percent of papers looked at right-wing extremism. As right-wing extremist terrorists in the post-2010 United States have launched more attacks than jihadists (Miller, 2017), and as this form of extremism is on the rise in several European countries as well (Koehler, 2017), this imbalance reflects poorly on the field's ability to take a broad perspective on pertinent forms of terrorism and extremism.

Schuurman's assessment also indicated a strong preference for terrorism research to mirror whatever states see as the most pressing or most novel iteration of the terrorist-threat landscape. As a result, topics like 'lone actor terrorism' or 'foreign fighters' would suddenly be among the top five most researched subjects, only to disappear again from this position of prominence the next year. Such a desire for contemporary policy relevance can make it difficult to go beyond descriptive studies on the latest iteration of a terrorist group, or the newest preferred method of attack, and to undertake more fundamental research projects. The dramatic and violent nature of terrorist attacks creates strong pressures from citizens, government and the media for explanations and assessments (Weinberg and Eubank, 2008). Researchers often appear ideally placed to provide answers, but this risks locking them in a cycle of scrambling to focus on the latest threat, promulgating not just a one-sided, largely state-determined perspective on what is seen as terrorism (Youngman, 2020), but also limiting the field's ability to look beyond the immediate or to address more fundamental questions, such as those about the how and why of involvement in terrorism.

The downsides of a research agenda influenced by state-centrism and a focus on the latest threat go beyond an overemphasis on descriptive work and limited topical diversity. As De Goede (2008) points out, thinking about likely future threats is strongly influenced by contemporary perceptions and biases.

Arguably, the scant attention that academics have, until relatively recently, paid to right-wing extremism is a result of precisely this mechanism. It is also striking to note that on the eve of the 9/11 attacks, Sunni extremist groups such as al-Qaeda did not feature in the top-10 most researched terrorist groups (Silke, 2004b; see also Czwarno, 2006). For terrorism research to increase its problem-solving potential, paying more attention to developments beyond the immediately apparent will be crucial. Broadening the field's research agenda to better reflect the multifaceted nature of extremism and terrorism is also important to provide balance to societal and political debates on this form of political violence. The current overemphasis on jihadism, for instance, not only allows other forms of extremism to develop in relative anonymity, but can also contribute to the impression that terrorism comes from one particular community only.

The extent of the field's orientation on the state and imbalances in its topical focus have been discussed for years (Schmid and Jongman, 1988; Silke, 2004a; Ranstorp, 2007; Horgan and Boyle, 2008). While the review conducted by Schuurman (2019) highlights ongoing grounds for concern, more positive developments must be mentioned as well. Scholars' topical focus does appear to be becoming more divergent, with increasing attention for issues such as right-wing extremism (Ravndal and Bjørgo, 2018), the role of gender dynamics (Cook, 2019) and media representations of different forms of terrorism (Kearns et al., 2019). Strengthening such trends will be crucial to ensuring the field's health in terms of a justifiable balance between applied problem solving and fundamental research, and between state-centrism and research that looks critically at how states themselves have viewed, dealt with and at times engaged in terrorism.

Conclusion

The 9/11 attacks brought the academic study of terrorism to unprecedented prominence. But the availability of new sources of funding, the influx of new researchers and exponentially growing research output was accompanied by widespread pessimism about the quality of work being done. Echoing concerns that had been around since the 1970s, scholars working on terrorism in the post-9/11 era noted the scarcity of primary data, the overreliance on the literature review method, few dedicated researchers and limited collaborative work. Numerous publications appearing in the early and mid-2000s deepened concerns about the ability of research on terrorism to overcome longstanding methodological obstacles. By the time of Sageman's (2014) indictment of the field as having stagnated, this pervasive sense of pessimism was beginning to loosen its hold. Numerous scholars challenged the view that terrorism researchers had failed to make significant progress.

Several reviews of the state of the art written in the late 2010s have lent empirical support to a more positive appraisal of the field. At least from a methodological standpoint, research on terrorism has made significant progress in terms of utilizing more primary data and relying on research designs other than the literature review. At the same time, the field has drawn criticism for the degree to which its research agenda mirrors states' views of and concerns about terrorism. Such state-centrism, and the desire to conduct applied, problem-solving research, has contributed to an overwhelming focus on jihadist terrorism and a tendency to continuously shift attention to the latest or most visible iteration of the terrorist threat, not only making it difficult to move beyond descriptive research, but also leading to marked imbalances in the field's topical focus. For instance, right-wing extremism has until recently received scant attention despite constituting a major source of extremist violence in countries like the United States.

There are numerous areas where research on terrorism can and should aim to improve itself. But that should not take away from the very real progress made, in particular on methodological issues. It also deserves emphasis that there is an increasingly widespread realization of the need to broaden the field's research agenda, to look in more detail at understudied subjects like right-wing extremism and to achieve a more equal balance between applied research on highly contemporary issues and more fundamental research on topics just shy of the limelight. Perhaps most important to the consolidation and further expansion of the progress that the field has made is attracting a greater number of scholars willing to make a career out of the study of terrorism. Strengthening the core of the research community will ensure that the field's shortcomings are not just recognized, but that they can be consistently addressed. Complementing such a push with more frequent collaboration between scholars would further improve the field's health and allow expansion into ever more ambitious research projects. There is much to look forward to.

References

Art, R. J. and Richardson, L. (2007) *Democracy and counterterrorism: lessons from the past.* Washington, DC: United States Institute of Peace Press.

Bell, J. B. (1977) 'Trends on terror: the analysis of political violence', *World Politics*, 29(3), pp. 476–488.

Blakeley, R. (2007) 'Bringing the state back into terrorism studies', *European Political Science*, 6(3), pp. 228–235.

Chaussy, U. (2020) *Das Oktoberfest-Attentat und der Doppelmord von Erlangen: wie Rechtsterrorismus und Antisemitismus seit 1980 verdrängt werden*. Berlin: Ch. Links Verlag.

Cook, J. (2019) *A woman's place: US counterterrorism since 9/11*. New York: Hurst.

Coolsaet, R. (2019) 'Radicalization: the origins and limits of a contested concept', in Fadil, N., De Koning, M. and Ragazzi, F. (eds), *Radicalization in Belgium and the Netherlands: critical perspectives on violence and security*. London: I.B. Tauris, pp. 29–51.

Crenshaw, M. (1986) 'The psychology of political terrorism', in Hermann, M. G. (ed.), *Political psychology*. San Francisco, CA: Jossey-Bass, pp. 379–413.

Crenshaw, M. (2014) 'Terrorism research: the record', *International Interactions*, 40(4), pp. 556–567.

Czwarno, M. (2006) 'Misjudging Islamic terrorism: the academic community's failure to predict 9/11', *Studies in Conflict and Terrorism*, 29(7), pp. 657–678.

De Goede, M. (2008) 'Beyond risk: premediation and the post-9/11 security imagination', *Security Dialogue*, 39(2–3), pp. 155–176.

Desmarais, S. L., Simons-Rudolph, J., Brugh, C. S., Schilling, E. and Hoggan, C. (2017) 'The state of scientific knowledge regarding factors associated with terrorism', *Journal of Threat Assessment and Management*, 4(4), pp. 180–209.

Duyvesteyn, I. (2007) 'The role of history and continuity in terrorism research', in Ranstorp, M. (ed.), *Mapping terrorism research: state of the art, gaps and future directions*. New York: Routledge, pp. 51–75.

Franzosi, R. (1987) 'The press as a source of socio-historical data: issues in the methodology of data collection from newspapers', *Historical Methods*, 20(1), pp. 5–16.

George, A. L. (1991) 'The discipline of terrorology', in George, A. L. (ed.), *Western state terrorism*. Cambridge: Polity Press, pp. 76–101.

Gordon, A. (2007) 'Transient and continuant authors in a research field: the case of terrorism', *Scientometrics*, 72(2), pp. 213–224.

Gordon, A. (2010) 'Can terrorism become a scientific discipline? A diagnostic study', *Critical Studies on Terrorism*, 3(3), pp. 437–458.

Gunning, J. (2007a) 'A case for critical terrorism studies?', *Government and Opposition*, 42(3), pp. 363–393.

Gunning, J. (2007b) 'Babies and bathwaters: reflecting on the pitfalls of critical terrorism studies', *European Political Science*, 6(3), pp. 236–243.

Gurr, T. R. (1988) 'Empirical research on political terrorism: the state of the art and how it might be improved', in Slater, R. O. and Stohl, M. (eds), *Current perspectives on international terrorism*. London: Macmillan Press, pp. 115–154.

Heath-Kelly, C. (2010) 'Critical terrorism studies, critical theory and the "naturalistic fallacy"', *Security Dialogue*, 41(3), pp. 235–254.

Hegghammer, T. (2013) 'The future of terrorism studies', EMC Chair Symposium, US Naval War College, RI. Available at: https://hegghammer.files.wordpress.com/2019/08/2013-hegghammer-nwc-remarks.pdf

Horgan, J. and Boyle, M. J. (2008) 'A case against "critical terrorism studies"', *Critical Studies on Terrorism*, 1(1), pp. 51–64.

Horgan, J. and Braddock, K. (2010) 'Rehabilitating the terrorists? Challenges in assessing the effectiveness of de-radicalization programs', *Terrorism and Political Violence*, 22(2), pp. 267–291.

Howell, J. and Lind, J. (eds) (2010) *Civil society under strain: counter-terrorism policy, civil society, and aid post-9/11.* Sterling, VA: Kumarian Press.

Jackson, R. (2008) 'An argument for terrorism', *Perspectives on Terrorism*, 2(2), pp. 25–32.

Jackson, R. (2012) 'Unknown knowns: the subjugated knowledge of terrorism studies', *Critical Studies on Terrorism*, 5(1), pp. 11–29.

Jacques, K. and Taylor, P. J. (2009) 'Female terrorism: a review', *Terrorism and Political Violence*, 21(3), pp. 499–515.

Jarvis, L. (2009) 'The spaces and faces of critical terrorism studies', *Security Dialogue*, 40(1), pp. 5–27.

Kearns, E. M., Betus, A. and Lemieux, A. (2019) 'Why do some terrorist attacks receive more media attention than others?', *Justice Quarterly*, 36(6), pp. 985–1022.

Kennedy-Pipe, C. (2018) '"Terrorism studies: what we have forgotten and what we now know"', *Government and Opposition*, 53(2), pp. 356–384.

King, M. and Taylor, D. M. (2011) 'The radicalization of homegrown jihadists: a review of theoretical models and social psychological evidence', *Terrorism and Political Violence*, 23(4), pp. 602–622.

Koehler, D. (2017) *Right-wing terrorism in the 21st century: the 'National Socialist Underground' and the history of terror from the far-right in Germany.* London: Routledge.

Koehler, D. (2019) 'Violence and terrorism from the far-right: policy options to counter an elusive threat'. The Hague: International Centre for Counter-Terrorism, 10, pp. 1–21.

Kowalski, M. (2014) 'Between "sousveillance" and applied ethics: practical approaches to oversight', *Security and Human Rights*, 24(3–4), pp. 280–285.

LaFree, G. and Freilich, J. D. (2012) 'Editor's introduction: quantitative approaches to the study of terrorism', *Journal of Quantitative Criminology*, 28(1), pp. 1–5.

Loadenthal, M. (2015) 'Introduction: like finding a needle in a pile of needles: political violence and the perils of a brave new digital world', *Critical Studies on Terrorism*, 8(3), pp. 456–465.

Lum, C., Kennedy, L. W. and Sherley, A. J. (2006) 'The effectiveness of counter-terrorism strategies', *Campbell Systematic Reviews*, 2, pp. 1–50.

Mahoney, C. W. (2018) 'More data, new problems: audiences, ahistoricity, and selection bias in terrorism and insurgency research', *International Studies Review*, 20(4), pp. 589–614.

McAllister, B. and Schmid, A. P. (2011) 'Theories of terrorism', in Schmid, A. P. (ed.), *The Routledge handbook of terrorism research.* Abingdon: Routledge, pp. 201–262.

Miller, E. (2017) *Ideological motivations of terrorism in the United States, 1970–2016.* College Park, MD: START, pp. 1–6.

Morrison, J. F. (2020) 'Talking stagnation: thematic analysis of terrorism experts' perception of the health of terrorism research', *Terrorism and Political Violence*. DOI: 10.1080/09546553.2020.1804879

Mueller, J. (2005) 'Six rather unusual propositions about terrorism', *Terrorism and Political Violence*, 17(4), pp. 487–505.

Neumann, P. and Kleinmann, S. (2013) 'How rigorous is radicalization research?', *Democracy and Security*, 9(4), pp. 360–382.

Phillips, B. J. (2021) 'How did 9/11 affect terrorism research? Examining arti-cles and authors, 1970–2019', *Terrorism and Political Violence*. DOI: 10.1080/09546553.2021.1935889

Pisoiu, D. and Ahmed, R. (2016) *Radicalisation research – gap analysis*. RAN Research Paper, pp. 1–25. Available at: https://ec.europa.eu/home-affairs/sites/homeaffairs/files/docs/pages/201612_radicalisation_research_gap_analysis_en.pdf

Quiggin, T. (2013) 'Words matter: peer review as a failing safeguard', *Perspectives on Terrorism*, 7(2), pp. 71–81.

Ranstorp, M. (2007) 'Introduction: mapping terrorism research – challenges and prior-ities', in Ranstorp, M. (ed.), *Mapping terrorism research: state of art, gaps and future direction*. London: Routledge, pp. 1–28.

Ranstorp, M. (2010) 'Introduction', in Ranstorp, M. (ed.), *Understanding violent radi-calisation: terrorist and jihadist movements in Europe*. London: Routledge, pp. 1–18.

Ravndal, J. A. and Bjørgo, T. (2018) 'Investigating terrorism from the extreme right: a review of past and present research', *Perspectives on Terrorism*, 12(6), pp. 5–22.

Reich, W. (1990) 'Understanding terrorist behavior: the limits and opportunities of psychological inquiry', in Reich, W. (ed.), *Origins of terrorism: psychologies, ideol-ogies, theologies, states of mind*. Washington, DC: Woodrow Wilson Center Press, pp. 261–279.

Reid, E. O. F. (1997) 'Evolution of a body of knowledge: An analysis of terrorism research', *Information Processing and Management*, 33(1), pp. 91–106.

Roach, K. (2011) *The 9/11 effect: comparative counter-terrorism*. Cambridge: Cambridge University Press.

Sageman, M. (2014) 'The stagnation in terrorism research', *Terrorism and Political Violence*, 26(4), pp. 565–580.

Sandler, T. (2014) 'The analytical study of terrorism: taking stock', *Journal of Peace Research*, 51(2), pp. 257–271.

Schmid, A. P. (1982) *Political terrorism: a research guide to concepts, theories, data bases and literature*. Amsterdam/New Brunswick, NJ: SWIDOC/Transaction Books.

Schmid, A. P. (2011a) '50 un- and under-researched topics in the field of (counter-) terrorism studies', *Perspectives on Terrorism*, 5(1), pp. 76–78.

Schmid, A. P. (2011b) 'The literature on terrorism', in Schmid, A. P. (ed.), *The Routledge handbook of terrorism research*. London: Routledge, pp. 457–474.

Schmid, A. P. (2014) 'Comments on Marc Sageman's polemic "The stagnation in ter-rorism research"', *Terrorism and Political Violence*, 26(4), pp. 587–595.

Schmid, A. P. and Forest, J. J. F. (2018) 'Research desiderata: 150 un- and under-researched topics and themes in the field of (counter-)terrorism studies – a new list', *Perspectives on Terrorism*, 12(4), pp. 68–76.

Schmid, A. P. and Jongman, A. J. (1988) *Political terrorism: a new guide to actors, authors, concepts, data bases, theories, and literature*. Amsterdam/New Brunswick, NJ: SWIDOC/Transaction Books.

Schulze, F. (2004) 'Breaking the cycle: empirical research and postgraduate studies on terrorism', in Silke, A. (ed.), *Research on terrorism: trends, achievements and failures*. London: Frank Cass, pp. 161–185.

Schuurman, B. (2019) 'Topics in terrorism research: reviewing trends and gaps, 2007–2016', *Critical Studies on Terrorism*, 12(3), pp. 463–480.

Schuurman, B. (2020) 'Research on terrorism, 2007–2016: a review of data, methods, and authorship', *Terrorism and Political Violence*, 32(5), pp. 1011–1026.

Silke, A. (2001) 'The devil you know: continuing problems with research on terrorism', *Terrorism and Political Violence*, 13(4), pp. 1–14.

Silke, A. (2004a) 'An introduction to terrorism research', in Silke, A. (ed.), *Research on terrorism: trends, achievements and failures*. London: Frank Cass, pp. 1–29.

Silke, A. (2004b) 'The road less travelled: trends in terrorism research', in Silke, A. (ed.), *Research on terrorism: trends, achievements and failures*. London: Frank Cass, pp. 186–213.

Silke, A. (2007) 'The impact of 9/11 on research on terrorism', in Ranstorp, M. (ed.), *Mapping terrorism research: state of the art, gaps and future directions*. New York: Routledge, pp. 76–93.

Silke, A. (2008) 'Holy warriors: exploring the psychological processes of jihadi radicalization', *European Journal of Criminology*, 5(1), pp. 99–123.

Silke, A. (2009) 'Contemporary terrorism studies: issues in research', in Jackson, R., Smyth, M. B. and Gunning, J. (eds), *Critical terrorism studies: a new research agenda*. New York: Routledge, pp. 34–48.

Silke, A. (2019a) 'State terrorism', in Silke, A. (ed.), *Routledge handbook of terrorism and counterterrorism*. London: Routledge, pp. 66–73.

Silke, A. (2019b) 'The study of terrorism and counterterrorism', in Silke, A. (ed.), *Routledge handbook of terrorism and counterterrorism*. London: Routledge, pp. 1–10.

Silke, A. and Schmidt-Petersen, J. (2017) 'The golden age? What the 100 most cited articles in terrorism studies tell us', *Terrorism and Political Violence*, 29(4), pp. 692–712.

Stampnitzky, L. (2014) *Disciplining terror: how experts invented 'terrorism'*. Cambridge: Cambridge University Press.

Stern, J. (2014) 'Response to Marc Sageman's "The stagnation in terrorism research"', *Terrorism and Political Violence*, 26(4), pp. 607–613.

Weinberg, L. and Eubank, W. (2008) 'Problems with the critical studies approach to terrorism', *Critical Studies on Terrorism*, 1(2), pp. 185–195.

Wieviorka, M. (1995) 'Terrorism in the context of academic research', in Crenshaw, M. (ed.), *Terrorism in context*. University Park, PA: Pennsylvania State University Press, pp. 597–606.

Wood, G. (2018) *The way of the strangers: encounters with the Islamic state*. New York: Random House.

Wright, L. (2011) *The looming tower: Al-Qaeda and the road to 9/11*. New York: Random House.

Young, J. K. and Findley, M. G. (2011) 'Promise and pitfalls of terrorism research', *International Studies Review*, 13(3), pp. 411–431.

Youngman, M. (2020) 'Building "terrorism studies" as an interdisciplinary space: addressing recurring issues in the study of terrorism', *Terrorism and Political Violence*, 32(5), pp. 1091–1105.

13 Gender issues in terrorism studies

Katherine E. Brown

Introduction

How did a schoolgirl become a threat to national security such that her citizenship was revoked by the United Kingdom (UK) home secretary? Answer: she joined Daesh,[1] had three children in Iraq, initially refused to apologise on international television while living in an internal displacement camp set up once the 'caliphate' fell. Such an outcome seems implausible, and yet it is the fate of Shamima Begum (Masters & Regilme 2020; Farnham 2019). We see gender working in multiple ways in this short account (Shepherd 2009). First, gender is socially constructed (as in men and women are 'made' not born), so the account is seen as incongruous because we recognised certain qualities and roles as associated with those identified as male and those identified as female but also as not identified with terrorism, for example her mothering. Second, gender is performative (we 'do' gender), although here Shamima Begum's initial refusal to act submissively and apologetically went against gender norms and expectations, such that she was viewed to have doubly transgressed. And third, gender is a significant feature that organises terrorism and government responses (it is structural) – state security is prioritised at the expense of women's security, in a form of a protection racket (Sjoberg & Peet 2011; Brown 2020). By seeing gender, we can also see that the answer is incomplete: it ignores the gender-specific vulnerabilities of young girls to radicalisation, it ignores how women's affiliation helps legitimise Daesh's agenda while not engaging in acts of terrorist violence, it ignores the racialised component of

---

[1]   I use the term Daesh to refer to the so-called Islamic State (ISIS) as this phrase challenges the legitimacy of the group. Daesh is an invented Arabic acronym formed from the initial letters of the group's previous name in Arabic – "al-Dawla al-Islamiya fil Iraq wa al-Sham". Although it does not mean anything as a word in Arabic, Daesh sounds similar to an Arabic verb that means to tread underfoot, trample down, or crush something. The group's supporters also object to its use (Irshaid, 2015).

citizenship revocation and it ignores how women's rights and security are often bypassed in favour of the state.

This chapter begins by demonstrating why a bespoke chapter on gender is needed. The chapter then outlines three core approaches to the study of gender and terrorism that have been used for the past 30 plus years. These are seeing gender as a category, as constitutive and as transformative of terrorism. Within the three approaches we discuss the issues of women and children affiliated to terrorist organisations and their rehabilitation, the process of 'gendered radicalisation', how gender operates in terrorist propaganda and ideologies and the use of gender-based violence (GBV) as a coercive strategy. It also looks at whether Incels[2] can be considered terrorists, and whether domestic violence should be viewed as terrorism via a continuum of violence. The third section of the chapter discusses three future approaches for research within the study of gender and terrorism: intersectional approaches; queer studies; and child studies. Finally, the chapter moves to a conclusion, stressing the diversity of approaches and research agendas in the study of gender and terrorism.

A quick note on terminology and the scope of this chapter: this chapter takes a broad approach to core terms. Research is included that touches on groups and organisations that are often described as 'violent extremists', 'extremists' or 'insurgents' rather than 'terrorists'. This is partly to offset a bias in the discipline towards researching Islamist-inspired terrorism. Debates about definition are attempts to establish 'who owns the words' (Rowlandson 2015, 20). In the second section of this chapter we highlight feminist questions regarding the mainstream boundaries on the definition of terrorism.

Why do we need this chapter anyway?

There are at least three compelling reasons: the mainstream of terrorism studies is gender blind; it tends to ignore feminist research; and counterterrorism practices continue to ignore or instrumentalise the human rights and security needs of women.

---

[2]   Incel is a compound word from the term 'involuntarily celibate' and refers to men who identify with a particular misogynist view of the world where they view themselves as disadvantaged due to a sexual culture that wrongfully allows women bodily, economic and political autonomy. It is discussed in more detail later.

Mainstream terrorism researchers and practitioners tend to adopt a 'gender-blind approach' and unreflectively see terrorism as properly the activity of men (Gasztold 2020). Consequently, gender is often ignored as a significant variable or explanatory factor in terrorism because men's experiences are assumed to be the 'human norm'. This means for example that theories of radicalisation presume men's journeys to terrorism are generalisable, and second, rarely see the men *as* men, thereby ignoring masculinity and gender relations in their modelling (Brown 2020; Pearson, Winterbotham & Brown 2021). This failure to integrate the subfield of 'women and terrorism' into the mainstream is noted by Davis, West and Amarasingam's (2021) review. They note 'Year after year, conflict after conflict, members of the public and the media greet the phenomenon of women engaging in terrorism with surprise, concern, and in some cases, denial' (2021, 58).

Consequently, and despite the evidence, when women are revealed as participants in terrorism, their participation is seen as exotic and deviant – novel, but also marginal (Davis et al. 2021, 58). In the iconic works in terrorism studies the role and motivations of women are minimised and trivialised (Gasztold 2020, 2–3). Schmidt (2020) confirms 'Unless women are specifically documented as *combatants*, many war and terrorism scholars do not consider women's roles seriously, writing them off as camp followers, "fan girls", supporters, or "jihadi brides"; or, more commonly, they do not mention women or gender at all'.

However, since Daesh, international policy and counterterrorism frameworks demonstrate an increased awareness of the importance of gender in combatting and preventing terrorism. Normatively at least, it seems that the policy agenda is further ahead than academia. In part, this is explained by the influence of the United Nations (UN)-driven Women, Peace and Security (WPS) agenda. Security practitioners acknowledge the importance of UN Resolutions 1325 (passed in 2000), 1889 (in 2013) and 2178 (in 2014), all of which relate to women's meaningful and equal participation in peace and security processes. Derived from these, international security policies and practices targeting women focus on empowering women either as a preventative measure to war and terrorism or to bring about more sustainable peace settlements in during-conflict and in post-conflict scenarios. The UN Secretary-General recognised women's participation in countering terrorism as essential in 2016, asserting that, 'to build counter-narratives and counterstrategies and pave the way for reparations and redress … it is critical to invest in the capacity of women's groups to lead grass-roots efforts to counter extremism and youth radicalization' (UNSG CRSV 2016, para 22).

There are however challenges in the policy application of WPS in relation to terrorism. This agenda links women's empowerment in politics and civil society as a core component to preventing violent extremism, but also sees women as natural 'preventers' of violent extremism through their private and public social identities and relationships – and often leads to 'women washing' and instrumentalising women's rights and lives (Giscard d'Estaing 2017; Heathcote 2018; Huckerby & Ní Aoláin 2018; Huckerby 2020; Lorentzen 2021). Thus, we move from 'gender blind' to gender sensitive, but these cannot be assumed to be working in favour of women's rights and equality; they are not gender responsive or transformative (Brown 2020). Indeed, 'women washing' is possible because it stems from widely held stereotypes about women and mothers. Stereotypes about peaceful mothers and responsible fathers are features of countries' anti-radicalisation programmes, regardless of their cultural framings. Women are seen as natural supporters of counterradicalisation initiatives because it is assumed that such initiatives benefit 'naturally peaceful' mothers and 'moderate' women (Brown 2020). Further, it is assumed that these programmes will automatically (whether targeting women or not) lead to a liberalising or moderating of the communities that will in turn benefit women and their rights. The evidence for these assumptions is sparse and questionable. First, it cannot be assumed that women are peaceful or moderate, and second, it cannot be assumed that the policies will lead to a liberalisation of communities to the benefit of women. Many programmes operating via or in consultation with community leaders reinforce patriarchal modes of governance within communities as they are often the most conservative and traditional men who are given voices and power as a result – because government outsiders assume they're the most 'representative' of that community.

The second core challenge with the application of gender in policy and practice is that commitments to WPS are frequently aspirational rather than reflective of frontline practices, funding and budgeting promises or operating procedures. Overall, there is a notable 'say-do-gap' (White 2022). As Schmidt notes, countering violent terrorism is a men's club (2020), and some practitioners continue to assert stereotypical views – such as explaining women's participation in ISIS as part of a 'zombification' process (Speckhard, Shajkovci & Esengul 2017). Fionnulla Ní Aoláin (2016) finds that women are rarely present in policymaking or in positions of leadership in counterterrorism fields. Women are therefore viewed as beneficiaries or supporters of countering violent terrorism and counterterrorism, rather than active in shaping the agendas or as bearers of knowledge about terrorism and counterterrorism.

Thus, although we have increased awareness of women and gender in response to the security threat of Daesh, it is insufficient. This insufficient understanding relies on gender-blind theories – due to the failure to integrate the longstanding subfield of 'women and terrorism' into the mainstream and practitioners and policymakers uncritically reflecting societal stereotypes about gender roles and norms. This chapter offers the opportunity to move beyond the continuous cycle of 'rediscovery' by building on 30 years of feminist and gender insights into terrorism.

Approaches to the study of gender and terrorism

This section is organised in line with True's (1996) initial tripartite division as gender relates to the wider field of international relations. The first takes gender as a variable, the second as constitutive and the third as transformative. A recent bibliography on 'women and terrorism' in *Perspectives on Terrorism* offers us over 600 resources since early 2000, with the majority published since 2015 (Tinnes 2020). This informs this section as well as work published since.

Gender as a variable

The first approach is a positivist and empirical matter of mapping and accounting for women's actions in relation to terrorism. In this approach, scholars are often 'adding women' into an already understood field of practice and theory, and this is the most common approach we see in the subdiscipline. They take up Cynthia Enloe's call that 'women have always been present, if we choose to see them'. This approach has three core questions about women in terrorism: who and how many; doing what; and why.

The first challenge is numerical. It has been argued that a feature of 'new terrorism' is a resurgence of women's participation (Jacques & Taylor 2013; Laster & Erez 2015); given numerous historical accounts of women's participation and failure of the field to take women's participation seriously, we can be sceptical of this claim. Nevertheless, regardless of whether there is an empirical increase, there is increased visibility and reporting of women's involvement in terrorist groups (Brown 2017). Even with this new awareness of women's activities, determining the exact number of women involved in terrorism remains problematic because large datasets and government data frequently do not record perpetrators' gender. This is evidenced by the two plus year study that Cook and Vale (2018, 2019) undertook, using open-source and unofficial data that they then had to verify and triangulate to determine who had participated in the so-called Islamic State, because of the lack of official and verified data. They found that 13 per cent of 41,490 foreign citizens who became affiliated with Daesh in Iraq and Syria between April 2013 and June 2018 were women. Examining online 'frontline' terrorist activities, we see women are present once we disaggregate that data. Of the 338 suicide bombing attacks claimed by Boko Haram, 244 (72 per cent) were carried out by women; across Europe (excluding the UK) in 2020, women represented 30 per cent of left-wing terrorists arrested on terrorism charges and 13 per cent for jihadi-related terrorism offences (Europol 2021). At first glance, these may not seem significant numbers – they remain a minority – however, women's participation in other struggles suggest some higher figures, especially if we think past the obsession with spectacular violence and define terrorist activities more broadly to include logistics, propaganda, intelligence gathering and recruitment.

There is considerable variability in the category of woman, and measuring participation alongside age, ethnicity, marital status, religiosity, education levels, criminal records, etc. is important to identify vulnerabilities and pathways for joining. For example, the types of women joining Daesh from overseas in the early years were often married women, and families travelled together to Iraq and Syria to be part of the new so-called Caliphate and to defend other Muslims against the tyranny of dictatorship and Shi'a rule.[3] Later, we saw younger women travelling independently and often against the wishes of their family to establish a 'new life' within the group, and who seemed empowered by their narrative of jihad rather than the Caliphate. This shift in the type of women is linked to the changing goals and narrative of the group as well as the environment in which it operates. Given that women are 'in terrorism', gender analysis demonstrates the extent and variability of women's participation.

The second challenge in mapping women's participation is due to the range of terrorist groups. The diversity of causes, longevity, wider socio-political contexts and so on makes it difficult to establish a taxonomy of women's roles. Within far-right extremist groups, for example, some groups accept women as Valkyrie-inspired warriors with active violent roles, while others prioritise more conservative ideas of women's roles being linked to 'Kinder, Kirche, Küche' (children, church and kitchen) (Mattheis 2018; Fangen & Lichtenberg 2021). Cook and Vale (2018, 2019) highlight how women are involved in terrorism for Daesh via women-only cells, family cells, as lone women perpetrating attacks or as part of a 'women's section'. Yet other researchers show how women also operate as an intrinsic part of terrorist groups rather than as complementary or parallel institutions, such as in the Kurdistan Workers' Party (PKK), where there are additional women-only structures and training but

---

[3]   I'm using here the language of the group rather than affirming it as accurate.

also full integration into the group. This is supported by the PKK ideology that promotes gender empowerment (Szekely 2020). In addition, the roles women play in any one organisation may change over time. For example, the role of women in the National Liberation Front (FLN) in Algeria changed; where they were initially not involved beyond caring duties, over time women would dress in more European styles (contrary to FLN gender ideals) so women could move about more freely and carry explosives, weapons or messages to places where men could retrieve them (Macmaster 2020). Similarly, Hamas initially resisted women's active participation in its violent activities but after the Al Aqsa Martyrs Brigade carried out a successful attack by a woman, they changed their stance (Ahmad 2019).

The third core question addressed by researchers in this approach concerns identifying motivation and agency. There is a tendency among media, policymakers, practitioners and in mainstream terrorism studies to stereotype women's participation according to assumptions about women's position in society in relation to men, their presumed passivity and prioritisation of emotional or personal motivations (Schmidt 2020). Research in this approach to the study of gender and terrorism demonstrates these are inaccurate accounts. Overall, for men and women any combination of factors may be driving participation and radicalisation, both personal and political (Sjoberg & Gentry 2015; Cook & Vale 2018; Pearson et al. 2021). Women's motivations and vulnerabilities are similar to those of men, and like men, they express and experience these in gendered ways (Gan, Neo, Chin & Khader 2019; Brown 2017, 2020). Additionally, this realisation of the complexity and multiple pathways to terrorism encourages us to focus on the group level of analysis rather than the individual level and allows us to avoid conducting ad hoc 'psychological autopsies' of women terrorists (Brunner 2007). This leads to new frameworks for understanding the decision making, pathways and agency of women in terrorism. One such approach is the development of 'gendered radicalisation' as a framework for understanding how women and men become involved in terrorism (Pearson et al. 2021). This framework explores how gender operates as a variable within the radicalisation process to influence women and men's journeys to violent extremism and terrorism. It serves as a corrective to models which ignore gender and uses feminist conceptualisations of agency.

Gender as constitutive

Gendered radicalisation as a model does more than count women in the data; it acknowledges how gender is constitutive of radicalisation. In this second approach, ideas about gender are viewed as components of terrorism and gender roles and relations shape terrorist activity. This approach to the study of terrorism and gender looks at how gender signifies relationships of power (Herschinger 2014).

Ideas about gender roles, such as motherhood[4] and marriage, give insight into how gender constitutes terrorism. For terrorist organisations, especially where their goal is to transform ordinary lives as well as the polity, narratives of motherhood link them to the nation and the land (Chatterjee 1989). Far from framing wives and mothers as passive or supportive, terrorist narratives presented these active choices as a means of female agency, as Mattheis and Winter (2019) show in the case of Daesh. Through identities Daesh imagine Muslim women as public agents of change in creating and shaping the global Caliphate (Biswas & Deylami 2019) and customs (Vale 2019). In recent interviews with women affiliated with Daesh, 97.4 per cent said their role was as a mother or wife (Speckhard & Ellenberg 2020) – women were praised and granted social standing upon bearing children, especially boys, and saw becoming mothers as a duty to the group. Mothering becomes a collective activity which fosters unity and intergenerational knowledge transmission. Women also mediated marriages to foster cohesion within the terrorist organisation, disrupting local marriage customs, and introduced new parenting norms, shifting local ideas about what was good mothering. Marrying into a terrorist group is about aligning public identities with 'private' roles and values, but it is also a means to acquiring physical and financial security in volatile environments, such as Libya and Tunisia (UNDP 2021). Recent research on Boko Haram for UN Women suggests a similar feature – women being coerced into marrying Boko Haram fighters but with the promise of safety if they agree. This is also the case for some foreign women in Iraq and Syria who 'married their way to the border' to escape Daesh (Speckhard & Ellenberg 2020). In this manner terrorist groups like Daesh are operating a protection racket (Brown 2018, 2020). Although most research on motherhood and terrorism focuses on Islamist groups, we can also see its significance in far-right movements and in some eco-terrorist narratives (D'Ascenzio 2017; Johnston & Johnston 2017). Keenan (2014) discusses how 'Big Mother' strategies are deployed in counterterrorism responses and security narratives in suburban America. Motherhood and marriage are part of terrorist (and counterterrorist) strategies, goals and activities. These insights about (women's) activities typically seen as outside the purview of terrorism studies show how terrorist group strategies and individual partici-

---

[4]   Here referring to motherhood is an organisational norm rather than a motivator or way of understanding individual women's motivation and experiences. This distinction is important because it has implications for preventing violent extremism and counterterrorism strategies that seek to prioritise women's role as mothers (Winterbotham 2018; Brown 2020).

pation need to be understood in the context of a wider gendered socio-political security environment.

Mothering and marriage are relational – they make sense only when we also consider men's roles. One of the main advances in terrorism studies has been the consideration of masculinity as intrinsic to terrorism. For example, women's direct participation and affiliation to terrorist groups is also a way of shaming men, because it suggests that men are not fulfilling their heroic, protective and breadwinner functions by standing apart from the cause. Women affiliated with Daesh in propaganda on social media will also emphasise the masculine and desirable qualities of male fighters for the group, and mock enemy and civilian men for their emasculation at the hands of the state or wider society (Ingram 2021). Daesh tends to vilify 'enemy' women in its media production, and sees women generally as inherently weak, with any exceptional feats of endurance or sacrifice due to exceptional faith and despite their feminine nature (Mehran, Imiolek, Smeddle & Springett-Gilling 2020). This helps us understand how 'toxic' masculinity and hegemonic masculinity (as well as other forms of masculinity) constitute terrorism (Duriesmith & Ismail 2019; Pearson 2020).

Typically seen as evidence of toxic masculinity is the presence of GBV. A rise in rates of domestic violence, violent attacks against women in public leadership roles, efforts to undermine women's rights and their human rights and the targeting of women's public spaces and women-based organisations in civil society are early warning indicators of extremism and terrorism within a community or country (Bigio & Vogelstein, 2019, 8; Huckerby 2020). Sexual violence and the broader category of GBV perpetrated by terrorist organisations and those opposing them are inherently linked to control over territory (Asal & Nagel 2021). The UN Commission of Inquiry found that 'ISIS's rules exacerbate the subordinate role of women in society, reinforcing patriarchal attitudes. Failure to abide by these rules is punishable by lashing' (UN Human Rights Council 2014, para. 49). Women's role as 'victims' here is clear, and is not accidental but a targeted governance campaign (Brown 2018). Terrorist groups also highlight GBV against women, and women's rights violations perpetrated by militaries and security actors, to justify their actions and to garner public support. For Daesh, this includes emphasising discrimination against Muslim women in Muslim-minority countries and using examples of Islamophobia and rape culture to support their own gender norms which seek to enforce strict gender segregation and women's traditional family roles (Lahoud 2018; Jacobsen 2019). Paradoxically, however, despite criticising the failures of the West to protect women, they then enslave and abuse 'enemy' women (Al-Dayel & Mumford 2020). In far-right and left-wing extremist groups, women also experience violence and sexual abuse from within (Winther 2018). Women's complicity in violence and support for the new gender norms gives further authority to terrorist groups.

Gender as transformative

The final approach is a consideration of gender and terrorism in such a way that the category of 'terrorism' is reconfigured. It also asks how and why gender is integral to terrorism in the way that it is. Most recently this is evident in the discussion about Incels.[5]

Incels are linked to lone actor terrorism and mass shootings. To date, approximately 50 people have been killed due to Incel violence in America and Canada (Hoffman, Ware & Shapiro 2020). These have included mass shootings and other terrorist violence, and they often leave manifestos and share ideas online with other like-minded individuals. A recent report by the Swedish Defence Research Institute found that the United States and UK were the most common nationalities across Incel forums, but that Sweden had the most participants on a per capita ratio (Fernquist, Kaati, Pelzer, Asplund Cohen & Akrami 2020). In a survey of 400 Incels, 50 per cent reported receiving an undergraduate or graduate degree, while 66 per cent identified as middle class or above (Hoffman et al. 2020). While they are racially diverse, they are united in their understanding of gender relations.

Incels and others who identify with 'ideological masculinity' perceive themselves to be victims who are denied access to privileges, power and women's bodies because of socio-economic and political changes in (Western) society (Cottee 2021). In contrast to other men who express sexual frustration, the distinction is with 'those seek to politicize their sexual frustration into a master status' rooted in misogyny (hatred of women) or femmephobia (Menzie 2020). Incels present as heterosexual and male. There are therefore debates about whether Incels represent a new form of terrorism because they seek to change society, use fear and violence to influence and have an underlying ideology and worldview that unites them. The Incel worldview exhibits 'clear traits of an extremist worldview whereby violence is not only seen as acceptable but also as the only possible way to solve the crisis endpoint in which society is supposedly stuck' (Baele, Brace & Coan 2019, 17). A January 2020 report by the Texas Department of Public Safety warned that Incels are an 'emerging domestic terrorism threat'. In contrast, Cottee (2021) argues that while the 'squeamish'

---

5   This section draws on Brown (2021).

or 'devoutly feminist' should probably not research or read Incel material, he reminds readers how law-abiding most Incels really are.

The fallback to 'law-abiding citizens' is a call not to tarnish all people associating with a violent ideology as terrorists, but it ignores the other statistical correlation that lone actor terrorists commonly have a history of committing GBV. As Shifman and Tillet (2015) argue, 'men who commit violence, rehearse and perfect it against their families first'. McCulloch, Walklate, Maher and Fitzgibbon (2019) show how the (mis)understanding of violence against women in lone actor terrorism can result in failures to realise the threats violent men pose. Joshua Roose also strongly advocates that Incels are a terrorist threat, noting how they draw on similar gendered ideas to Daesh by exploiting the fault lines of masculinity (cited in Constantinou 2019). Recognising the correlation between attacks on women and terrorism has led to new indicators or drivers of terrorism and a reassessment of what constitutes terrorism. Feminist peace research further opens what 'counts' as terrorism, as Sara Merger (2018) opined: 'When is terrorism not terrorism? When it is targeting women.'

To address this criticism, a new term, 'misogynist terrorism', has emerged. It describes not only Incels but a broader phenomenon of cultural violence targeting women. Misogyny, or ideological misogyny, is 'a political phenomenon that polices and enforces women's subordination and men's domination' (Díaz & Valji 2019). Men demand a variety of services from women, but if those are not forthcoming or women occupy public space normally occupied by men, women are often targeted for misogynist abuse or violence. A United Nations Development Programme (UNDP) report explicitly links misogyny and gendered hate speech to violent extremism and terrorism regardless of the political cause (2021). Aside from noting correlation and perhaps causality, linking it to existing groups and affiliations in Incel movements, some feminist peace researchers have pushed further and conceptualised domestic abuse and violence in the home as terrorism. Intimate (partner) terrorism is part of a spectrum of intimate violence mostly perpetrated by men against women; it includes threats of violence, isolation, emotional and psychological abuse. This has also been framed as 'patriarchal terrorism', sometimes leading to 'self-help murder' among women who have been victims of this violence (Harper 2017). However, UNDP notes 'the very ubiquity of misogyny means the problem remains hidden in plain sight' (2021, 2). Rachel Pain (2014) brought together 'everyday terrorism' and the 'war on terror' in her geographical work. Examining the different emotions of fear operating, she finds the difference between these terrorisms is a matter of how trauma, fear and entrapment operate in these interrelated sites. She concludes that there are intimate connections between global, local and intimate securities. The connectivity is further theorised by Gentry in her work *Disordered Violence* (2020), as she explores the underlying power inequalities that structure violence.

Future trends and conclusion

There are three trends in research on gender and terrorism, where there is both a growing intellectual curiosity and a clear policy need: addressing intersectionality; including queer studies; and reflecting on child rights and child-centric approaches.

Although transformational approaches to the study of gender and international relations have opened the category 'woman', within the study of terrorism, this element has yet to fully take root. Intersectional theories show us how different socio-economic markers, such as race, gender, class, age and sexuality, consistently interact and overlap as 'intersecting oppressions' (Crenshaw 1991). Approaches to intersectionality have featured in terrorism studies mostly through consideration of media representation vis-à-vis Islamophobia – for example, Auer, Sutcliffe and Lee's (2019) consideration of the British woman dubbed the 'white widow', Samantha Lewthwaite, who is affiliated with Al-Shabaab by the media following the Westgate Mall (Nairobi) attack in 2013. However, there are more opportunities to use intersectional analysis to consider how terrorist groups operate and their narratives, and to unpack the categories of men and women within terrorism. Petrich and Donnelly (2019) apply such an approach to recognise how Al-Shabaab have different relationships with different categories of women. Ghabra (2020) also uses intersectional analysis to break down the gendered ethics of whiteness in response to the 2019 Christchurch terrorist attacks.

Gentry (2020) acknowledges in her work that although she takes an intersectional approach, one area which needs further consideration is that of sexuality. She is not alone here, and greater consideration of how threats to LGBTQ rights and transphobia intersect with terrorism and violent extremism is an important consideration. Much like approaches to the study of gender, this is more than a call for simply adding other variables (sexuality) – it is also a request to 'queer the field' to understand terrorism differently. As an example of the first approach, Carastathis (2018) explores homophobic and transphobic violence in Greece, linking it to terrorism. Puar in *Terrorist Assemblages* considers how homophobia constitutes the 'war on terror', and this is a canonical work when considering the intersectionality at work in countering violent extremism and counter terrorism. Harris and Holman Jones (2017) discuss how working in an intersectional manner is both an empirical and normative endeavour, such that in response to the terrorist attack in Orlando in 2016 they 'believe that all our futures, "our human dignity, our lives, are connected to the liberation of Black people, Muslim people, of women, of trans people, and so we cannot move forward without working with these communities to end White Supremacy [and] patriarchy"' (citing Ogles 2016).

Looking to the future also raises the spectre of child terrorists. Children born in Iraq and Syria to international Daesh-affiliated parents number approximately 6,500, in addition to children who were taken there by their parents. This raises the question of childhood in terrorism and how this is gendered. We know that the experiences of children born to Daesh parents are varied, and with a significant difference between girls and boys. Boys have been treated as adults, in some cases literally weaponised, and in all cases rhetorically so (Almohammad 2018), and they have been subject to violence at the hands of Daesh. Girls find their life experiences narrowed to the domestic sphere, with examples of child marriage, GBV and witnessing violence. There are also examples of children rebelling against Daesh and refusing to accept their indoctrination (Cook & Vale 2019). Additionally, it is not only terrorist groups who differentiate on the grounds of gender and age. The UN Special Rapporteur criticises how states are discriminating against boys on the threshold of adulthood by treating them as adults – as especially risky and unworthy of repatriation – even where in law they are children, and victims. Looking at child rights and agency in radicalisation cases also highlights questions about the continuation of violence in terms of child abuse and terrorism and challenging the consequences of such linkages. Addressing the rehabilitation and long-term reintegration of children born and raised in violent extremism contexts is a vital component of future terrorism research (UNICEF & International Alert 2016; Ahdash 2018).

Gender approaches, like feminism generally, are not a singular response to policy, practices or theory. They are diverse in foundations, methodologies and normative goals. Gender approaches to the study of terrorism have been successful in highlighting how terrorism operates, its differential harms and the stereotypes in efforts to counterterrorism. As a subfield it shows us who, why and how individuals participate in terrorism, it reveals how gender norms and roles influence how groups operate and it exposes assumptions and the power at work in how terrorism and counterterrorism are constituted and put into practice. It offers new avenues for enquiry and offers critiques of policy and practice by transforming categories of analysis. However, while gender approaches to understanding and responding to terrorism have become accepted by international and regional organisations – including NATO and the UN – the academic field of terrorism studies must overcome its blind spots.

References

Ahdash, F. (2018). The Interaction between Family Law and Counter-Terrorism: A Critical Examination of the Radicalisation Cases in the Family Courts. *Child and Family Law Quarterly*, 30(7), 389–413.

Ahmad, A. (2019). 'We Have Captured Your Women': Explaining Jihadist Norm Change. *International Security*, 44(1), 80–116.

Al-Dayel, N. & Mumford, A. (2020). *ISIS and Their Use of Slavery*. The Hague: International Centre for Counter-Terrorism.

Almohammad, A. (2018). *ISIS Child Soldiers in Syria: The Structural and Predatory Recruitment, Enlistment, Pre-Training Indoctrination, Training, and Deployment*. The Hague: International Centre for Counter-Terrorism.

Asal, V. & Nagel, R. U. (2021). Control over Bodies and Territories: Insurgent Territorial Control and Sexual Violence. *Security Studies*, 30(1), 136–158.

Auer, M., Sutcliffe, J. & Lee, M. (2019). Framing the 'White Widow': Using Intersectionality to Uncover Complex Representations of Female Terrorism in News Media. *Media, War and Conflict*, 12(3), 281–298.

Baele, S. J., Brace, L. & Coan, T. G. (2019). From 'Incel' to 'Saint': Analyzing the Violent Worldview behind the 2018 Toronto Attack. *Terrorism and Political Violence*. DOI: 10.1080/09546553.2019.1638256

Bigio, J. & Vogelstein, R. (2019). *Women and Terrorism: Hidden Threats, Forgotten Partners*. New York: Council on Foreign Relations.

Biswas, B. & Deylami, S. (2019). Radicalizing Female Empowerment: Gender, Agency, and Affective Appeals in Islamic State Propaganda. *Small Wars and Insurgencies*, 30(6–7), 1193–1213.

Brown, K. E. (2017). Gender and Terrorist Movements, in C. Duncanson & R. Woodward (Eds), *Handbook of Gender and the Military*. Basingstoke: Palgrave, pp. 419–435.

Brown, K. E. (2018). Gendered Violence in the Making of the Proto-State Islamic State, in S. Parashar, J. A. Tickner & J. True (Eds), *Revisiting Gendered States*. Oxford: Oxford University Press, pp. 174–190.

Brown, K. E. (2020). *Gender, Religion, and Extremism: Finding Women in Anti-Radicalisation*. Oxford: Oxford University Press.

Brown, K. E. (2021). Feminist Responses to Violent Extremism, in C. Confortini & S. Parashar (Eds), *Routledge Handbook of Feminist Peace Research*. New York: Routledge, pp. 136–147.

Brunner, C. (2007). Occidentalism Meets the Female Suicide Bomber: A Critical Reflection on Recent Terrorism Debates: A Review Essay. *Signs*, 32(4), pp. 957–971.

Carastathis, A. (2018). 'Gender Is the First Terrorist': Homophobic and Transphobic Violence in Greece. *Frontiers: A Journal of Women Studies*, 39(2), 265–296.

Chatterjee, P. (1989). Colonialism, Nationalism, and Colonialized Women: The Contest in India. *American Ethnologist*, 16(4), 622–633.

Constantinou, M. (2019). Is the Hate Fuelled Ideology of Misogynists a Form of Terrorism? *Impact*. www .impact .acu .edu .au/ community/ is -the -hate -fuelled -ideology-of-misogynists-a-form-of-terrorism

Cook, J. & Vale, G. (2018). From Daesh to 'Diaspora': Tracing the Women and Minors of Islamic State. International Centre for the Study of Radicalisation, July.

Cook, J. & Vale, G. (2019). From Daesh to 'Diaspora' II: The Challenges Posed by Women and Minors after the Fall of the Caliphate. *CTC Sentinel*, 12(6). https://ctc .usma.edu/daesh-diaspora-challenges-posed-women-minors-fall-caliphate/

Cottee, S. (2021). Incel (E)motives: Resentment, Shame and Revenge. *Studies in Conflict and Terrorism*, 44(2), 93–114.

D'Ascenzio, A. (2017). Resistance Materials: Female Antagonism in the No-TAV Case. *Identities: Journal for Politics, Gender and Culture*, 14(1–2), 155–161.

Davis, J., West, L. & Amarasingam, A. (2021). Measuring Impact, Uncovering Bias? Citation Analysis of Literature on Women in Terrorism. *Perspectives on Terrorism*, 15(2), 58–75.

Díaz, P. & Valji, N. (2019). Symbiosis of Misogyny and Violent Extremism: New Understandings and Policy Implications. *Journal of International Affairs*, 72(2), 37–56.

Duriesmith, D. & Ismail, N. (2019). Militarized Masculinities beyond Methodological Nationalism: Charting the Multiple Masculinities of an Indonesian Jihadi. *International Theory*, 11(2), 139–159.

Enloe, C. (1989). *Bananas, Beaches and Bases: Making Feminist sense of International Politics*. Los Angeles: University of California Press.

Europol (2021). *European Union Terrorism Situation and Trend Report*. Luxembourg: Publications Office of the European Union.

Fangen, K. & Lichtenberg, L. (2021). Gender and Family Rhetoric on the German Far Right. *Patterns of Prejudice*. DOI: 10.1080/0031322X.2021.1898815

Farnham, H. (2019). What the Media Circus Surrounding Shamima Begum Can Teach Us about Gender and Nation. *Genderings*, 3 April. https://blogs.lse.ac.uk/gender/ 2019/04/03/gender_and_nation/

Fernquist, J., Kaati, L., Pelzer, B., Asplund Cohen, K. & Akrami, N. (2020). *Hope, Cope and Rope: Incels i digitala miljöer*. FOI Memo 7040.

Gan, R., Neo, L. S., Chin, J. & Khader, M. (2019). Change Is the Only Constant: The Evolving Role of Women in the Islamic State in Iraq and Syria (ISIS). *Women and Criminal Justice*, 29(4–5), 204–220.

Gasztold, A. (2020). *Feminist Perspectives on Terrorism: Critical Approaches to Security Studies*. Cham: Springer.

Gentry, C. (2020). *Disordered Violence: How Gender, Race and Heteronormativity Structure Terrorism*. Edinburgh: Edinburgh University Press.

Ghabra, H. S. (2020). Don't Say His Name: The Terror Attacks in New Zealand and the Ethics of White Allyship. *Journal of International and Intercultural Communication* . DOI: 10.1080/17513057.2020.1849773

Giscard d'Estaing, S. (2017). Engaging Women in Countering Violent Extremism: Avoiding Instrumentalisation and Furthering Agency. *Gender and Development*, 25(1), 103–118.

Harper, S. B. (2017). No Way Out: Severely Abused Latina Women, Patriarchal Terrorism, and Self-Help Homicide. *Feminist Criminology*, 12(3), 224–247.

Harris, A. & Holman Jones, S. (2017). Feeling Fear, Feeling Queer: The Peril and Potential of Queer Terror. *Qualitative Inquiry*, 23(7), 561–568.

Heathcote, G. (2018). Security Council Resolution 2242 on Women, Peace and Security: Progressive Gains or Dangerous Development? *Global Society*, 32(4), 374–394.

Herschinger, E. (2014). Political Science, Terrorism and Gender. *Historical Social Research/Historische Sozialforschung*, 39(3), 46–66.

Hoffman, B., Ware, J. & Shapiro, E. (2020). Assessing the Threat of Incel Violence. *Studies in Conflict and Terrorism*, 43(7), 565–587.

Huckerby, J. (2020). In Harm's Way: Gender and Human Rights in National Security. *Duke Journal of Gender Law and Policy*, 27, 179–202.

Huckerby, J. & Ní Aoláin, F. (2018). Gendering Counterterrorism: How to, and How Not to – Part II. *Just Security*. www.justsecurity.org/55670/gendering-counterterrorism -to-part-ii/

Ingram, K. M. (2021). An Analysis of Islamic State's Gendered Propaganda Targeted towards Women: From Territorial Control to Insurgency. *Terrorism and Political Violence*. DOI: 10.1080/09546553.2021.1919637

Irshaid, F. (2015). Isis, Isil, IS or Daesh? One group, many names. *BBC News*, https:// www.bbc.co.uk/news/world-middle-east-27994277

Jacobsen, S. (2019). Calling on Women: Female-Specific Motivation Narratives in Danish Online Jihad Propaganda. *Perspectives on Terrorism*, 13(4), 14–26.

Jacques, K. & Taylor, P. J. (2013). Myths and Realities of Female-Perpetrated Terrorism. *Law and Human Behaviour*, 37(1), 35–44.

Johnston, G. & Johnston, M. S. (2017). 'We Fight for All Living Things': Countering Misconceptions about the Radical Animal Liberation Movement. *Social Movement Studies*, 16(6), 735–751.

Keenan, K. (2014). Gender Aspects of Terrorism in Urban Spaces. *Historical Social Research*, 39(3), 100–114.

Lahoud, N. (2018). Empowerment or Subjugation: An Analysis of ISIL's Gender Messaging. UN Women. https:// arabstates .unwomen .org/ en/ digital -library/ publications/2018/6/empowerment-or-subjugation

Laster, K. & Erez, E. (2015). Sisters in Terrorism? Exploding Stereotypes. *Women and Criminal Justice*, 25(1–2), 83–99.

Lorentzen, J. (2021). Women as 'New Security Actors' in Preventing and Countering Violent Extremism in Mali. *International Affairs*, 97(3), 721–738.

Macmaster, N. (2020). The FLN and the Role of Women during the War, in *Burning the Veil: The Algerian War and the 'Emancipation' of Muslim Women, 1954–62*. Manchester: Manchester University Press.

Masters, M. & Regilme, Jr., S. (2020). Citizenship Revocation as a Human Rights Violation: The Case of Shamima Begum. *E-IR*, 28 November. www.e-ir.info/2020/ 11/28/citizenship -revocation -as -a -human -rights -violation -the -case -of -shamima -begum/

Mattheis, A. (2018). Shieldmaidens of Whiteness: (Alt) Maternalism and Women Recruiting for the Far/Alt-Right. *Journal of DeRadicalisation*, 17, 128–162.

Mattheis, A. & Winter, C. (2019). The Greatness of Her Position: Comparing Identitarian and Jihadi Discourses on Women. *ICSR Report*, 15 May. https:// icsr .info/2019/05/15/the-greatness-of-her-position-comparing-identitarian-and-jihadi -discourses-on-women/

McCulloch, J., Walklate, S., Maher, J. & Fitzgibbon, K. (2019). Lone Wolf Terrorism through a Gendered Lens: Men Turning Violent or Violent Men Behaving Violently? *Critical Criminology*, 27(3), 437–450.

Mehran, W., Imiolek, D., Smeddle, L. & Springett-Gilling, J. (2020). The Depiction of Women in Jihadi Magazines: A Comparative Analysis of Islamic State, Al

Qaeda, Taliban and Tahrik-e Taliban Pakistan. *Small Wars and Insurgencies.* DOI: 10.1080/09592318.2020.1849898

Menzie, L. (2020). Stacys, Beckys, and Chads: The Construction of Femininity and Hegemonic Masculinity within Incel Rhetoric. *Psychology and Sexuality.* DOI: 10.1080/19419899.2020.1806915

Merger, S. (2018). When Is Terrorism Not Terrorism? When the Political Motivations Are Misogyny. Gender and War. www.genderandwar.com/ 2018/ 04/ 26/ when -is -terrorism-not-terrorism

Ní Aoláin, F. (2016). The 'War on Terror' and Extremism: Assessing the Relevance of the Women, Peace and Security Agenda. *International Affairs,* 92, 275–291.

Pain, R. (2014). Everyday Terrorism: Connecting Domestic Violence and Global Terrorism. *Progress in Human Geography,* 38(4), 531–550.

Pearson, E. (2020). Gendered Reflections? Extremism in the UK's Radical Right and al-Muhajiroun Networks. *Studies in Conflict and Terrorism.* DOI: 10.1080/1057610X.2020.1759270

Pearson, E., Winterbotham, E., & Brown, K. E. (2021). *Countering violent extremism: Making gender matter.* Springer Nature.

Petrich, K. & Donnelly, P. (2019). Worth Many Sins: Al-Shabaab's Shifting Relationship with Kenyan Women. *Small Wars and Insurgencies,* 30(6–7), 1169–1192.

Rowlandson, W. (2015). *Imaginal Landscapes: Reflections on the Mystical Visions of Jorge Luis Borges and Emanuel Swedenborg.* London: Swedenborg Society.

Schmidt, R. (2020). Duped: Examining Gender Stereotypes in Disengagement and Deradicalization Practices. *Studies in Conflict and Terrorism.* DOI: 10.1080/1057610X.2020.1711586

Shepherd, L. J. (2009). Sex or gender? Bodies in world politics and why gender matters. In L. Shepherd, (Ed). *Gender Matters in Global Politics* (pp. 29-42). London: Routledge.

Shifman, P. & Tillet, S. (2015). *To Stop Violence, Start at Home.* www.nytimes.com/ 2015/02/03/opinion/to-stop-violence-start-at-home.html

Sjoberg, L. & Gentry, C. (2015). *Beyond Mothers, Monsters, Whores: Thinking about Women's Violence in Global Politics.* Manchester: Zed Press.

Sjoberg, L. & Peet, J. (2011). A(nother) Dark Side of the Protection Racket. *International Feminist Journal of Politics,* 13(2), 163–182.

Speckhard, A. & Ellenberg, M. D. (2020). ISIS in Their Own Words: Recruitment History, Motivations for Joining, Travel, Experiences in ISIS, and Disillusionment over Time: Analysis of 220 In-Depth Interviews of ISIS Returnees, Defectors and Prisoners. *Journal of Strategic Security,* 13(1), 82–127.

Speckhard, A., Shajkovci, A. & Esengul, C. (2017). *Women and Violent Extremism in Europe and Central Asia: The Roles of Women in Supporting, Joining, Intervening in, and Preventing Violent Extremism in Kyrgyzstan.* New York: UN Women.

Szekely, O. (2020). Exceptional Inclusion: Understanding the PKK's Gender Policy. *Studies in Conflict and Terrorism.* DOI: 10.1080/1057610X.2020.1759265

Tinnes, J. (2020). Bibliography: Women and Terrorism. *Perspectives on Terrorism,* 14(2). www.universiteitleiden.nl/ binaries/ content/ assets/ customsites/ perspectives -on-terrorism/2020/issue-2/12.-tinnes-2.pdf

True, J. (1996). Feminism, in S. Burchill & A. Linklater, with R. Devetak, M. Paterson & J. True (Eds), *Theories of International Relations.* New York: St Martin's Press.

UN Human Rights Council (2014). *Rule of Terror: Living under ISIS in Syria.* Report of the Independent International Commission of Inquiry on the Syrian Arab Republic, 19 November. UN Doc. A/HRC/27/CRP.3.

UNDP (2021). Misogyny: The Extremist Gateway. *Extremism in Focus Issue Brief*, 2. Oslo: UNDP Governance Centre.

UNICEF & International Alert (2016). 'Bad Blood': Perceptions of Children Born of Conflict-Related Sexual Violence and Women and Girls Associated with Boko Haram in Northeast Nigeria. www.international-alert.org/publications/bad-blood

United Nations Security Council (2016). *Report of the Secretary-General on conflict-related sexual violence. S/2016/361/REV.1.* New York: United Nations.

Vale, G. (2019). *Women in Islamic State: From Caliphate to Camps*. The Hague: International Centre for Counter-Terrorism.

White, J. (2022). *Gender Mainstreaming in Counter Terrorism Policy*. London: Routledge.

Winterbotham, E. (2018). Do Mothers Know Best? How Assumptions Harm CVE. Global Institute Global Challenges. https://institute.global/policy/do-mothers-know-best-how-assumptions-harm-cve

Winther, K. (2018). *Exit: Leaving Extremism Behind*. Oslo: Norwegian Film Institute.

14   Collaborative approaches to countering terrorism

Lara A. Frumkin and Paul Ford

On 3 June 2017, eight people were killed and 48 injured in a pre-planned attack by three terrorists who used a vehicle to ram pedestrians on London Bridge in the United Kingdom's (UK) capital city, killing two. The van used then crashed onto Borough High Street, close to London Bridge, where the terrorists got out and began attacking citizens with knives. Off-duty police officers and civilians engaged the attackers and were stabbed during the attack, with the terrorists killing five people in the adjoining market and one slightly thereafter. Armed officers arrived eight minutes after the initial emergency call was made and the terrorists were shot dead within 20 seconds of the police arriving at the scene. The entire event lasted only 10 minutes. This attack came fewer than three months after the Westminster attack (March 2017) and under two weeks after the Manchester Arena bombing during an Ariana Grande concert (May 2017).

Of the three attackers on 3 June 2017, two were known to the police. Khuram Shazad Butt had been questioned by the police previously and was investigated but ultimately classed as a low police priority. Youssef Zaghba was being monitored continuously while residing in Italy by Italian law enforcement who informed the UK authorities about Zaghba and their concerns. Rachid Redouane was the only one of the three not known to the police.

Success in countering terrorism is often borne of tragedy, and the terrorist attacks at London Bridge are no exception. The police operational tactics employed during this attack were formulated through the application of Operation Plato (London Government, 2016), a strategy created to respond to terrorist firearm attacks in which the assailants move at fast pace. This policy application was a significant step up for law enforcement agencies in the UK and moved policing from a 'threat containing and negotiation resolution' position to one of 'confronting and neutralising'. The application of this policy remains a proportionate response to an extreme terrorist threat which was independently evaluated and confirmed by Lord Toby Harris, the Independent Reviewer of Terrorism and Member of the Joint Committee on

National Security Strategy within the UK Parliament. Although the tragedy at London Bridge resulted in loss of life, the operation itself was largely reported as successful in preventing a higher number of deaths (Harris, 2017). This was the first time that UK police had used these tactics to eliminate a terrorist threat. The subsequent 'Run, Hide, Tell' strategy was launched as a result of this incident.

The 2011 Blackett Review of High Impact Low Probability Risks undertook an extensive consultation with both subject matter experts and the intelligence community. This yielded 11 recommendations designed to strengthen government approaches to terrorist threats. Interestingly, six of the recommendations are related to greater collaboration between intelligence communities and those external to them who hold subject area expertise, such as academics. According to the Blackett Review (2011), academics could lend their expertise to the credibility of key risk assumptions held by the intelligence community, support analysis, aid detection of early signs of threat, consider the best way to engage in communication regarding risk and provide scrutiny to risk assessment. All in all, these are positive steps for academics who are interested in working with law enforcement personnel with respect to data analysis.

We do not know if the London Bridge attack would have ended differently, or not have occurred at all, had academic researchers been involved in tracking Zaghba or Butt. We do know that many academics are keen to work alongside law enforcement on counterterrorism (CT) strategy and many in law enforcement welcome such overtures to progress their own work, reinforcing the Blackett Review (2011) recommendations.

The relationship between academics and law enforcement agencies has improved recently with efforts to provide sound evidence-based research, securing fresh perspectives in sustainable strategic and operational CT outcomes. Forces in the United States (US), UK, New Zealand, Australia and Canada have developed evidence-based processes, applying rigorous academic research techniques to measure what works in CT strategy.

The UK College of Policing defines evidence-based policing (EBP) as 'an approach in which police officers and staff work with academics and other partners to create, review, and use the best available evidence to inform and challenge policing policies, practices, and decisions'. Law enforcement is well equipped to devise strategies and operations to respond quickly to terrorist attacks, and in some cases to prevent them, e.g., the UK has an extensive history in dealing with Irish Republican, far right and Islamist extremism (Sinclair, 2014). Academic CT researchers often have the luxury of time and rigorous research methods to investigate how and why a terrorist might undertake an attack, so combining efforts might yield even better CT outcomes.

Cultivating relationships

Studying concepts as broad as terrorism has always been challenging and considering the different approaches law enforcement and academics take when researching terrorism only further muddies the waters. The key factors that complicate relationships between academia and CT policing remain trust, confidence, access to sensitive data and competing interests (Lum and Kennedy, 2012). These often serve as barriers for undertaking targeted research and until the value of EBP is realised across law enforcement, effective collaboration remains limited (Lum and Koper, 2017). It is therefore important to develop and cultivate relationships with law enforcement agencies who are engaging in relevant work which complements and furthers the existing terrorism literature. It is also worth reflecting on how particular researchers work with policymakers, law enforcement or government to inform agendas on terrorism research.[1] Without external perspectives, law enforcement is at risk of isolation of thought, stagnation of policy development and limited application of methodological rigour to achieve strong operational outcomes.

One of Sageman's (2014) critiques is that there is an 'unbridgeable gap' (p. 565) between academic researchers and the intelligence community. Since this critique, the Centre for Research and Evidence on Security Threats and the Defence and Security Accelerator were formed in the UK, and the National Counterterrorism Innovation, Technology, and Education Center in the US, all of which bring together academics, government and other stakeholder groups. These join a few other centres which were in operation prior to Sageman's critique, such as the US Minerva Research Initiative and the National Consortium for the Study of Terrorism and Responses to Terrorism. Centres such as these help link researchers, stakeholders and analysts, though more might be needed to help bridge the gap that Sageman highlights. Data hubs are also an emerging trend in policing and many forces have established Strategic Insight Teams dedicated to EBP, such as the one developed by the Metropolitan Police Service in 2018.

---

[1]   It should be noted that critical terrorism studies researchers may be opposed to this kind of collaboration. Please see the chapter by Achieng et al. in this book for a full discussion.

Government agencies are more interested in preventing people from engaging in terrorism than understanding the pathway to and through it. It should be noted that some police forces have established EBP research groups, bringing together academics and police officers to develop shared understandings, and might be interested in looking at the 'why' in addition to the 'prevent' approach. For example, Societies of Evidenced Policing that exist in the US, UK, Australia and New Zealand and the UK College of Policing do just that. Another such group is the UK CT Evidence-Based Review Group established in 2021 in partnership with the Counter Terrorism Policing Headquarters. This group seeks to support CT legitimacy and effective policing outcomes by liaising with multi-disciplinary academic researchers and is key in developing a vanguard of academic and CT partnerships.

Targeting, Testing and Tracking (Sherman, 2015) is a model where academic-style systematic analysis aids law enforcement in identifying high-priority problems. This is similar to an academic inductive methodological approach initially searching for patterns in data, for example, suspected terrorists' behavioural indicators of attack preparation. Once the analysis of the behavioural indicators is completed, results are disseminated to see if tracking could be implemented. Foiled attacks would establish the impact of the findings. If they are found to be useful, a result might be the implementation of a new method of detecting individuals engaging in reconnaissance for attack planning. The relationships between academia and law enforcement in using EBP such as the Targeting, Testing and Tracking model remain critical both in devising methodological approaches and interrogating incoming data.

When researchers from different disciplines such as psychology and political science work together, they must adapt and find a common language to communicate with each other. Interdisciplinarity of this sort has allowed for cross-fertilisation of research and approaches to data analysis. Research projects that might have otherwise not been undertaken could be considered in those interdisciplinary cracks and crevices (Silke, 2004). A common thread among CT academics across disciplines is the tendency to delve into the underlying reasons someone might engage in terrorism or political violence. The emphasis is to seek to understand why something is happening, how a person got to a particular point and what the triggers were for those behaviours. Academic and law enforcement collaborations similarly need to find a common language. Indeed, this is noted by Anderson (2017), though he also states that terminology is important when information is shared as academics and law enforcement may use similar words to mean different things, for example, data.

The importance of data

Fundamental to effective CT research is access to good-quality and accurate data. UK policing is not currently in a position to capture accurate, measurable and valid data sets. This means that considerable time is required to assess, identify limitations and clean data where appropriate. Police collect most demographic data on a voluntary basis and therefore these data are often skewed and have gaps (such as ethnicity or age reporting) (Ford, 2021). The operating parameters of CT policing make it both difficult to access primary data to conduct research on suspected terrorists and assess useful secondary data contained within police databases as it is often incomplete. Accurate data are key to undertaking good-quality research, and Ford's (2021) study identified several shortcomings in how data were collected, recorded and analysed. The police service should consider how to improve data collection as this would provide better opportunities for quality research.

Even if good data are available, in intelligence community research analysts provide findings to law enforcement as finished products. This does not foster a culture where other analysts may access and interrogate data to see if they reach the same conclusions as the original researcher. Furthermore, intelligence analysts do not always describe the analytical method used, and data often come from multiple, inconsistent sources and via different collection processes (e.g., interviews, crime reporting, witness statements) which may impact the rigour of a study. This makes it challenging to conduct analysis with the level of scrutiny that academic research mandates. Using data in this way tends to rely on the analyst's own analytical skills, which may or may not use meticulous methodological techniques, and depends on the analyst's own interpretation of the data to draw conclusions.

From an academic standpoint, the term 'data' usually means empirical evidence gathered in furthering the understanding of a given research question. This is done in a standardised way, with the study having been through a university ethics committee review to ensure anonymity, confidentiality and lack of deception where possible. Academics typically expect a full description of the methods used, excerpts of the data and, with increasing regularity, access to the raw data for themselves. This approach to data analysis, reporting and availability of data for interrogation is therefore at odds with CT analytical methods.

The types of CT data that law enforcement and academics use are different as well. Historically, much of the academic research used secondary data when researching terrorism or writing theoretical pieces on the subject (Silke, 2001); law enforcement on the other hand has access to primary data. This allows for quite different forms of analysis and the ability to draw theoretical versus more concrete conclusions. As Schuurman points out in his chapter in this book, recently there has been an increase in the use of primary data in terrorism studies with almost 60 per cent of articles now using some form of it. This shift provides a valuable opportunity for a bridge between practitioners and academics, if data are to be shared.

In government, evidence gathering may take an unsystematic approach that drives forward a CT agenda which is at odds with the academic promotion of knowledge. For example, government data collection may involve a case study approach of gathering background information on a person of interest with some evidence to predict what sorts of actions the person might undertake. There is, however, no ethics committee or concern with protecting participants, primarily because the participants are those suspected of engaging in nefarious activities. Law enforcement will gather empirical evidence by interviewing suspects or persons who can provide information about a suspect. They may look at crime reporting or use information collected covertly. This approach of collecting primary data should broadly resonate with academics (perhaps not the covert data collection part). Both academics and law enforcement begin their research with a question to answer; for academics the question stems from findings of prior studies which help to direct the next steps in research. For law enforcement, research questions are most often based on reporting about a suspect. However, law enforcement data collection may not be done in a way academics would consider sufficiently rigorous. Furthermore, law enforcement data are not always stored in a single database (Anderson, 2017). They may be found in regional databases which officers will need to access, search and then collate with other information about a particular suspect.

This allows for data to be broadly accessible by those in law enforcement, though they have been collected in different ways by different people and this might be problematic to meet academic data requirements. Additionally, academics are trained on various methodological and data analytic techniques which are not required for all CT analyst careers. Thus, academics could engage in a thorough analysis of the data but might not be willing to if they cannot evidence that the data were collected in an ethical and consistent manner. As Sageman (2014) points out, there are instances when the intelligence community data are sufficiently thorough, collected in a rigorous way and credible but the community is unable to use it to its full potential due to inadequate training in data analysis. On the other hand, academics possess the skills to engage in thorough methodological data analysis but the quantity and quality of data available to them once cleaned may be insufficient to draw valuable conclusions (Knight and Keatley, 2019), partly evidencing Sageman's 'unbridgeable gap' (Sageman, 2014: 565).

Academics endeavour to use data to target and test existing theories, or develop new theories, based on findings from rigorous research (Sherman, 2015). The findings are then shared in the academic community and beyond, including with policymakers and those in law enforcement. Academics disseminate their findings and sometimes make available their data, so that others may scrutinise their work. Law enforcement's goals are to bring a person to justice so providing a version of academia's open science practices into the CT fray might lead to cooperation challenges. This is hardly surprising as many traditional organisations such as policing retain a 'status quo bias' (Kahneman, 2013) maintaining current practice over innovation. Even when intelligence analysts engage in strategic projects they do not typically publish and share their findings, rather they use that information to better understand how to refine their tradecraft.

A possible key to cooperation in analysis is shared trust and having a pool of academics who are security cleared to work with law enforcement researchers. This is under way in some circles and Davies (2017) argues this enhances beliefs that law enforcement research can be trusted. A focus on what academic research could do in assisting law enforcement analysis needs to be undertaken broadly. Much academic CT research takes a problem-solving approach (Al-Kassimi, 2019) which fits well with the requirements of law enforcement. Reliance on evidence and the scrutiny of that evidence by external parties is crucial. Allowing academics and external reviewers to look at raw data, support analysis and interrogate findings is essential. This approach could lead to a working partnership, albeit a one-way relationship.

There has been a convergence between insider (law enforcement) and outsider (academic) research in the context of key developments to law enforcement research and policing more generally (Davies, 2017). On the one hand, 'outside' law enforcement scholars are incentivised to work collaboratively with insiders as part of knowledge exchange funding schemes. On the other hand, the police in particular have become increasingly driven by an evidence-based approach encouraging greater analytical capabilities of insiders. This blurring of outsiders and insiders brings a series of advantages to law enforcement research, including enhancing methodological techniques, opportunities for knowledge exchange, wider dissemination of results and greater policy impact. In order to continue down this cooperative path, law enforcement needs to adopt a reflexive approach asking wider research questions than simply 'what works' (Davies, 2017).

Analytical approaches

In both academic and intelligence-focused research, a key goal is to use data to draw conclusions about an initial question. In academia, the questions could be 'what do we notice about behaviour when people are lying' or 'what political ideologies lead us to suspect someone is a terrorist'. In law enforcement, we may come across similar questions but the way they are phrased might be 'why did a suspect engage in particular behaviours' or 'is that a sign of terrorist activity'. Some intelligence analysis techniques are similar to academic research methods, but there are others that are specific to intelligence researchers. Three intelligence-specific analytic approaches are discussed here.

Intelligence cycle

A common model used in law enforcement research is called the intelligence cycle. This may also be used by military analysts, who sometimes overlap with law enforcement, especially if it comes to looking at suspected terrorist activities overseas. The intelligence cycle is more commonly used by intelligence and law enforcement agencies (e.g., FBI) than the other models and information about it is readily available online (e.g., www.intelligencecareers .gov/icintelligence.html). It has less psychological science behind it than the Assessment of Competing Hypotheses (described below) though it is effective in delivering conclusive pieces of intelligence. There are some variations in labels used within the cycle, though most feature the same general ideas. The cycle discussed here covers the following: planning, collection, processing, analysis and dissemination. Others might use the term 'direction' instead of 'planning' or include a review component at the end. A commonality across these modules is that they are cycles, implying that intelligence analysis and research are never ending. Just like with academic research, we need to consider the data and then go back and reassess them. It could be a political change that alters the conclusions, more refined methodological techniques or new data that had not been previously used.

The first stage in the cycle, planning, is about learning what the big questions are that need to be addressed. Unlike with academia, these are questions that are generated at high levels in law enforcement or by policymakers, including the prime minister or president. The questions will guide what sort of hypotheses researchers consider and will help to form a plan about how to engage in data gathering and analysis.

The second stage is collection, which is similar to when academic researchers engage in data collection. Most law enforcement research questions are derived from practical topics that need answering. These could be things such as 'why do some people follow a radicalisation pathway' or 'how can buildings be made more secure from terrorist threats'. In both cases, there are specific data necessary to address the research question. Some data collected will come from interviews with suspected terrorists, or they may come from physical or technical surveillance. Human sources can provide a plethora of useful information, but law enforcement needs to go through a lengthy vetting process with human sources. They also need to determine if the source could know the information and is willing to provide it or is serving as a double agent. Too often law enforcement believed a source who was not acting in good faith and sometimes this has resulted in the death of law enforcement personnel.

In addition to desk research and human intelligence, technical and physical surveillance comes from a range of sources. These can come from signals, such as phones or other technology. They may also come from images, such as satellites or even social media. Open sources may provide useful information in research. Much like an academic who uses discourse analysis to investigate news reporting, a law enforcement researcher might review open-source information for data about a particular threat or hot spot for terrorist activity. Neither ethics applications nor approval are needed for intelligence data collection, unlike academic work, though sometimes a request for data needs to be approved by a court.

In processing, researchers need to take the data they have collected and develop them into something useable. At one level this means simply organising the data in a way that allows them to be analysed. With quantitative data, it may require cleaning and depositing them into one database. With qualitative data, it might involve transcribing the data or getting them translated into the researcher's own language. Satellite or social media data might need to be standardised such that synthesis with other pieces of data can all be put together.

Analysis in law enforcement is similar to, but encompasses more than, academic analysis. At one level, law enforcement analysis involves evaluating and analysing the data to produce a coherent picture to answer the research question. It is usually the discussion section of academic research where researchers fit their analysis into the larger research picture, linking it back to theory. For law enforcement, analysis does that but goes further; it asks for alternative explanations for the data. Is there a possibility that even though the data seem to point to X event, it could be that event Y will take place instead? In addition, rather than thinking about how the findings from the data fit into the larger theoretical picture, law enforcement researchers must think about the threat picture and if there are opportunities for intervention. This may not sit comfortably with academic researchers who are used to using their findings to contribute to knowledge. Law enforcement research is about finding the threat, warning the appropriate people and stopping it.

Dissemination, or finished intelligence, may be thought of as having an academic paper published. The distribution list is far narrower, usually law enforcement analysts disseminate their final reports to the person who requested it and into the intelligence community. The finished product could deliver a warning about a potential threat, or it could provide technical assistance, such as how to secure bridges from potential terrorist attacks. It could simply provide information about day-to-day events, such as unrest in particular communities that might be susceptible to extremist behaviours. The information may be used to guide policy, judicial or military action; it may be used to refine the research question, in which case the analyst starts on the intelligence cycle again.

Assessment of Competing Hypotheses

A well-known method amongst intelligence analysts is the Assessment of Competing Hypotheses (ACH) proposed by Richard Heuer (1999). It is used when people need to make decisions where an error could lead to a disastrous outcome. The goal of ACH is to lessen the risk, avoid confirmation bias and encourage critical thinking by comparison of various hypotheses.

This method allows for analysts to generate hypotheses from their research questions and to test them against the evidence available. When using ACH, the analyst needs to engage in four steps:

1. undertake a search for information/data;
2. organise the information/data to assist with its analysis;
3. analyse the data; and
4. write the findings for dissemination.

Broadly speaking this matches what academic research does with the exception of step 3, 'analyse the data'. Analysing the data in ACH is the stage where the analyst uses the data to refute, rather than simply test, a hypothesis. The hypothesis that is considered to be the truth (note in ACH a hypothesis is 'true' while in academia a hypothesis is supported) is the one with the least amount of data refuting it (Heuer and Pherson, 2010).

Dhami, Belton and Mandel (2019) argue that ACH requires the researcher to rate the data as consistent (or inconsistent) with each hypothesis, lending support to the hypothesis that has the greatest credibility as it has the least evidence against it. There is space to reassess the hypothesis as more data become available, thereby allowing for an iterative process in hypothesis support.

The way that data are organised and presented can influence how individuals process that information (Gigerenzer and Hoffrage, 1995). In fact, most information that comes in about potential terrorist attacks is fraught with what-ifs. ACH works by considering all the data against each of the hypotheses. If the data do not support the hypothesis, the hypothesis is rejected. If the data do support the hypothesis, it is retained. The researcher will continue to look for data to refute the hypothesis and if that occurs, the hypothesis may then be rejected. The hypothesis which has no data points disconfirming it is the one to be considered the truthful hypothesis (in intelligence terms), so a law enforcement team use it to proceed with their operation.

Analytical judgement is crucial in ACH; decisions about rejection and acceptance of hypotheses is based on numerical totals of data supporting each hypothesis, which is in turn based largely on an analyst's judgement. Further, it requires analysts to consider every piece of data in order to reject or continue to accept hypotheses. This is time-consuming and potentially ignores some context around the data, which could help elucidate whether it supports or rejects hypotheses. ACH might be problematic then if there is a reliable terrorist threat and answers are needed rapidly.

PESTEL model

Several police forces employ randomised control trials to evaluate the outcomes of academic research undertaken within policing. The opportunity to evaluate academic rigour to policing operations is broadly welcomed by law enforcement agencies that use several planning frameworks to assess strategic objectives. The PESTEL model (Frue, 2017) was originally developed by Francis J. Aguilar in 1964 and involves the collection and portrayal of information about external factors which have, or may have, an impact on law enforcement objectives. It is an analysis of the political, economic, social and technological factors in the external environment of an organisation, which can affect its activities and performance. However, the model is not without its limitations as it does not consider the internal factors of policing and is used to explore its listed factors externally rather than internally. So, if an organisation uses the model in isolation, the analysis will not provide an opportunity to match organisational strengths to existing requirements. Some PESTEL users oversimplify the amount of data used for decisions as it is easy to use insufficient data. The risk of capturing too much data may lead to 'paralysis by analysis'. The data used may be based on assumptions that later prove to be unfounded.

More recently, development and application of the National Decision Model (College of Policing, 2013) by UK law enforcement agencies focuses on building an information and intelligence picture to determine activity underpinned by a defined Code of Ethics. The key to effective outcome evaluation is the academic rigour to the research proposal and methodology that is applied. Utilising systematic and meta-analytic techniques enables effective scrutiny of qualitative and quantitative research design and assures a high-quality review of material.

Conclusion

We started this chapter by exploring the collaborative approaches between academics and CT analysts, recognising existing limitations to enhancing partnerships. Those early EBP trailblazers such as Sherman have empowered an effective route to strengthen and progress further collaboration. As society moves towards the use of data hubs, analysis of big data and innovative scientific research to provide solutions to CT strategy, there remains a clear case for further collaboration between academics and CT law enforcement. The rise of EBP as a model in which CT organisations can access the best possible research to deliver strong operational and strategic outcomes is compelling. Increased awareness amongst senior law enforcement decision makers of underpinning decision-making processes with a sound research-based approach leads to enhanced internal and external legitimacy and secures credible responses to the external scrutiny of associated policy and policing tactics.

Collaborative law enforcement and academic work is already established, and new CT researchers are in a good space to further this work. Academics have the skills and methodological knowledge but need to learn the law enforcement side. Linking with existing law enforcement–academic research frameworks will further strengthen collaboration. For example, at Arizona State University the Centre of Problem-Orientated Policing has been developed. The University of Michigan supports an Inter-University Consortium for Political and Social Research and at George Mason University, the Centre for Evidence-Based Crime Policy is focused on applying scientific research to policing policy. Law enforcement needs to be made aware of the value academics can bring to policing, especially as there is greater and greater emphasis on EBP academic research groups. The key to good law enforcement research is not only the collection of data but rigorous analysis and telling the story associated with those data.

Ensuring a consistent and applied approach requires persistence and buy in from all parties. It may be realised through improved familiarisation of what works and the opportunity to research emerging and topical issues, resolving the question often posed by senior law enforcement professionals of 'so what'. Through highlighting the mutual benefits of access to enhanced targeted research and to rich sources of data for both CT law enforcement and academics, we collectively may focus with precision on delivering an approach that both informs and protects society from the worst that terrorism intends.

References

Al-Kassimi, K. (2019). Critical Terrorism Studies (CTS): (State) (Sponsored) Terrorism Identified in the (Militarized) Pedagogy of (US) Law Enforcement Agencies. *Cogent Social Science, 5(1)*. https://doi.org/10.1080/23311886.2019.1586813

Anderson, D. (2017). Attacks in London and Manchester March–June 2017 Independent Assessment of MI5 and Police Internal Reviews Unclassified Report. https://assets .publishing.service.gov.uk/government/uploads/system/uploads/attachment_data/ file/664682/Attacks_in_London_and_Manchester_Open_Report.pdf

Blackett Review (2011). Government Office for Science, Blackett Review of High Impact Low Probability Risks. https://assets.publishing.service.gov.uk/government/ uploads/system/uploads/attachment_data/file/278526/12-519-blackett-review-high -impact-low-probability-risks.pdf

Davies, M. (2017). To What Extent Can We Trust Police Research? Examining Trends in Research 'on', 'with', 'by' and 'for' the Police. *Nordisk Politiforskning, 3(2)*, 154–164.

Dhami, M.K., Belton, I.K. and Mandel, D.R. (2019). The 'Analysis of Competing Hypotheses' in Intelligence Analysis. *Applied Cognitive Psychology, 33(6)*, 1080–1090.

Ford, P. (2021). A Study of Citizen Complaints about Counter Terrorism Policing. *UK College of Policing National Library*.

Frue, K. (2017). Who Invented PEST Analysis and Why It Matters. https://pestleanalysis .com/who-invented-pest-analysis/

Gigerenzer, G. and Hoffrage, U. (1995). How to Improve Bayesian Reasoning without Instruction: Frequency Formats. *Psychological Review, 102(4)*, 684–704.

Harris, T. (2017). Harris Review into London's Preparedness to Respond to a Major Terrorist Incident: Progress Report – One Year On. www.london.gov.uk/sites/

default/ files/ progress _report _ - _harris _review _into _londons _preparedness _to
_respond_to_a_major_terrorist_incident.pdf

Heuer, R.J. (1999). *The Psychology of Intelligence Analysis*. Washington, DC: CQ Press.

Heuer, R.J. and Pherson, R.H. (2010). *Structured Analytic Techniques for Intelligence Analysis*. Washington, DC: CQ Press.

Kahneman, D. (2013). *Thinking, Fast and Slow*. New York: Farrar, Straus and Giroux.

Knight, S. and Keatley, D.A. (2019). How Can the Literature Inform Counter-terrorism Practice? Recent Advances and Remaining Challenges. *Behavioral Sciences of Terrorism and Political Aggression*, *12(3)*, 217–230.

London Government (2016). *An Independent Review of London's Preparedness to Respond to a Major Terrorist Incident*. London Government. www .london .gov .uk/ sites/ default/ files/ londons _preparedness _to _respond _to _a _major _terrorist _incident_-_independent_review_oct_2016.pdf

Lum, C. and Kennedy, L.W. (2012). *Evidence-Based Counterterrorism Policy*. New York: Springer.

Lum, C. and Koper, C. (2017). *Evidenced Based Policing: Translating Research into Practice*. Oxford: Oxford University Press.

Sageman, M. (2014). The Stagnation in Terrorism Research. *Terrorism and Political Violence*, *26(4)*, 565–580.

Sherman, L.W. (2015). A Tipping Point for 'Totally Evidenced Policing': Ten Ideas for Building an Evidence-Based Police Agency. *International Criminal Justice Review*, *25(1)*, 11–19.

Silke, A. (2001). The Devil You Know: Continuing Problems with Research on Terrorism. *Terrorism and Political Violence*, *13*(4), 1–14.

Silke, A. (2004). An Introduction to Research on Terrorism. In A. Silke (Ed.), *Research on Terrorism: Trends, Achievements, and Failures*. London: Frank Cass.

Sinclair, G. (2014). Confronting Terrorism: British Experiences Past and Present. *Crime, History and Societies*, *18(2)*, 117–122.

15   Terrorism research practices in the private sector: context and considerations

Ross Frenett, Meghan Conroy, Carolyn Hoyle, Celia Davies, Nic Rees, Ludovica Di Giorgi and Catriona Scholes

Introduction

Although 'terrorism research' brings to mind prestigious journals and learned institutions, the majority of research in this sector takes place outside the academic context. However, the research outputs of talented analysts operating within government and the private sector are rarely placed in the public domain. As such, students and those wishing to better understand how terrorism research links to practice can sometimes have a limited understanding of how this is carried out in the private sector.

High-quality private-sector terrorism research shares many attributes with analysis within the academy. That said, there are a number of distinctive challenges faced by terrorism researchers within the private sector. This chapter will explore some of those challenges, drawing on examples and experiences of the authors as employees of Moonshot. Moonshot is a private company that specializes in countering violent extremism and other online harms. The company carries out paid terrorism research on behalf of a wide range of clients including the United States Agency for International Development, the United States State Department, the United Kingdom (UK) Home Office, Public Safety Canada, Google, and Facebook. This research includes deploying tools developed in house to collect and analyze relevant data from search engines, social media platforms, and encrypted messaging apps. Moonshot provides clients and partners with rapid analyses on evolving threat environments, and long-term monitoring of possible threats. It carries out monitoring and evaluation work to assess the efficacy of counter-extremism programming funded by our partners. In addition to executing research and analysis, Moonshot delivers campaigns and online interventions and undertakes capacity-building work with frontline practitioners. Each of these programmatic efforts is underpinned by rigorous research. This chapter will draw heavily on the processes and procedures Moonshot has developed over six years in operation as private-sector terrorism researchers attempting to balance analytical excellence with the profit motive.

Specifically, this chapter addresses the nature of decision maker-focused research and ethical safeguards in a client-centric industry. We will also explore the methodologies and processes used in rapid response research, a type of research common in the private sector but rare in the academy. We aim to grant students and practitioners some insight into the unique challenges faced by private-sector terrorism researchers.

Decision maker-focused research

Terrorism research carried out in the private sector has always been commissioned by an organization or individual for an explicit purpose. Although this may seem so obvious as to be unworthy of mention, it is highly relevant. Each piece of research is likely to impact a decision. For example, police departments that commission research might allocate scarce resources on the basis of a heat map deliverable. Meanwhile, technology companies may opt to update their terms of service based on analysis of threats on the platforms they manage, affecting millions. While much high-quality academic research languishes behind paywalls in journals, decision makers are often consuming the unpublished outputs of private-sector terrorism research to inform their choices.

Private-sector researchers in this field must take the time to understand the audience for the research outputs they're producing. If the audience has a very low level of knowledge around a given subject, conveying that information in a clear way is crucial. While some research is commissioned by organizations with large teams of subject matter experts who will devour 90-page reports in an afternoon, this is the exception. Many clients are time-poor. It's the job of the private-sector researcher to convey the key points in a way that will land with the reader.

Write for who your clients are, not who you'd like them to be.

If a chief executive officer, member of parliament, or senior civil servant is only likely to allocate three minutes to thinking about a problem, then your research output should fit on one page. If they are likely to allocate 30 seconds to thinking about an issue, you should consider a visual way of conveying your key findings. If a private-sector researcher writes journal-quality, longform pieces that the client cannot quickly and easily digest, the researcher is failing at one of their most basic duties: to convey information clearly to decision makers and empower them to make ethical, effective judgments.

This decision maker-focused research leads to private-sector terrorism researchers having a disproportionate reliance on visualizations and info-graphics compared with their academic counterparts. That, when coupled with the power of our clients to cause real harm to communities should they misunderstand our findings, means that we need to treat these visualizations with great care. To address this, Moonshot has developed documentation and training for all analysts on how to process, analyze, and present data to time-poor clients. Analysts are instructed to ask five key questions when planning a visualization:

- Where is this visualization going? Who will see it?
- Have I provided context?
- Can the visualization stand alone?
- Could a viewer misinterpret the visual?
- What story am I trying to tell?

Not every piece of data can be safely, accurately, and ethically visualized. If there is a risk that time-poor clients and decision makers could misinterpret data, it is the responsibility of the private-sector researcher to find a form of expression that works for the client or simply to provide recommendations without the underlying data.

Although in general private-sector terrorism researchers operate with greater data access and a larger degree of freedom than their academic counterparts, this is not always the case. The client relationship can create legal obligations for private-sector terrorism researchers. An example of this is the Regulation of Investigatory Powers Act (RIPA) in the UK. RIPA is the UK law governing the use of covert techniques by public authorities. It requires that when public authorities, such as the police or government departments, need to use covert methods to obtain private information about someone, they do it in a way that is necessary, proportionate, and compatible with human rights. Crucially, this legislation covers contractors, so private-sector organizations like Moonshot must be RIPA compliant in our research carried out on behalf of any UK government clients. Similar laws exist in other jurisdictions, and often place private-sector researchers in the somewhat unusual situation of considering themselves arms of the state for compliance purposes.

Ethical safeguards in a client-focused industry

A fundamental difference between research carried out in an academic context and that carried out in the private sector is the client–customer relationship. The dynamic establishment between researcher and client is imbalanced; terrorism researchers operating in the private sector need to be conscious of the common pitfalls which can bedevil the ethical and effective private-sector terrorism researcher. In an era of large-scale data extraction, private-sector terrorism researchers and their clients run the risk that their role is understood to be the mining and visualization of data at scale. It is not. The role of the private-sector terrorism researcher is to provide expertise *underpinned* by data.

Clients, be they government agencies or private-sector organizations, often hire researchers not to gain true insight but to grant credibility to pet theories. This can manifest itself in subtle ways, such as attempting to set up the terms of reference in a way likely to produce one set of results. However, sometimes it's more obvious. Moonshot researchers have in the past been asked to gather data to back up client suppositions that a certain percentage of a given population was sympathetic to extremism. Although we – of course – did not do this, any researcher entering the private sector must be prepared to push back when clients make these kinds of requests. This pushback could lead to contract termination and, naturally, loss of profit.

Paid projects involving qualitative research with vulnerable individuals are fraught with ethical hazards. In particular, private-sector clients funding research will sometimes attempt to tie payment milestones to numbers of interviews conducted with certain types of vulnerable individuals. This commoditizing of personal stories must be resisted at the contract stage by private-sector terrorism researchers, whether they are freelancers or large companies. Should a payment be linked to an arbitrary number of interviews conducted with former extremists or survivors, researchers could be forced to choose between placing undue pressure on potential subjects to consent to interviews and the financial wellbeing of their firm.

Business development

Private-sector terrorism researchers who fail to secure new work will not be terrorism researchers for long. The demands of business development are relentless. With this in mind, strict rules surrounding business development are required for terrorism researchers and practitioners in the private sector. Indeed, the source of funding must be closely scrutinized; for example, the potential client may be a government with a poor human rights record. Reports from organizations such as Human Rights Watch and Freedom House can and should be used to guide these conversations and decisions. Moreover, the project's thematic focus must be probed: Does the scope of work raise ethical concerns relating to the client's political or economic interests? What is the intended use of any outputs we provided? What unintended, but foreseeable, uses could our findings be put to?

The pressures of the profit motive often encourage private-sector companies to exaggerate their capabilities – and private-sector terrorism research is no exception. However, this temptation to exaggerate poses great ethical challenges. If the client believes that a data snapshot is a comprehensive picture of the threat landscape, they may make policy decisions – including enforcement decisions – on the basis of flawed data. Finally, the risks to local partners must be closely considered. Too often private-sector terrorism researchers partner with local experts and subsequently place them in danger and fail to provide long-term support.

Although in the short term ethical constraints on client acquisition by private-sector terrorism researchers can lead to reduced business, in the long term researchers who obey strict ethical standards can benefit from the 'ethical advantage'. Most obviously, if a private-sector terrorism researcher or company gains a reputation for high ethical standards, clients for whom this is a priority will seek to work with them. A more subtle competitive advantage enjoyed by ethical private-sector terrorism researchers involves data quality. Much unethical terrorism research involves gathering data on large groups of people perceived to be 'at risk' due to a protected characteristic, rather than any actions they have taken. Firms that accept work monitoring innocent people are not only engaging in unethical and harmful behavior that could make the world less safe, they are also gathering wholly useless data that grant them no insight into how radicalization actually works. Ethical terrorism researchers, on the other hand, only gather useful data, and therefore build their understanding of the complexities of radicalization and develop their own in-house expertise in a way that becomes a competitive advantage.

Internal controls

Given the myriad harms that could emerge from terrorism research in the private sector, firm ethical procedures should be established and strictly adhered to. To meet this challenge, Moonshot appointed a Director of Ethics and established an internal Ethics Committee. The director and committee have a mandate to provide guidance and support to Moonshot staff in designing and implementing ethically sound and responsible work while simultaneously fostering a culture of challenge. The Ethics Committee is drawn from across different bands and areas of subject matter and organizational expertise, and excludes the companies' co-chief executive officers. The team members who comprise the Ethics Committee rotate periodically – with the exception of Moonshot's Director of Ethics – in order to ensure diverse perspectives are integrated into our ethical framework.

The Ethics Committee convenes regular ethics workshops and drop-in sessions that allow a safe space for colleagues to discuss ethical issues related to our work. Given the time-sensitive nature of our work, the committee makes itself available for one-to-one or group sessions to talk through ethical questions that may arise on a day-to-day basis and can provide rapid feedback, oversight, and approval. The Ethics Committee provides a channel for ethical concerns from team members to be raised to leadership and develops process documents to support ethical decision making and tool design.

Although ethics committees are still not common in private-sector terrorism research, more and more clients are demanding that contractors reach high ethical standards. A dynamic, representative, and rapid response ethics team is one way of achieving this.

External controls

Beyond internal systems, Moonshot commissions an annual audit of the overall policy and operational framework within which the company manages its approach to ethics. The auditors review organizational policies and procedures, specifically documentation relating to ethics, values, and human rights. Additionally, staff from across the organization are interviewed without management present. The outcomes of the audit are published.[1] As above, this is not yet common practice, but as firms with strict ethical controls continue to capture market share, it is growing in popularity.

---

[1]   https://moonshotteam.com/adapt-ethics-audit/

Peer review

In the academy, peer review is a useful tool to ensure self-regulation of a discipline's intellectual and evidential standards. Typically, this manifests in the form of several select reviewers editing a manuscript within their remit before it is published. While rigorous peer review doubtless helps ensure quality control, we have found that having one or two reviewers from the same field does not beget the same quality as bringing diverse reviewers into the fold. The greatest contributor to private-sector quality control is the hiring of individuals from diverse backgrounds, including racial, ethnic, gender, educational, socioeconomic, geographic, and professional backgrounds. Diversity in every possible category is essential to the health of private-sector terrorism research and the broader counterterrorism and countering violent extremism space.

Risk assessment, risk mitigation, and 'do no harm'

Because so many private-sector research projects are experimental, risk assessment and mitigation is a significant consideration in project design and implementation. A risk is an unwanted event resulting from actions or behaviors. Private-sector researchers can have impact and produce risks depending on how they interact with their context. To identify risk, researchers need to place activities in context and understand both audience and environment. This should be done through research, research, research. There are several types of risks that private-sector terrorism researchers must grapple with before, during, and after the completion of a project:

- legal risks;
- reputational risks;
- ethical risks; and
- security risks.

Knowing about risk is not the same as mitigating risk. Once a risk is identified researchers must make a conscious decision to take one of the below actions:

- *Accept.* In some cases, researchers may accept the risk and not act on it, maybe because of its low impact/likelihood. Always monitor and track these risks where possible in case things change.
- *Reduce.* Take action to control or minimize the risk, but without changing the research strategy.
- *Avoid.* Proactively change your strategy to avoid the risk, such as canceling an activity to ensure risk does not occur.
- *Transfer.* Move the risk onto another person or organization, or decide to share the risk with them. All parties must agree to this approach.

What level of risk researchers are willing to accept depends on the organizational culture as well as the rules and regulations under which it operates. It is important to bear in mind that even after researchers have reduced risks by planning control and mitigation measures, there will always be a certain amount of risk remaining that cannot be controlled. These are called the residual risks, and researchers should remain aware of these throughout a project. With that in mind, risks are not only posed to the researchers involved, but also to the subjects of the research being carried out.

'Do no harm' is not just an ethical principle to bring conflict sensitivity to policies and programs. Rather, it is a tool to turn principle into practice. Specifically, in the context of Moonshot's work, it is a set of techniques used to avoid causing inadvertent harm through actions or behaviors. Private-sector researchers in every stage of their projects should use the 'Do no harm' principle to avoid facilitating inadvertent harm. A way to ensure adequate risk assessment and mitigation is to follow the 'Do no harm' cycle as outlined in Figure 15.1.

Figure 15.1   The 'Do no harm' cycle

Timescales: Rapid response research

Private-sector terrorism researchers often operate on enormously different timescales to those in academia. Although medium-term and long-term analysis carried out over weeks or months are common, rapid response reports due within hours of an event are core features of terrorism research practices in the private sector. This brings with it unique challenges.

Analysts conducting rapid response research need to be meticulously trained and have well-established processes and procedures if they are to yield useful insights in the midst of uncertainty. Before a team can carry out rapid response work, they must prepare. An unprepared rapid response researcher is useless at best and dangerous at worst.

Preparation

Rapid response research is, by its nature, unpredictable. It can often take place at unsociable hours or on holidays. Those planning on carrying out rapid response research in the private sector need to ensure that teams are available when an incident takes place. This involves agreed-upon rotas and remuneration as well as clearly defined expectations. Researchers on call need to be reachable at all hours. To safeguard against the possibility that a key researcher is unavailable when called upon, a backup team should also be rostered. The requirement to have teams on standby at all times, with backup researchers, makes rapid response research highly resource intensive.

A team operating in the midst of a crisis needs clarity as to who is due to carry out what role and where decision-making power is vested. In a crisis, rapid judgments will need to be made as to what data to include, what to leave out, what to draw the client's attention to, and what recommendations to make. These can only be made by one person who has been agreed upon ahead of time. Other roles to consider include client manager, data extraction specialist, subject matter expert, and lead writer, among others. In small teams, some of these roles will be merged, though this should be clear from the outset. Additionally, each team must assign a quality assurance lead regardless of team size. The quality assurance lead acts as a type of rapid peer reviewer, and must not have involvement in any other part of the research.

Modern rapid response research mostly involves the gathering and analysis of social media and other online data. While manual analysis of these platforms is theoretically possible, doing so at scale and at pace is only possible with the use of specialized data-gathering tools. There are myriad tools available that claim to grant insight into conversations on social media.

While private-sector terrorism researchers often have the funds available to purchase access to these tools, very few are actually suitable for terrorism researchers. Many tools only cover mainstream platforms such as Twitter, where a dwindling proportion of extremist communication takes place. Other tools have rate limits, which make them unsuitable for rapid research, or only allow broad queries, which are of very little use to terrorism researchers interested in niche movements and ideas. These limitations have led to many private-sector terrorism researchers – including those at Moonshot – to develop bespoke data-gathering tools suitable for our use cases. All tools, whether bespoke or off the shelf, need to be prepared and maintained if they are to be of use to rapid response researchers.

Rapid response research takes place in highly unstable information environments, where disinformation and wild speculation are the norm. Researchers hoping to produce useful outputs need to have prepared an agreed-upon indicator database, which allows them to cut through the noise and identify conversations taking place among those sympathetic to or openly engaging with extremist movements. The exact nature of these indicators will vary depending on the platforms being analyzed, the data extraction tools available, and the language and types of terrorism being studied. What is certain is that these databases cannot be improvised *during* an incident; preparation is critical to successful rapid response.

It is imperative to expect that data extraction systems and tools often don't work as expected. Teams hoping to successfully carry out this form of research need to practice regularly between incidents. Practice sessions should include sub-optimal conditions, for example removing the use of individual platforms. Teams engaging in this type of research need to be trained in how to use data extraction platforms, how to write in the in-house style, and simple data visualization and quantitative measures. Because of the very nature of rapid response work, researchers responsible for the work may be tired and under emotional stress. The only way to ensure quality output is to engage in regular structured training exercises.

Process

Once an incident has taken place and rapid response research has been requested the client manager should make contact with the client and seek to reconfirm key information such as deadline, scope, and purpose. It is vital that there is no confusion as to any of the above points. Scope and purpose can and will vary greatly depending on the client type. A government agency may be interested in reaction to an attack within other extremist groups, perhaps fearing escalation or retaliation. A social media company on the other hand may be solely focused on the effect of an attack on their platform and ensuring robust enforcement of terms of service.

Although passionate researchers will often want to dive straight into data extraction and analysis, it's essential that rapid response research teams are all briefed on deadlines, communication channels, scope, responsibilities, and check-in points before they begin their work. Particular attention should be paid to ensuring that teams are aware of any disturbing material they may come across in the course of the analysis.

If you have prepared, you should already have lists of indicators ready and properly formatted for the data extraction tools you plan to use. Now that an incident has taken place, you will likely need to update these indicators. In order to do this, you will need to rapidly workshop incident-specific indicators with the relevant subject matter experts. Categories to consider include location names, names of individuals connected to the incident, and hashtags used on social media to discuss the incident.

As discussed, rapid response teams must ensure that data extraction tools, off the shelf or in house, are working properly. All tools should be checked to ensure they are gathering data and that download functions are working as expected. At the beginning of a piece of rapid response research, a glitch in your systems can be resolved; however, if it is discovered later on, this could be disastrous for both the researchers and the client.

When carrying out rapid cross-platform data extraction, there are a number of pitfalls researchers need to avoid, mitigate, and manage. The most serious of these involve risks to the researchers themselves and possible threats to the public. As rapid response research often takes place while an incident is unfolding, content that breaches social media platforms' terms of service is often readily available for collection and analysis.

Researcher wellbeing

Researchers engaged in rapid response research must be made aware that they are at heightened risk of coming into contact with graphic material. In the hours after an attack or other incident requiring monitoring, many platforms contain graphic material that will later be removed for breach of terms of service. Clear processes to manage the impact of this must be established. These include short-term mitigating tactics such as viewing material in pairs, on black and white screens, and making clear that researchers can and should step away at any time. Longer-term mitigating measures must also be put in place, in particular the supply of counseling services to any researcher likely to come into contact with graphic material.

Public safety

In the aftermath of incidents, threats of further attacks or retaliatory violence are commonplace. Rapid response researchers who come across threats to public safety must assume these have not been seen by others and respond immediately to protect public safety. Researchers should follow a clear and pre-established escalation procedure such as the one outlined in Table 15.1.

In the case of organized trolling or doxing where there is no obvious threat of violence, the targets should be directly informed if contact information can be found. This should include an overview of what was observed and a recommendation that the targeted person makes their social media profiles private for protection purposes.

Data hygiene

While incidents are unfolding, there are often attempts by malign actors to amplify certain hashtags or narratives. It is vital that researchers scrutinize their data and do not report inauthentic activity to decision makers as fact. Beyond malign actors, data can sometimes be inaccurate simply due to dual-use phrases and words. For example, in the aftermath of the 2020 Nice stabbing, Moonshot was tasked by a client to assess the conversation surrounding the attack on a global scale. As Nice has the same spelling as 'nice', initial extracts showed the conversation gaining unprecedented traction among global audiences.

Upon completion of data extraction, analysis, writing, and quality assurance, rapid response teams must hold wash-up meetings. The purpose of these meetings is to note any challenges encountered and create clear action plans to address them. These meetings should be held immediately on completion of rapid response research projects and before memories of faulty extraction techniques or unclear processes fade.

Once this has been done, rapid response teams should return to their usual cadence of practice and drills while patiently awaiting the next time they are called upon.

Conclusion

Private-sector terrorism research should not be unduly exceptionalized; high-quality research methods translate across sectors. However, the context in which private-sector terrorism research takes place does place distinctive pressures on researchers for which those considering it as a career should be prepared.

Table 15.1 Risk escalation procedure

Risk tiers	Definition	Qualifiers	Escalate to	Request removal from platform	Time of escalation/ reporting
Tier 1: Threat to Life (with identifiable time frame)	A threat to life happens when, because of a deliberate intention or the criminal act of another, a researcher identifies a: • real and immediate threat to a loss of life • threat to cause serious harm • threat of injury to another A threat to life also includes: • serious sexual assault • rape 'Real and Immediate' means: • a risk that is reasonably assessed to be real • the potential assailant has the intention and current ability to carry out the threat	Identifiable time frame, e.g. where the intended victim is attending a specified event Severity of threat Identified suspect Identified victim	Police via the appropriate emergency number for jurisdiction 911, 999, or 112	Yes	Immediate upon analyst identification

Risk tiers	Definition	Qualifiers	Escalate to	Request removal from platform	Time of escalation/ reporting
Tier 2: Threat to Life (without identifiable time frame)	A threat to life happens when, because of a deliberate intention or the criminal act of another, a researcher identifies a: • real and immediate threat to a loss of life • threat to cause serious harm • threat of injury to another A threat to life also includes: • serious sexual assault • rape 'Real and immediate' means: • a risk that is reasonably assessed to be real • the potential assailant has the intention and current ability to carry out the threat	Time frame is not indicated/identifiable Severity of threat Identified suspect Identified victim	Report via appropriate online police portals in your jurisdiction	Yes	Immediate upon analyst identification

Risk tiers	Definition	Qualifiers	Escalate to	Request removal from platform	Time of escalation/reporting
Tier 3: Encouraging violence against another/ encouraging suicide	Encouraging violence Intentionally encouraging the commission of an offense, in this case violence upon another person Encouraging suicide An act that is capable of encouraging or assisting the suicide of another person	Encouraging violence to be committed against an identifiable person Encouraging an identifiable person to commit suicide Identified suspect Identified victim	Report via appropriate online police portals in your jurisdiction	Yes	Once daily

Drawing on examples from Moonshot, a private company that tackles online harms including but not limited to violent extremism, this chapter briefly touches upon the unique dynamics of the client relationship and the nature of ethical safeguards in the private sector, as well as offering some suggestions to overcome the challenges created by rapid response research.

For any more detail, we'll have to charge you.

16 Ethics and terrorism research: the rights, safety and vulnerability of participant and researcher

John F. Morrison, Eke Bont and Andrew Silke

Introduction

In recent years we have seen a significant increase in primary research in terrorism studies (Schuurman, 2020). With this proliferation comes a growing need for us all to consider how this primary data collection and analysis can be carried out in the most ethical manner. Having comprehensive ethical considerations as a cornerstone of modern terrorism research protects the research subjects and the researcher, and in turn safeguards the autonomy of the research areas, emphasising the integrity of knowledge. The development of ethically sound research designs can streamline the data collection process, as advanced ethical and risk planning is much easier than resolving ethical dilemmas in the midst of the data collection process.

However, up until recently ethics was an often ignored aspect of terrorism research. Methods sections of empirical papers have too often overlooked the importance of outlining how ethical issues were considered, the ethical frameworks followed and/or the ethics review process preceding data collection. In a recent systematic review of contemporary disengagement and deradicalisation research, two of the present authors observed a dearth of consideration of research ethics. Of the 54 pieces of empirical disengagement and deradicalisation research between 2017 and 2020 identified for consideration in the review, only nine made any mention of gaining ethical approval for the research. This is not to say that ethical approval was not gained for the other 45 pieces of research. It may be that the authors and/or editors did not deem this to be important enough information to be included in the final publication. If this is in fact the case, then they are mistaken. Notification of ethical approval *is* important information to transfer to the reader. It demonstrates the fidelity and efficacy of the research and researchers alike.

It does appear though that the tide is slowly turning, and there is now a growing appreciation of the importance of ethics within our research. This is exemplified by the publication of a 2021 special issue of the journal *Terrorism and Political Violence* on the topic of ethics in terrorism research. Within that special issue the present authors proposed the development of the Framework for Research Ethics in Terrorism Studies (FRETS) (Morrison, Silke & Bont, 2021). This was developed to assist chairs and reviewers of university research ethics committees in completing reviews of terrorism studies ethics proposals, in as objective a manner as possible. It is also envisaged that this framework could and should be used by researchers to guide the development of their research designs, methodologies and ethics proposals. Within FRETS (see the Appendix for a full copy) we proposed six core areas which needed to be taken into consideration by all interested parties. These are:

1. participant's rights, safety and vulnerability;
2. informed consent;
3. confidentiality and anonymity;
4. researcher's rights, safety and vulnerability;
5. data storage and security-sensitive materials; and
6. the ethical review process.

There is nothing inherently unethical about terrorism research. Rigorous, ethical and low-risk data collection is a possibility, and is in fact the norm. As with all areas of research, including analogous subjects such as criminology and conflict studies, there are fundamental ethical guidelines which researchers should follow. Research into these topics does not inevitably imply sympathy for any set of actors or their actions, just as criminological research, for example, does not necessarily carry an implication of sympathy or support for the criminal actors or police policies.

That said, researchers of terrorism have at times resisted being pigeon-holed as neutral on issues related to the subject. It is well worth reflecting on the 2022 experience of the Centre for Analysis of the Radical Right (CARR), for example. Early in the year, over a dozen researchers affiliated with CARR publicly resigned in protest following the publication of a controversial blog, 'Beware of Anti-Fascists', on the CARR website. CARR initially defended the publication, arguing that the Centre 'will always be non-aligned'. This, however, only intensified matters and provoked a letter of protest signed by 27 current and former CARR members which rejected such an interpretation of CARR's orientation. The signers argued instead that they explicitly 'oppose the rise of the far right and we work to support unequivocally anti-fascist values'. Shortly afterwards, CARR's director resigned from the organisation, the original offending blog was removed from the CARR website, the CARR fellowship of the blog's author was terminated and a public apology over what had happened was released. CARR also committed to a period of reflection and review in terms of the organisation's working practices, processes and orientation. Inevitably, CARR's reputation took some damage as a result of the affair.

Writing in 1988, Schmid and Jongman famously observed that the terrorism researcher's 'role is not to "fight" the terrorist fire; rather than a "firefighter", [the researcher] should be a "student of combustion"' (p. 179). It is worth reflecting on how that principle applies to much if indeed not most terrorism research? Terrorism research has consistently included applied research focused on real-world problems and issues. One consequence of this has been that much research has had a direct or indirect function of helping to produce solutions to such problems. Similar trends have been seen in other fields of research with strong applied foci on real-world problems such as criminology and forensic psychology. Neutrality, of course, is not the same as objectivity, and bias has long been recognised as a potential problem in terrorism research (just as it can be for all research). These issues, however, are very much live in the context of contemporary terrorism studies and add an important element for reflection in the context of research ethics.

Ultimately, at the heart of all areas of research has to be a concern that the research should do no undue harm to the participants, researchers or any other actors either directly or indirectly linked to the research. This needs to be a guiding principle at all stages of the research from design to data collection, analysis to dissemination of results. In order to be successful in achieving this we need to first be aware of any general and unique issues relating to participants' and researchers' rights, safety and vulnerability. Building on the development of FRETS this chapter will primarily focus on the safety and vulnerability of both participant and researcher. This has been designed to emphasise both the contrasts and similarities between these two areas. This in no way should be seen as a value judgement in terms of the importance of these ahead of any other factors outlined in the FRETS guidelines. Each and every one of those aspects are of significant importance in our consideration of research ethics in terrorism studies and are in fact all interconnected. For example, if the storage of sensitive interview or observational data is breached or compromised, this can in the most extreme circumstances have a significant impact on the safety of both the participant and the researcher. This, or any other ethical breach, can in turn have a detrimental impact on the trust which participants may have in engagement in future academic research.

The impact of Boston College

This deterioration of trust in the research process has been witnessed first hand by authors of this chapter. Each of us engages in primary research in the context of Northern Ireland. This involves interviewing former republican paramilitary actors about the Troubles and their involvement within it. Traditionally this has been a population who have been willing to engage in the research process. However, in recent years we have observed a growing distrust of academic research, and a reticence to be as openly involved as before. It has been commented time and time again that this growing reticence and distrust dates back to Boston College's 'Belfast Project'. This was an oral history research project which ran from 2001 to 2006. The study involved researchers interviewing a series of individuals who had been involved in paramilitary activity during the Troubles. Participants were guaranteed by the interviewers that their interviews would not be published or made public in any way until they had passed away. This was designed to allow participants to be upfront and open in their recollections and their views without fear that this could have an impact on their own person safety.

In 2010 the book *Voices from the Grave* was published, and contained within it was the analysis of the interviews with two of the participants, David Ervine and Brendan 'Darkie' Hughes. Both men had passed away, thus allowing for their interviews to be published. In the same year another participant, Dolours Price, gave a media interview where she acknowledged her participation in the project, intimating that she had given details in her interviews on those who had participated in the unsolved murder of Jean McConville. With these assertions being made the Police Service of Northern Ireland (PSNI) called for the release of the interviews to assist them in their ongoing investigations into the conflict. While the individual researchers on the project have continuously resisted and challenged the legislative pressure being placed, the PSNI have been able to gain access to at least some of the recordings, some of which have subsequently been used in criminal investigations and as evidence in court cases in Northern Ireland.

Although well intentioned, the researchers involved in the Belfast Project were not able to fulfil the assurances given to participants and at the time of writing significant legal issues connected to the research are still ongoing (16 years after the research itself finished). The case demonstrates that without iron-clad and consistent clarity with respect to the rights of the participants and what their involvement precisely entails, this can negatively impact not just one's current research. It can also have significant long-lasting impacts on the willingness that participants have to be involved with future research and their overall trust in the academic research process. Each of the three of us have heard through our own independent research potential participants intimating that prior to the Boston College affair they would have been more than willing to engage in the research process. But the impact of Boston College has made them reticent to engage, and even if they did, they would not be able to be as open and honest as they may previously have been.

All of this goes to show that while we need to take research ethics seriously, a lax and inconsistent approach to research ethics can also have a detrimental impact on existing researchers and participants, as well as future research and researchers' opportunities. With this the possibilities we have in gaining a more in-depth understanding of terrorism and terrorist involvement will diminish.

Thinking about how we assess ethical risks

Assessing ethical risks in terrorism studies research, what the potential impact might be and how these risks can be mitigated requires definitional and conceptual clarity. Overall, risk captures the potential harm caused by an event in light of its likelihood and expected consequences. A useful way to conceptualise ethical risk in terrorism research is to see it as the product of three factors:

- *Threats*: the likelihood of specific ethical issues being realised, given the research focus and methodology.
- *Vulnerability*: relative exposure of proposed research to ethical issues or the likelihood of a negative impact occurring should an issue occur.
- *Consequence*: harm that would result if ethical issues materialise.

Figure 16.1 illustrates one way for illustrating these relationships.

To start with, it is worth considering the specific threats faced by terrorism/violent extremism research. Many of these threats will be faced to some degree by research on other topics (e.g. organised crime research) though not always to a similar extent. Some threats include the type of problems which came to plague the Boston College Belfast Project – police and criminal justice agencies seizing or attempting to seize research material. Boston College represented a case of interview transcripts/recordings being the target, though other research material can also be targeted. For example, in 2015 the International Centre for the Study of Radicalisation (ICSR) based at King's College London

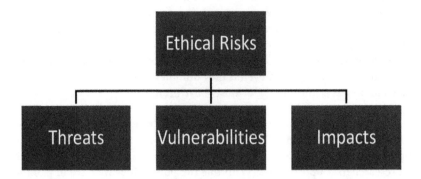

Figure 16.1   Ethical risks in a threat-vulnerability-impact model

was forced to hand over a video to the police (Burrell, 2015). The video had been filmed by fighters in Syria and uploaded to a public online platform but was subsequently deleted. The video had been collected from the website by ICSR researchers but was then deleted on the original platform. The police were granted a court order under the Terrorism Act, and King's College was compelled to provide the video. It is also possible for researchers to be arrested or detained for possessing/downloading terrorist-related material or because they are perceived to be a potential terrorist or terrorist sympathiser. This was the experience of Rizwaan Sabir in 2008 who was arrested and detained by police under the Terrorism Act. Sabir was a postgraduate student at Nottingham University and had downloaded an Al-Qaeda training manual and emailed it to a member of staff at the university. Sabir was conducting research on terrorist tactics as part of his programme, and the manual had been downloaded from a publicly available United States government website. He was held for seven days before being released without charge and later discovered he was subsequently wrongly included on a police database of terrorist offenders (Sabir, 2022).

More bureaucratic threats can include research being refused permission to start (or finding such approval very difficult to obtain) because university ethics/research committees are averse to terrorism-related research. Such aversion may relate to a political bias against such research, or because it is perceived as too dangerous/risky; or perhaps just because it is seen as too sensitive/contentious a topic for research (bearing in mind the experience of Boston College, for example). It is worth noting that FRETS was designed to assist with this issue (Morrison et al., 2021) and can help Institutional Review

Board/Human Research Ethics Committee[1] chairs and reviewers in completing reviews of terrorism studies ethics proposals in as objective a manner as possible (for more on this see below).

Threats may also be focused directly on the researchers and colleagues. This might take the form of physical threats potentially from terrorists and their supporters/sympathisers, but also there have been cases involving threats from state security organisations/individuals and their supporters/sympathisers. Similarly threats can take other forms, including psychological harassment (e.g. through social media) as well as legal harassment in the form of threats to sue either on an individual or institutional basis or through Freedom of Information requests which are intended to be harassing or attritional.

It is perhaps not surprising in such contexts that when we think of vulnerabilities, researcher burnout is increasingly being recognised as an issue in terrorism studies. This can result from a range of factors including the type of threat and harassment flagged above, but also can relate to issues such as the harmful effects of exposure to extremist content online, for example, or exposure to psychologically harmful real-world events connected to some types of field research.

Negative impacts can apply across a wide range of domains. This can include impacts on the individual researcher who suffers professional and personal reputational damage, to the research institutions which have housed or sponsored work (with both Boston College and CARR examples of different ways in which organisations can be affected). Potential impacts to participants in terrorism research loom especially large and it is to that subject that we now turn.

Participants' rights, safety and vulnerability

At the foundation of ethical research is the tenet that we as researchers should do no undue harm. However, the concept of harm is objectively difficult to assess. How do we measure degrees of harm, and to whom? When considering the aim of doing no undue harm we need to ask 'to whom?' Should we be only considering harm to the participant or the researcher? Or should we also be considering broader society, participants' families or even theonceptt of

---

[1] These are the institutional bodies mandated to assess ethical issues relating to research projects.

democracy (Taylor & Horgan, 2021)? Grossman and Gerrand (2021) challenge us to consider research the intersection between ethical and moral responsibility, and that we should not consider ethical terrorism research as a dyad of researcher and participant. But it is in actual fact a triad where we also need to consider the end user and consumer of the research.

For research to be truly ethical we must be able to consider the potential impact of the research on as wide a population as possible. In doing so though we must be realistic, and not overexaggerate the potential impact and/or reach of the research. While acknowledging the need to consider the potential impact of research on a broad population the present chapter considers the rights, safety and vulnerability of the two most distinct groups: participants and researchers.

Participants in terrorism research have the same rights as participants in any other form of research. This includes the right to confidentiality and anonymity, giving their informed consent before participating in the research and the right to withdraw/revise it after completion of the research. They also have the right to withdraw their participation at any time or refuse to answer any specific question without having to give a reason for this. No matter who the participant is, terrorist, practitioner or victim, they have these rights (e.g. British Psychological Society, 2018). It does not matter what an individual researcher's own personal beliefs are about the participant or the subject of the research, these basic rights of the participant must be constant. This can be most challenging when interviewing those who have been involved in illegal and/or violent activity. As Booth (2008) emphasises we need to acknowledge and recognise 'the human behind the "terrorist label"'. Following on from this we also need to recognise the human behind the victim, police, soldier, countering violent extremism practitioner and other such labels.

A large part of ethical research is the assessment of risks. The risks posed by any research are context and subject dependent. Many of the participants in terrorism research may in fact have a significant degree of risk in their lives to begin with. This is true for those who had previously been terrorist actors, victims of terrorism or members of the security services. These are not your 'traditional' participants in social science research. Therefore, rather than asking 'is there any risk for the participants in the research?' we need to ask 'is there significantly greater risk of harm to the participants than if the research was not conducted?'. In order to answer that we need to consider risk at all stages of the research process, from design to sampling, data collection to write-up. When considering the degrees of harm we need to consider their context and perspective, as well as our own. If we are to take an example of this we could ask, is it 'harmful' to discuss a terrorist attack with victims of terrorism? Would this bring about risk of retraumatising the victims, or their families? An Institutional Review Board/Human Research Ethics Committee may, understandably, perceive an interview about victimisation from terrorism as posing a risk of retraumatisation, and therefore class the research as unethical. However, research suggests that trauma victims may, at times, in fact benefit from sharing their experiences (Baele, Lewis, Hoeffler, Sterck & Slingeneyer, 2018). Just because a participant may endure emotional pain this does not mean that they are unwilling to participate in the research, or should be prevented from participating. In their analysis of the histories of 'the disappeared' in Northern Ireland, Lundy and McGovern (2006) observed that participants *wanted* to engage in the research process. This allowed them to tell their story and to raise awareness. In their eyes the benefits outweighed any emotional costs. This does not mean that structures of support should not be in place for these participants. But, it does demonstrate that the possibility of negative emotional effect should not in itself be a reason to consider research to be unethical. Added to this, when we are considering the emotional effect of participation in the research process we must not solely focus on the victims of terrorism and their families. Security officials and 'terrorists' can also be retraumatised by involvement in some form of research.

When we consider the rights, safety and vulnerability of participants, we need to be aware of the specific populations participating in the research and avoid any generic consideration of risk or harm. Within traditional social science research one of the most basic ethical issues is gaining informed consent from the participant. Within this process we as researchers have to provide the participants with adequate information for them to be able to come to a decision as to whether they wish to participate or not (Paluck, 2009). Traditionally this is obtained by getting written consent from the participant. Yet, for the populations participating in terrorism research this process may in its own way bring risk. For a range of reasons the notion of giving written consent may be deemed an unjustifiable risk for terrorists (both former and current), security officials and victims of terrorism. As researchers we therefore need to ask ourselves if a proposed process of gaining informed consent can pose a risk to participants. If it does then a safer approach needs to be established. This can be a form of oral consent or other more innovative methods. We should not feel tied to a traditional process just because of its prevalence of use. In order to be truly ethical researchers we must ask ourselves what is best within this specific situation for this/these specific participant/s.

As part of the informed consent process participants should be assured of the rights to anonymity and confidentiality. When we are actually anonymising the data of an interview, focus group or any other data collection technique we must do so much more than simply excluding or changing a participant's name. All identifiable aspects of the research must be removed or anonymised. This can include not disclosing the location of the research (Aldridge, Medina & Ralphs, 2008), or any mention of identifiable individuals, events or locations, unless relevant. The reason this is done is not just to protect the participants and the researchers, it is also to protect others indirectly impacted by the researcher. Following on from this if a participant asks for their contribution to be deanonymised we should not automatically agree to this, as it is not only for their own purposes that their data are anonymised. We must therefore take into account the potential impact of this process on all of those indirectly affected by the research.

Confidentiality and anonymity are not guarantees of data sources never being revealed. In the extremely rare situations where the participants reveal details relating to planned future illegal activity, or participants' involvement in an unsolved crime, the researcher is obliged to inform the police of their involvement. Always remember that the central tenet of ethical research is to do no undue harm to anyone either directly or indirectly impacted by the research. This includes potential victims of future criminality. Therefore, these caveats to confidentiality and anonymity need to be clearly outlined during the informed consent process.

Researchers' rights, safety and vulnerability

The psychological risks for terrorism researchers are under-researched, underestimated and often overlooked during ethical review processes (e.g. Sluka, 2015; Winter, 2019), likely due to a predominant focus on the psychological risks for participants (Baele et al., 2018). Most commonly suggested to affect researchers' emotional wellbeing are vicarious trauma and secondary traumatic stress, which arise as a consequence of empathically engaging with the narratives of trauma survivors (Devilly, Wright & Varker, 2009; Pearlman & Caringi, 2009; Pearlman & Saakvitne, 1995). While the impact of these concepts is increasingly recognised in helping professions and emergency services, their occurrence in researchers remains largely unexplored (Moran & Asquith, 2020; Nikischer, 2019; van der Merwe & Hunt, 2019).

Based on experiences of researching the militant jihad, extremism and suicide terrorism, Anne Speckhard described that upon returning home from fieldwork she often experiences 'a flood of feelings, flashbacks of terrifying events, as well as emotions expressed in terrifying nightmares' as well as, at times, an 'intense hyper-aroused state' (Speckhard, 2009, p. 218). Even months after a research trip, she says she sometimes finds herself upset and shaking when reading her notes. Speckhard mentions she finds comfort in 'not being alone in [her] responses to the material' (2009, p. 218), which suggests the importance of researchers sharing these experiences with one another. Researchers of similarly sensitive topics outside of terrorism research have also published personal reflections on how they were psychologically impacted, with resulting symptoms of secondary traumatic stress and/or vicarious traumatisation (Doná, 2014; Eades, Hackett, Raven, Liu & Cass, 2020; Moran & Asquith, 2020; Nikischer, 2019; Ratelle, 2013; Taylor, 2019; van der Merwe and Hunt, 2019; Williamson et al., 2020). Transcription may be especially affecting, given the repeated exposure to distressing narratives (Kiyimba & O'Reilly, 2016). Research using qualitative methods to analyse secondary data may also increase risk, as it involves closer engagement with the traumatic material (Meth & Malaza, 2003; Moran & Asquith, 2020; Whitt-Woosley & Sprang, 2018). Researchers can also experience emotional burnout, with one terrorism researcher admitting that despite his interest, he became 'emotionally weary and moody' from hearing about the lived experiences of some participants (Adeloye, Carr & Insch, 2020). William McGowan (2020) similarly experienced 'researcher burnout' following fieldwork for his doctoral research project on political violence and terrorism.

The potential emotional harm of exposure to violent or distressing online content and imagery has recently received attention following a publication by Charlie Winter (2019), where he reflected on his research on violent extremist material from jihadist groups. In a separate National Public Radio article which included interviews with various researchers on this topic, Winter disclosed there are moments his 'everyday life is invaded' by these images (Allam, 2019). Other terrorism researchers in this article, such as Seamus Hughes and Amarnath Amarasingam, shared similar experiences of this content 'haunting' them or 'permeating' their personal lives. While little is known on the effects of this content on researchers (Winter, 2019), other occupations such as war journalists and online content moderators have been found to be at risk for psychopathology and severe distress following frequent exposure to distressing and violent content (Arsht & Etcovitch, 2018; Cambridge Consultants, 2019; Feinstein, Audet & Waknine, 2014). This is also illustrated in the outcomes of court cases and lawsuits initiated by former content moderators. For example, Facebook agreed in May 2020 to pay $52 million to United States content moderators as compensation for mental health issues, such as post-traumatic stress disorder, that developed as a result of their work (BBC News, 2020).

In his publication, Winter stressed that the psychological risks of researching distressing materials must be foregrounded and factored into research designs due to this research becoming increasingly common following the proliferation of online terrorist and extremist content, and that further research must be conducted on this as existing evidence is largely anecdotal. Winter (2019) also shared recommended advice from an independently sought counsellor which 'worked for' himself personally, including the need for researchers to fully process distressing information and to stay grounded during the analysis process (pp. 11–12). The fact that Winter sought out this counsellor himself further illustrates the urgent need for terrorism researchers to have better support made available if and when they engage in potentially distressing research.

Researchers may encounter emotional issues that are not related to trauma, but objectivity. Terrorism researchers have reflected on the difficulties of regulating or concealing emotional responses while interviewing (e.g. Dolnik, 2013; Feenan, 2002; McGowan, 2020; Morrison, n.d.; Nilsson, 2018; Speckhard, 2009), and the challenges of emotional distancing and maintaining neutrality (e.g. Chaitin, 2003; Gallaher, 2009). This may be especially relevant when a researcher interviews a 'terrorist' actor, given their (prior) involvement in violence or their extremist views (e.g. Sluka, 2015). For example, in a Talking Terror podcast episode, Vidhya Ramalingam reflected on the 'emotional toll' of interviewing the far-right movement as a woman of colour (Morrison, n.d.). Similarly, Gallaher (2009, p. 128) stated she was surprised 'by the intensity' of her emotional reactions to her research on a far-right movement, and would feel anger, anxiety and an 'urge to tell [her] informants just how wrong' she thought they were. In situations like this, it is helpful for the researcher to recognise the humanity and the person behind the label of 'terrorist' (Booth, 2008).

An alternative issue is that researchers may develop empathy for those studied (Breen-Smyth, 2009; Feenan, 2002). As a result, researchers may fear being accused of supporting terrorism or legitimising violence, despite that research into this topic does not imply sympathy for the actors or their actions (Jones & Bhui, 2008). Nonetheless, due to the charged political nature of terrorism and political violence, it may be impossible to claim complete research objectivity (Breen-Smyth, 2009; Lee, 1995) and further reflection on this topic is required. Researchers have also described feelings of guilt and shame arising due to perceptions of not making a perceived positive difference or being powerless to help victims, for exposing others (e.g. research assistants) to the content or for generating 'data' and 'profiting' from other people's traumas (Allam, 2019;

Drozdzewski & Dominey-Howes, 2015; Nikischer, 2019; Speckhard, 2009; Taylor, 2019; Williamson et al., 2020).

Given that research is largely anecdotal, empirical exploration of this topic is urgently required. Support should also be made available to researchers, as well as adequate training, psychoeducation and monitoring (Dickson-Swift, James, Kippen & Liamputtong, 2008, 2009; Loyle & Simoni, 2017; Whitt-Woosley & Sprang, 2018). This responsibility should fall to those leading research projects, funders and research institutions, as it would benefit them in turn given that researcher wellbeing will minimise ethical problems and enhance the quality of important research (Baele et al, 2018; Dickson-Swift et al., 2008; Winter, 2019).

Conclusion

With the welcome proliferation of data-driven terrorism research it is an imperative that parallel to this must be the continued evolution and development of how we ensure that the research carried out is of the highest ethical standard possible. These ethical approaches must take into consideration the rights and safety of participants, researchers and those others who could potentially be directly or indirectly impacted by the research. While the research and data analysis must be objective, so too must the ethical review process. We believe that the FRETS presented here provides a model which can assist in the review process.

This chapter has emphasised ethical issues which researchers have encountered in their research. These were not presented to criticise the researchers. On the contrary, these were presented to illustrate how a robust, clear and objective ethical review process can support researchers in the development of ethically sound and viable research. Inherently our ethics does, and should, concentrate on the rights and safety of our research participants. Participants in terrorism research have the same rights as participants in any form of research. This includes, but not exclusively, the right to confidentiality and anonymity, giving their informed consent before participating in the research and the right to withdraw/revise it after completion of the research. These rights hold irrespective of affiliation, viewpoints or identity. In our efforts to ensure these rights we need to consider the specific contexts in which participants find themselves and assess the most appropriate ways to proceed in the securing of these rights, while not impinging on the rights and/or safety of others.

Alongside this must be a continued emphasis on the rights and safety of the researchers. Within terrorism research many of us engage with disturbing topics and data. It is inherent on us to acknowledge this and to put in place mechanisms and structures of support to ensure that engagement in this research does not impinge on our physical and/or psychological wellbeing. For this to be most effective we believe that there is space for future research projects to be focused on gaining an in-depth understanding of terrorism researcher welfare. This should consider all forms of terrorism research and data. Such a data-driven approach to researchers' welfare can help to build on the foundations of knowledge presented here. It can assist in developing well-grounded protocols which can in turn assist in the continued development of a hospitable environment for us to carry out our research.

References

Adeloye, D., Carr, N., & Insch, A. (2020). Conducting qualitative interviews on sensitive topics in sensitive places: the case of terrorism and tourism in Nigeria. *Tourism Recreation Research*, 45(1), 69–79.

Aldridge, J., Medina, J., & Ralphs, R. (2008). Dangers and problems of doing 'gang' research in the UK. In F. Van Gemert, D. Peterson & I. Lien (Eds). *Street Gangs, Migration and Ethnicity* (pp. 44–59). Cullompton: Willan.

Allam, H. (2019). 'It gets to you': extremism researchers confront the unseen toll of their work. *National Public Radio*, 20 September, www.npr.org/ 2019/ 09/ 20/ 762430305/it-gets-to-you-extremism-researchers-confront-the-unseen-toll-of-their -work?t=1605092512189

Arsht, A., & Etcovitch, D. (2018). The human cost of online content moderation. *Harvard Journal of Law and Technology*, 2 March.

Baele, S. J., Lewis, D., Hoeffler, A., Sterck, O. C., & Slingeneyer, T. (2018). The ethics of security research: an ethics framework for contemporary security studies. *International Studies Perspectives*, 19(2), 105–127.

BBC News (2020). *Facebook to Pay $52m to Content Moderators over PTSD*. www.bbc .co.uk/news/technology-52642633

Booth, K. (2008). The human faces of terror: reflections in a cracked looking-glass. *Critical Studies on Terrorism*, 1(1), 65–79.

Breen-Smyth, M. (2009). Subjectivities, 'suspect communities', governments, and the ethics of research on terrorism. In R. Jackson, M. Breen-Smyth & J. Gunning (Eds). *Critical Terrorism Studies: A New Research Agenda* (pp. 194–215). Abingdon: Routledge.

British Psychological Society (2018). *Code of Ethics and Conduct*. www.bps.org.uk/news -and-policy/bps-code-ethics-and-conduct

Burrell, I. (2015). Police use anti-terrorism laws to seize video material from King's College, London. *Independent*, 30 October, www.independent.co.uk/ news/ uk/ crime/police-use-anti-terrorism-laws-to-seize-video-material-from-king-s-college -london-a6715086.html

Cambridge Consultants (2019). Use of AI in online content moderation. www.ofcom
.org .uk/ research -and -data/ internet -and -on -demand -research/ online -content
-moderation

Chaitin, J. (2003). 'I wish he hadn't told me that': methodological and ethical issues in
social trauma and conflict research. *Qualitative Health Research*, 13(8), 1145–1154.

Devilly, G. J., Wright, R., & Varker, T. (2009). Vicarious trauma, secondary traumatic
stress or simply burnout? Effect of trauma therapy on mental health professionals.
Australian and New Zealand Journal of Psychiatry, 43(4), 373–385.

Dickson-Swift, V., James, E. L., Kippen, S., & Liamputtong, P. (2008). Risk to researchers in qualitative research on sensitive topics: issues and strategies. *Qualitative
Health Research*, 18(1), 133–144.

Dickson-Swift, V., James, E. L., Kippen, S., & Liamputtong, P. (2009). Researching sensitive topics: qualitative research as emotion work. *Qualitative Research*, 9(1), 61–79.

Dolnik, A. (2013). Up close and personal: conducting field research on terrorism in
conflict zones. In A. Dolnik (Ed.). *Conducting Terrorism Field Research: A Guide*
(pp. 228–254). New York: Routledge.

Doná, G. (2014). The psychological impact of working in post conflict environments:
a personal account of intersectional traumatisation. *Intervention: Journal of Mental
Health and Psychosocial Support in Conflict Affected Areas*, 12(1), 91–94.

Drozdzewski, D., & Dominey-Howes, D. (2015). Research and trauma: understanding
the impact of traumatic content and places on the researcher. *Emotion, Space and
Society*, 100(17), 17–21.

Eades, A. M., Hackett, M., Raven, M., Liu, H., & Cass, A. (2020). The impact of vicarious
trauma on indigenous health researchers. *Public Health Research and Practice*, 31(1).

Feenan, D. (2002). Researching paramilitary violence in Northern Ireland. *International
Journal of Social Research Methodology*, 5(2), 147–163.

Feinstein, A., Audet, B., & Waknine, E. (2014). Witnessing images of extreme violence: a psychological study of journalists in the newsroom. *JRSM Open*, 5(8),
2054270414533323.

Gallaher, C. (2009). Researching repellent groups: some methodological considerations
on how to represent militants, radicals, and other belligerents. In C. L. Sriram, J.
King, J. Mertus, O. Martin-Ortega & J. Herman (Eds). *Surviving Field Research:
Working in Violent and Difficult Situations* (pp. 127–146). New York: Routledge.

Grossman, M., & Gerrand, V. (2021). Terrorism confidential: ethics, primary data
and the construction of 'necessary fictions'. *Terrorism and Political Violence*, 33(2),
242–256.

Jones, E., & Bhui, K. (2008). The new ethics of research into terrorism. *BMJ*, 337(1),
a3069–a3069.

Kiyimba, N., & O'Reilly, M. (2016). The risk of secondary traumatic stress in the qualitative transcription process: a research note. *Qualitative Research*, 16(4), 468–476.

Lee, R. (1995). *Dangerous Fieldwork*. Thousand Oaks, CA: Sage.

Loyle, C. E., & Simoni, A. (2017). Researching under fire: political science and
researcher trauma. *PS: Political Science and Politics*, 50(1), 141–145.

Lundy, P., & McGovern, M. (2006). The ethics of silence: action research, community
'truth-telling' and post-conflict transition in the north of Ireland. *Action Research*,
4(1), 49–64.

McGowan, W. (2020). 'If you didn't laugh, you'd cry': emotional labour, reflexivity and
ethics-as-practice in a qualitative fieldwork context. *Methodological Innovations*,
13(2), 2059799120926086.

Meth, P., & Malaza, K. (2003). Violent research: the ethics and emotions of doing research with women in South Africa. *Ethics, Place and Environment*, 6(2), 143–159.

Moran, R. J., & Asquith, N. L. (2020). Understanding the vicarious trauma and emotional labour of criminological research. *Methodological Innovations*, 13(2), 2059799120926085.

Morrison, J. F. (n.d.). Vidhya Ramalingam: researching the far right. *Talking Terror*, podcast.

Morrison, J., Silke, A., & Bont, E. (2021). The development of the Framework for Research Ethics in Terrorism Studies (FRETS). *Terrorism and Political Violence*, 33(2), 271–289.

Nikischer, A. (2019). Vicarious trauma inside the academe: understanding the impact of teaching, researching and writing violence. *Higher Education*, 77(5), 905–916.

Nilsson, M. (2018). Interviewing Jihadists: on the importance of drinking tea and other methodological considerations. *Studies in Conflict and Terrorism*, 41(6), 419–432.

Paluck, E. (2009). Methods and ethics with research teams and NGOs: comparing experiences across the border of Rwanda and DRC. In C. L. Sriram, J. King, J. Mertus, O. Martin-Ortega & J. Herman (Eds). *Surviving Field Research: Working in Violent and Difficult Situations* (pp. 38–56). New York: Routledge.

Pearlman, L., & Caringi, J. (2009). Living and working self-reflectively to address vicarious trauma. In C. A. Courtois & J. D. Ford (Eds). *Treating Complex Traumatic Stress Disorders: An Evidence-Based Guide* (pp. 202–224). New York: Guilford Press.

Pearlman, L., & Saakvitne, K. (1995). *Trauma and the Therapist: Counter-Transference and Vicarious Traumatisation in Psychotherapy with Incest Survivors*. London: Norton.

Ratelle, J. F. (2013). Making sense of violence in civil war: challenging academic narratives through political ethnography. *Critical Studies on Security*, 1(2), 159–173.

Sabir, R. (2022). *The Suspect: Counterterrorism, Islam, and the Security State*. London: Pluto Press.

Schmid, A., & Jongman, A. (1988). *Political Terrorism: A Research Guide to Concepts, Theories, Data Bases, and Literature*, 2nd ed. Amsterdam: North-Holland.

Schuurman, B. (2020). Research on terrorism, 2007–2016: a review of data, methods, and authorship. *Terrorism and Political Violence*, 32(5), 1011–1026.

Sluka, J. A. (2015). Managing danger in fieldwork with perpetrators of political violence and state terror. *Conflict and Society*, 1(1), 109–124.

Speckhard, A. (2009). Research challenges involved in field research and interviews regarding the militant jihad, extremism, and suicide terrorism. *Democracy and Security*, 5(3), 199–222.

Taylor, M., & Horgan, J. (2021). Primum non nocere – first do no harm. *Terrorism and Political Violence*, 33(2), 221–224.

Taylor, S. (2019). The long shadows cast by the field: violence, trauma, and the ethnographic researcher. *Fennia*, 197(2), 183–199.

van der Merwe, A., & Hunt, X. (2019). Secondary trauma among trauma researchers: lessons from the field. *Psychological Trauma: Theory, Research, Practice, and Policy*, 11(1), 10–18.

Whitt-Woosley, A., & Sprang, G. (2018). Secondary traumatic stress in social science researchers of trauma-exposed populations. *Journal of Aggression, Maltreatment and Trauma*, 27(5), 475–486.

Williamson, E., Gregory, A., Abrahams, H., Aghtaie, N., Walker, S. J., & Hester, M. (2020). Secondary trauma: Emotional safety in sensitive research. *Journal of Academic Ethics*, 18(1), 55–70.

Winter, C. (2019). *Researching Jihadist Propaganda: Access, Interpretation, and Trauma.* Washington, DC: Resolve Network.

Appendix: Framework for Research Ethics in Terrorism Studies

Participants' rights, safety and vulnerability

1. Is there evidence that human participants, or those indirectly influenced by the research, are being put in significantly greater physical or psychological risk than if the research was not conducted? *If yes, answer question 2.*
2. Has the researcher provided an adequate mitigation plan to assuage any research-based risks for the participant(s)? *If no, the ethics application cannot be approved until the researchers have developed an appropriate mitigation plan. If an appropriate mitigation plan is deemed not to be achievable the proposal cannot be approved.*
3. Have the researchers provided adequate information on how they will recruit and contact participants, demonstrating where necessary how the participants' safety has been taken into consideration? *If no, clarification should be sought from the researcher.*
4. Could participation in the research potentially negatively emotionally affect/retraumatise participants? *If yes, answer question 5.*
5. Are adequate support structures in place? *If no, the ethics application cannot be approved.*

Informed consent

1. Is there a process in place to gain informed consent? *If no, answer question 2.*
2. Has an appropriate reason (e.g. participant's or researcher's safety) been given for not seeking informed consent? *If no, researchers need to be recommended to develop a procedure for securing informed consent.*
3. Does the informed consent process pose any potential risks to the researcher, participant or anyone else? *If yes, researchers need to develop a new approach to gaining informed consent.*

Confidentiality and anonymity

1. Will participants' data be anonymised and confidential? *If no, answer question 2.*
2. Has an adequate reason been given not to anonymise and/or treat the data confidentially? *If no, researchers should be asked to revisit this.*
3. For those projects with anonymised and confidential data, is there a comprehensive anonymisation and confidentiality process in place? *If no, the researchers must be asked to revisit this process.*
4. Has an appropriate mitigation strategy been adopted to protect participants' confidentiality bearing in mind legal requirements? *If no, the researchers must be asked to revisit this process.*
5. Have participants, if relevant, been informed of the fact that they forgo their right to confidentiality if they give information relating to planned criminal activity, or their criminal involvement in a live case? *If no, researchers need to be asked to include this in their informed consent processes, if relevant to the research and participants.*

Researchers' rights, safety and vulnerability

1. When considering the research methodology, topic and research context combined, is there considered to be any level of risk to researcher(s)? *If yes, answer question 2.*
2. Have appropriate mitigation protocols been put in place? *If no, ethical approval cannot be granted until appropriate protocols are in place.*
3. Will any of the research team have to view violent or disturbing imagery? *If yes, answer question 4.*
4. Are appropriate structures in place institutionally, or external from the institution, to support researchers' welfare? *If no, ethical approval cannot be granted until these structures are in place.*
5. Is it deemed safe for the researcher(s) to disclose full information about their research to participants and other significant individuals and bodies? *If no, answer question 6.*
6. If relevant, has the concealment of any research information from participants or other relevant actors been ethically justified? *If no, further clarification on concealment must be sought from the research team.*
7. Do researchers have the appropriate experience and/or are appropriately trained to carry out the research safely? *If no, ethical approval cannot be granted until training has been completed.*

Data storage and sensitive materials

1. Will the research involve the analysis of security-sensitive materials? *If yes, answer questions 2, 3 and 4.*
2. Will the security-sensitive materials be stored securely and legally? *If no, the ethical approval cannot be granted.*
3. If the security-sensitive material requires dissemination are there secure and legal means to do this? *If no, the ethical approval cannot be granted.*
4. Will the security-sensitive materials only be accessible to the designated researchers? *If no, the ethical approval cannot be granted.*

The ethical review process

1. Is there clear evidence that the reviewers' decisions have been based on the specific research proposal submitted? *If no, this proposal requires a new independent review.*
2. Is there any evidence of external biases influencing the reviewers' decisions? *If yes, this proposal requires a new independent review.*
3. [If the proposal was rejected] Would this research have been approved if the research subject was not related to 'terrorism'? *If yes, answer question 4.*
4. Has there been clear, and appropriate, rationalisation as to why the terrorism studies nature of the research has led to the proposal's rejection? *If no, this proposal requires a new independent review.*
5. Would any adjustments proposed be deemed appropriate for non-terrorism research utilising the same methodologies? *If no, answer question 6.*
6. Has there been clear, and appropriate, rationalisation as to why the terrorism studies nature of the research has led to these adjustments? *If no, these adjustments need to be reconsidered, changed or rationalised.*

PART IV

The future of terrorism studies

17 Interdisciplinarity, globality and downsizing: aspirations for the future of terrorism studies

Harmonie Toros

There are few exercises more likely to lead to embarrassment than publishing a prediction of the future. Indeed, I have little doubt that the future will look nothing like what I predict. As such, when faced with the challenge of writing a chapter on 'the future of terrorism studies', the only path is to focus on *aspirations* for the future rather than *predictions*. This chapter therefore examines what one scholar of terrorism and political violence aspires to see in future terrorism research. Aspirations are more than hopes though, they are also a call to all scholars of terrorism and political violence – from the undergraduate student taking their first class in international security to the veteran professor – to work toward better, fairer, more inclusive and more balanced scholarship. Achieving this requires slow, painstaking work from all of us.

I have many aspirations for scholarship on terrorism but I will focus on what I believe are the three most pressing. The first is a long-standing question that has been at the heart of this research since the 1970s, i.e. interdisciplinarity. Indeed, terrorism studies has always made a claim to interdisciplinarity, drawing particularly from political science (and its sub-disciplines of strategic and security studies), psychology, criminology, sociology and law. The future, however, requires us to look at the advantages and challenges of expanding beyond these 'core' disciplines as well as adopting a more thorough approach to interdisciplinarity that goes beyond 'borrowing' frameworks or empirical findings and actually developing long-term collaborative projects between disciplines.

The second aspiration is also one of expansion, this time from a scholarship that is largely produced by researchers from, or educated in, the Global North to a truly global scholarship. This is no doubt a challenge facing all areas of study but in the study of terrorism, I will argue, it is a particularly pressing problem. A vast majority of terrorist attacks take place outside the Global North yet theoretical frameworks and empirical findings continue to be produced within the Global North. This must change. *How* it can be changed, however, is a question of the politics, economics and sociology of knowledge and involves a true challenge for us all.

The final argument is counterintuitive. Most aspirational papers argue that their area of study needs greater attention because it is being overlooked. I am making the opposite claim here. After more than two decades of what John Mueller and Mark G. Stewart (2017) call 'misoverestimating terrorism', it is high time for the study of terrorism and its ranking as a major threat to national and international security to be scaled back. My third aspiration is thus that terrorism be brought back to being a sub-sub-discipline, similar to and connected with the study of insurgency.

Before I address each of these aspirations in turn, it is important to recognize the position from which they have come to be. Indeed, my work so far is clearly positioned in the sub-sub-sub-field called critical terrorism studies (CTS), which has long argued that terrorism needs to be 'de-exceptionalized' (Jackson, Breen-Smyth and Gunning 2009). This means that when I speak of the study of terrorist violence, I understand it as meaning state and non-state violence. I would like to believe, however, that these three aspirations – of deeper and broader interdisciplinarity, of greater access for scholars beyond the Global North and of recalibration – are likely to be shared beyond those identifying with CTS to include the much broader group of scholars who value better scholarship, better academic practice and better policymaking.

When you say 'interdisciplinary', mean it!

Although dominated by political scientists and International Relations (IR) scholars, the study of terrorism has always been interdisciplinary. Walter Laqueur was a historian, Martha Crenshaw is a political scientist, Grant Wardlaw studied psychology and law and Richard Jackson comes from a conflict resolution background. The key journals in the field – *Terrorism and Political Violence, Critical Studies on Terrorism* and *Studies on Conflict and Terrorism* – invite papers from 'many disciplines and theoretical perspectives' (*Terrorism and Political Violence* n.d.) and specifically note that 'research on terrorism employing methodological and disciplinary perspectives from outside political science and IR paradigms are especially encouraged' (*Critical Studies on Terrorism* n.d.). This has indeed led to considerable contributions from fields beyond politics and IR, particularly from psychology, criminology, history and law.

My first aspiration, however, is for the study of terrorism to press further down the road of interdisciplinarity by establishing real engagement across disciplines and by expanding the range of disciplines it is engaging with. Indeed, many have lamented that interdisciplinarity has often only gone skin deep in the study of terrorism. This is the result of two recurring problems. First, scholars of terrorism, particularly those coming from politics and IR, have often 'borrowed' frameworks and empirical findings from other disciplines without thoroughly engaging with those disciplines. As Marc Youngman (2020, p. 1101) laments in a powerful critique of terrorism studies, 'too often, researchers display only a cursory knowledge of the rich literatures relevant to a given theory, and therefore present findings as novel that are far from it'. The second recurring problem is the very high proportion of one-time contributors to the study of terrorism. Building on the work of Andrew Silke (2004), who found that more than 80 per cent of papers published in *Terrorism and Political Violence* and *Studies in Conflict and Terrorism* in the 1990s were produced by 'one-timers', Bart Schuurman (2020) found that this only came down to 74.8 per cent when examining research-based output of nine terrorism-focused journals from 2007 to 2016. Although this does not necessarily mean that this research is unsound, it is particularly at risk of suffering from the opposite problem as the first one raised above. Here, scholars with deep knowledge of their discipline are potentially simply engaging with terrorism as a 'case study' and often fail to place the terrorist violence within its broader historical, political and social context.

One pathway to addressing these recurring failings is to recognize that a single scholar often cannot be knowledgeable in a wide variety of fields. I was trained as a historian (BA, MA) and then as a conflict scholar (MA, PhD). I have some knowledge of sociological frameworks through my reading of Bourdieu and have looked at literature in psychology on the primacy effect of first impressions among others. I am not however a sociologist or a psychologist and I will never have the depth of knowledge of those trained in their respective fields. I am increasingly convinced therefore that true interdisciplinary work is best undertaken by engaging in collaborations and real dialogue with scholars in other disciplines. Considerable amounts of important collaborative work already exist, of course, but they remain a minority, as Schuurman (2020) found that 72.6 per cent of papers published in the nine main terrorism journals were single authored.

Such collaborations are particularly important when engaging with fields outside the social sciences and humanities. If there is some overlap in the social sciences in terms of methods, theoretical frameworks for understanding agency and structure, for example, such overlap becomes exceedingly slim when confronted with the natural sciences, mathematics, engineering or medicine. Such a collaboration is becoming increasingly important for a variety of reasons. One obvious one is that research into the terrorist use of cyber for messaging and recruiting requires interdisciplinary projects involving computing and engineering. In terms of counterterrorism practices, there is also an increased need for knowledge of automated weapons systems – research that would again benefit from engagement with engineers. The debate on 'bioterrorism' that came shortly after 9/11 would have no doubt benefited from a true collaboration between IR scholars and bioscientists, while the increased use of online messaging has led to extremely large datasets – the latest one I had to work with consisted of more than 80 million words – making collaborations with linguists and forensic linguists invaluable.

This broadened and deepened interdisciplinarity requires institutional support. Co-authored papers have to be valued just as single-authored papers; when small pots of money from interdisciplinary research are stretched thin to include many scholars, institutions need to recognize the time and effort that scholars (particularly early-career researchers) put into these collaborations. Cross-faculty and cross-research council funding should be increased and take into account that such projects may require longer initial discussions for scholars to decipher their respective concepts, frameworks, methods and practices. This first aspiration thus requires imagination and open-mindedness from scholars across a host of disciplines and real funding and support from universities and research councils.

Who sets the standards? Who writes the frameworks?

IR as a discipline has recently witnessed a push to break down some of the high walls that have long separated wealthy powerful institutions and academic circles of the Global North from financially precarious and often (but not always) marginalized scholarship from the Global South. These walls are built on economic, social and political privilege as well as on an epistemic violence that privileges theorizing from these centres of institutional power (Van Milders and Toros 2020). From post-colonial projects aimed at decolonizing the academy, to the International Studies Association (ISA) initiatives aimed at financially supporting the participation of scholars from the Global South and highlighting their scholarship, initial steps have been taken in the past few years aimed at breaking down these long-standing divides.

In the study of terrorism and political violence, this move is crucial for numerous reasons. To start with, a vast majority of terrorist violence today takes place in the Global South. As Gary LaFree, Laura Dugan and Erin Miller (2014) demonstrate, it is not since the 1970s that a region of the Global North (Western Europe) has been the scene to the largest proportion of recorded terrorist attacks.

> By contrast, attacks in Latin America (both Central America/the Caribbean and South America) dominated the 1980s with over 55 percent of the total. There are more dramatic regional shifts in the 1990s, when more than 80 percent of all terrorist attacks were spread somewhat evenly across South America, the Middle East/North Africa, South Asia, and Western Europe. Finally, from 2000 to 2012, attacks were highly concentrated in the Middle East/North Africa and South Asia, which jointly accounted for over 70 percent of all attacks among the top five regions. (LaFree et al. 2014, p. 55)

Considering such a high concentration of the field's primary object of investigation is outside the Global North, it is particularly problematic that most scholarship in the field is produced in the Global North by scholars from the Global North (Jackson, Toros, Jarvis and Heath-Kelly 2017). This invariably leads to theoretical frameworks, epistemological standpoints and methodologies developed in the Global North being *deployed* (my choice of military language here is not unintentional) into and onto empirical terrain from the Global South.

This constitutes epistemic violence that 'privileges the Western mode of knowledge production as the only viable way of producing knowledge that is universal, objective, neutral and scientific' (Van Milders and Toros 2020, p. 122). Drawing from Cynthia Weber's groundbreaking work in *Queer International Relations* (2016), it also allows for the persistence of ongoing representations of '"terrorist" as the out-of-place "underdeveloped" or "undevelopable", whose movements in relation to space, time and desire mark him as a civilisationally and sexually out-of-place global Southerner who holds developmental and/ or security risks for the "developed" Western /global Northern home/land' (Weber 2016, pp. 241–242). Crucially, such a violence silences important theoretical contributions from the Global South, where scholars have long developed a variety of alternative conceptualizations and frameworks through which to understand and investigate terrorism and counterterrorism (see the work of Furtado 2015, for example). It blinds terrorism scholarship and limits

its capacity to grasp the complex processes that lead to, constitute and eventually end terrorist and counterterrorist violence.

How to address this, however, is not an easy question to answer. Although the institutional initiatives of associations, funding councils and universities and the personal efforts of numerous scholars are important and laudable, the challenge should not be underestimated. Recent initiatives by scholarly journals, including *Critical Studies on Terrorism*, to support scholars from the Global South in strengthening their submissions to improve their chances of publication are worth looking at briefly. As one of the journal's editors working on this project, I have realized that such a support requires more than proofreading or supporting scholars in constructing their arguments in a 'journal article' way. It requires economic support such as providing access to journal articles from behind prohibitive paywalls and support in navigating informal practices of journal submissions, such as writing letters to editors and responses to reviewers. More concerning, however, is the realization that requiring scholars from the Global South to conform to practices established and set out in the Global North can be another path toward epistemic violence. What happens when a submission does not cite any 'established literature' on a topic? Is not asking the scholar to look at the canon – even simply to reject it – another way of sustaining the canon? Is the standard format of a research article – an introduction, a clearly stated research question, a literature review, a theoretical framework, empirical findings and a conclusion (or a variation of this) – the only way to present an original contribution to knowledge?

A politics of diversity and inclusivity in the study of terrorism and political violence should require other than the training of scholars from the Global South into practices of the Global North. It requires entering into a real dialogue across economic, social and political divides in order to create new academic practices and standards rather than spreading standards and practices developed for a minority of privileged scholars. This may mean changing how we understand what an article looks like and it certainly means changing the 'canon' upon which we build new knowledge. This is far more difficult than extending support to scholars outside the Global North and demands a real calling into question of what we understand as valuable knowledge, what we view as reliable methods and how open we really are to other ways of framing research in terrorism.

Downsizing terrorism

Several scholars have since the attacks of September 11, 2001 on United States landmarks denounced the extraordinary attention granted in policy circles, the media and the academy to terrorist violence. 'The terrorism studies literature demonstrates a persistent tendency to treat the current terrorist threat facing certain Western states as not only objectively "real", but as unprecedented, highly threatening, and exceptional,' Jackson et al. (2009, p. 219) lamented a decade ago. The scale of the attacks of 9/11 of course supported such a position, turning it into a powerful temporal marker that continues to separate a before and after for scholars of terrorism, political violence and IR, from both critical and traditional viewpoints (Toros 2017). The attacks were an outlier though in ambition and scale – an outlier that thankfully has never been repeated.

Many have examined the impact this focus on terrorism has had across the world on policymaking, in the media and in popular culture (see for example in starkly different fields Neal 2010 and Frank 2017). What is most relevant here is the impact on the academy. Indeed, this focus has not only led to an extraordinary proliferation of publications, workshops, courses, etc. on the topic (see the work of Lisa Stampnitzky 2013 analysing terrorism studies), but has also led to a change in the recording of acts of terrorist violence (Mueller and Stewart 2017).

> While it is not true that 9/11 'changed everything', the tragedy did have a powerful impact in some areas. Terrorism's apparent incidence and intensity, and therefore its seeming importance, has been multiplied by effectively conflating it with insurgency. Accordingly. The category *civil war* may be going out of existence – and the same could even happen for much international war. (Mueller and Stewart 2017, p. 21)

With increased attention and research in terrorism came an expansion of how the term was commonly defined. Mueller and Stewart (2017, p. 25) note that previously 'when terroristic violence by substate actors (or elements) became extensive within a country, the activity was no longer called terrorism but rather civil war or insurgency'. This more restrictive approach was replaced, Virginia Fortna (2015, p. 522) agrees, by definitions that are 'so broad as arguably to encompass all rebel groups in all civil wars'. The result is that 'the post-9/11 conflation of insurgency (or even all warfare) with terrorism makes it seem that the world is awash in terrorism, something that stokes unjustified alarm outside war zones' (Mueller and Stewart 2017, p. 28). Indeed, when one notes that the majority of recently recorded terrorist attacks occurred in Iraq,

Afghanistan, Syria and Nigeria – in violence that would previously have quali-
fied as insurgencies or civil wars due to its extensive and ongoing nature – the
impact becomes clear.

Scholarship has not only overestimated the occurrence of terrorist violence
and its salience in IR, it has often also overestimated the skill of groups engaging in terrorist violence. Michael Kenney (2010) investigates the errors of those
who have carried out successful and unsuccessful terrorist acts, arguing that
their capacities are often overestimated. Giving a detailed account of a series
of obvious blunders carried out by renowned terrorists, these 'have not shown
themselves to be terrorist "supermen", and many do not appear to be capable
of significantly improving their operational capacity over time' (Kenney
2010, p. 926). Furthermore, skill in one area – such as hijacking – tends to be
translated into skill in other areas. 'There have been widespread worries that,
because the 9/11 terrorists were successful with box cutters, they might soon
be able to turn out and detonate nuclear weapons' (Mueller and Stewart 2017,
p. 29).

What this imaginary of a 'world awash with terrorism' and of 'terrorist supermen' has done is turn terrorism, particularly Islamist-inspired terrorism, into
'a grave, even existential, threat to the West' (Kenney 2010, p. 926). From global
superpowers such as the United States to small island nations such as Barbados,
states declared terrorism a major security threat (Arthur 2007). Such a trend
had powerful institutional backers. For example, in the first five years after
the 9/11 attacks, 14 African countries passed counterterrorism legislation in
what is seen as a 'largely externally-driven' (Knudsen 2015) push by the United
Nations Counter-Terrorism Committee and donor governments following
'United Nations Security Council adopted Resolution 1373 calling on member
states to become party to all relevant international conventions on terrorism
and to enact the necessary domestic legislation to enforce these agreements'
(Whitaker 2007, p. 1018). Thousands have been arrested, international law has
been bent into a shape many struggle to recognize (Blakeley 2018) and entire
peace processes have been threatened or undermined (Haspeslagh 2021).

To counter this, what is needed is a recalibration – a downsizing – of terrorism
from its current place as 'exceptional' threat and form of political violence, to
one of the threats and *one of the* forms of political violence. It is not, of course,
a question of ignoring terrorist violence but of recognizing that not all political
violence should be classified or examined as terrorism. Even if one examines
a sub-section of political violence – for example, the widely used distinction
that terrorism involves only political violence against civilians – one still finds
oneself including violence that may be best understood as war – civil or inter-

national – or insurgency. As argued by Fortna (2015, p. 522), 'civilian targeting is ubiquitous; almost all rebel groups (and almost all government involved in civil wars) target individuals as a form of "control" to force cooperation and deter civilians from providing aid to the opponent. Violence against civilians is thus too broad a criterion by itself to distinguish terrorist rebel groups from others.' Similarly, not all political violence aimed at convincing third parties to change their behaviour through fear – another widespread way of defining terrorism – is terrorism. Wars also 'do not involve the annihilation of the enemy, but the breaking of the enemy's will in order to generate surrender or policy change' (Mueller and Stewart 2017, p. 24). Are all wars then terrorism?

Trying to avoid another run at the endless definitional debate that has plagued terrorism research for the past 40 years, I would like to propose two alternative potential pathways for the future. First, terrorism can be reduced back to political violence that is aimed at a larger audience than its immediate target but crucially that is *sporadic*. Here, extensive violence would 'no longer be called terrorism but rather civil war or insurgency' (Mueller and Stewart 2017, p. 25). Prolonged sustained campaigns of violence – such as in Iraq, Afghanistan, Syria and elsewhere – would not be understood as terrorist conflicts, although they may be seen as emerging from a campaign of terrorist violence and possibly returning to such a campaign of sporadic violence. This would help to put an end to the 'misoverestimation' of terrorism that has marked its study in the past two decades.

Such a move would not necessarily improve the research that is being undertaken on this reduced understanding of terrorism. For this, the second pathway is necessary: re-embedding the study of terrorism in the broader fields of conflict studies and strategic studies. The study of terrorism tells us something about contemporary political conflict and about contemporary strategy. I would argue it does not tell us much in isolation, or rather it makes claims that it is unable to ground in broader social and political theory or in its longer-term social, economic and political context. For those coming from a conflict studies background, the study of terrorism tells us something about conflict. The same works for those coming from a strategic studies background. Disembedded – which is how much terrorism studies has often lived in the past two decades – it can only hover in the zone of misoverestimation.

Can we imagine the study and practice of IR in which terrorism does not count for more than insurgency – in which it returns to be a sub-field of either conflict or strategic studies? This would mean an end to masters programmes on terrorism, possibly even to modules on terrorism which would be restored to a one- or two-week topic in a module on international security or conflict analysis. It would mean a slow reduction of submissions to journals specialized in the study of terrorism, less relevance in policy circles and no doubt a reduction of policy and academic jobs. Counterintuitively, I believe this is something to look forward to – a downsized but stronger sub-field.

Conclusion

Twenty years after 9/11 and the inexorable rise of terrorism in policy, the media, popular culture and the academy, there are small indications that we are finally beginning to tire of terrorism – no doubt to be replaced by another misoverestimated threat, be it Russia or cyberattacks. Such a move should be encouraged but also carefully reflected upon and managed so that what remains of terrorism studies is its best variation: a theoretically grounded, contextualized and empirically rich research programme. This requires that terrorism studies be truly interdisciplinary and global. Such aspirations are cheap, however, if they are not backed up by a determination to challenge the economics, sociology and politics of terrorism research.

Long-term interdisciplinary projects involving teams from different dis-ciplines and employing mixed methods and frameworks require financial support and the recognition that such work is not 'an easy way to get quick publications' but rather often complex relationships in which scholars need to learn new theoretical frameworks, new methods and new disciplinary lan-guages from one another. Such interdisciplinary work can rarely be carried out by a single scholar who, however much they may seek to reach into disciplines beyond their own, are unlikely to achieve the depth of knowledge acquired by those trained for years if not decades in those fields. It also requires expanding beyond the social sciences and humanities to computing, engineering, bio-sciences, linguistics and forensic science, among others.

Research in terrorism also needs to recognize that most terrorist violence takes place outside the Global North and needs to find a means to listen to the challenging voices investigating, analysing and conceptualizing terrorist vio-lence in the Global South. This movement has begun recently with small but growing institutional support from professional associations, funding councils and journals, aside from the hard work of individual scholars. The next step is to establish a true dialogue in which the frameworks, methods and format of research on terrorism is transformed. This again requires time and space where such dialogues can take place – and funding to support them – and it requires the relationship between Global North and Global South scholars to be understood as truly dialogical, that is, one in which both sides listen and learn from each other.

Finally, terrorism studies needs to shrink. This can be done by reducing terrorism to the study of *sporadic* political violence rather than ongoing and systematic political violence. Such a move will immediately reduce its salience – there will be many fewer cases of terrorism – and force scholars to once again ground the study of terrorist violence in either conflict analysis (for conflict scholars and those emerging from critical approaches) or in strategic studies (from those coming from a more traditional IR or security studies background). This will lead to more anchored research, to more contextualized research and to research that moderates rather than feeds susceptible policymakers in their dangerous tendencies to 'misoverestimate' security threats.

References

Arthur, O. (2007). Economic and financial policies of the government of Barbados. www .barbadosparliament .com/ uploads/ document/ dd fd976f0200 ee092a9ad8 149798f134.pdf

Blakeley, R. (2018). Drones, state terrorism and international law. *Critical Studies on Terrorism*, 11(2), 321–341.

Critical Studies on Terrorism (n.d.). Aims and scope. www .tandfonline .com/ action/ journalInformation?show=aimsScope&journalCode=rter20

Fortna, V. (2015). Do terrorists win? Rebels' use of terrorism and civil war outcomes. *International Organization*, 69(3), 519–556.

Frank, M. (2017). *The Cultural Imaginary of Terrorism in Public Discourse, Literature and Film*. Abingdon: Routledge.

Furtado, H. (2015). Against state terror: Lessons on memory, counterterrorism and resistance from the Global South. *Critical Studies on Terrorism*, 8(1), 72–89.

Haspeslagh, S. (2021). *Proscribing Peace: How Listing Armed Groups as Terrorists Hurts Negotiations*. Manchester: Manchester University Press.

Jackson, R., Breen-Smyth, M. and Gunning, J. (Eds) (2009). *Critical Terrorism Studies: A New Research Agenda*. Abingdon: Routledge.

Jackson, R., Toros, H., Jarvis, L. and Heath-Kelly, C. (2017). Introduction: 10 years of *Critical Studies on Terrorism. Critical Studies on Terrorism*, 10(2), 197–202.

Kenney, M. (2010). 'Dumb' yet deadly: Local knowledge and poor tradecraft among Islamist militants in Britain and Spain. *Studies in Conflict and Terrorism*, 33(10), 911–932.

Knudsen, D. (2015). A new wave of African counterterrorism legislation: Contextualizing the Kenyan security laws. *Georgetown Journal of International Affairs*. www .georgetownjournalofinternationalaffairs.org/online-edition/a-new-wave-of-african -counterterrorism-legislation-contextualizing-the-kenyan-security-laws

LaFree, G., Dugan, L. and Miller, E. (2014). *Putting Terrorism in Context: Lessons from the Global Terrorism Database*. Abingdon: Routledge.

Mueller, J. and Stewart, M. G. (2017). Misoverestimating terrorism. In M. Stohl, R. Burchill and S. Englund (Eds). *Constructions of Terrorism: An Interdisciplinary Approach to Research and Policy* (pp. 21–37). Oakland, CA: University of California.

Neal, A. (2010). *Exceptionalism and the Politics of Counter-Terrorism: Liberty, Security and the War on Terror.* Abingdon: Routledge.

Schuurman, B. (2020). Research on terrorism, 2007–2016: A review of data, methods, and authorship. *Terrorism and Political Violence*, 32(5), 1011–1026.

Silke, A. (2004). The devil you know: Continuing problems with research on terrorism. In A. Silke (Ed.). *Research on Terrorism: Trends, Achievements and Failures* (pp. 57–71). London: Frank Cass.

Stampnitzky, L. (2013). *Disciplining Terror: How Experts Invented 'Terrorism'.* Cambridge: Cambridge University Press.

Terrorism and Political Violence (n.d.). Aims and scope. www.tandfonline.com/action/journalInformation?show=aimsScope&journalCode=ftpv20

Toros, H. (2017). '9/11 is alive and well' or how critical terrorism studies has sustained the 9/11 narrative. *Critical Studies on Terrorism*, 10(2), 203–219.

Van Milders, L. and Toros, H. (2020). Violent international relations. *European Journal of International Relations*, 26(S1), 116–139.

Weber, C. (2016). *Queer International Relations.* Oxford: Oxford University Press.

Whitaker, B. (2007). Exporting the patriot act? Democracy and the 'war on terror' in the Third World. *Third World Quarterly*, 28(5), 1017–1032.

Youngman, M. (2020). Building 'terrorism studies' as an interdisciplinary space: Addressing recurring issues in the study of terrorism. *Terrorism and Political Violence*, 32(5), 1091–1105.

Index